Confederate Home Front

William Warren Rogers, Jr.

Confederate Home Front

MONTGOMERY DURING

THE CIVIL WAR

THE UNIVERSITY OF ALABAMA PRESS

Tuscaloosa and London

Library of Congress Cataloging-in-Publication Data

Rogers, William Warren, 1955–
Confederate home front : Montgomery during the Civil War /
William Warren Rogers, Jr.
p. cm.
Includes bibliographical references (p. 185) and index.

ISBN 0-8173-0962-4 (alk. paper)
1. Montgomery (Ala.)—History—19th century. 2.
Alabama—History—Civil War, 1861–1865.   I. Title.
F334.M757 R64 1999
976.1′4795—ddc21   98-58028

British Library Cataloguing-in-Publication Data available

For Mary Ann Neeley,

who loves and appreciates Montgomery

and has preserved its history

Contents

Illustrations

Preface

At the Southern Historical Association meeting in November 1995, the most attended session was a round-table discussion of Emory Thomas's recently published biography of Robert E. Lee. The session's popularity reflects less a revival of interest in the Civil War than the conflict's sustained fascination. Scholars have charted and recharted military campaigns. Historians continue to analyze, dispute, disparage, and resurrect the reputations of the various generals and the armies they commanded. Yet comparatively little attention has been devoted to the Southern home front. Some 900,000 soldiers served in Confederate armies. Over 9 million civilians lived in the seceding slave states.

In recent years historians have begun to focus on the Southerners who never wore a uniform. Drew Faust's 1996 book, *Mothers of Invention: Women of the Slaveholding South in the American Civil War,* reflects this trend. Gender was also the subject of George Rable's *Civil Wars, Women, and the Crisis of Southern Nationalism* (1989) and Catherine Clinton's *Tara Revisited: Women, War, and the Plantation Legend* (1996). Mary DeCredico focuses on market forces and business operations in her analysis of entrepreneurism in Georgia. Clarence Mohr examines how the war affected Georgia's slave population. Other historians have increased our knowledge of the experiences of people living in occupied territory. Stephen Ash chronicled events in Memphis, New Orleans, Nashville, and other areas controlled by the Union in *When the Yankees Came* (1995). Such scholarly ventures into hitherto uncharted areas have given us a fuller understanding of the war.

This book concerns the residents of Alabama's capital and their world between 1861 and 1865. Montgomery changed dramatically during the conflict and changed again afterward as a result of emancipation. William Davis has ably described Montgomery during this period as the capital of the Confederate States in his book *"A Government of Our Own": The Making of the Confederacy* (1994). In contrast, this work focuses on the experience of Montgomerians during the war. While Montgomery's residents had much in common with other Southerners as the war came, these Alabamians responded to four years of conflict in ways that importantly reflect their own sense of time and place. How residents perceived and adjusted to the conflict forms the basis of this study. No segment of home-front society was so affected as women. A large slave population, comprising half the city's residents, provides a basis for more conclusions. Although the details of life in wartime Southern cities differed, the contours were much the same. In a larger sense, in the context of the greater Confederacy, Montgomery takes on more relevance.

My approach is chronological and topical. Chapter 1 provides an overview of the city in 1860 and describes on a national level the sectional differences leading to Alabama's secession and Montgomery's establishment as the Southern capital. Chapter 2 deals with Montgomery's period as capital of the Confederacy, from February to May 1861. The subsequent six chapters concern city administration, business patterns, and citizens' attempts to maintain order. I pay attention to efforts to promote the Confederate cause and protect Montgomery from the enemy and to the various government departments in the city. Although Montgomerians were generally patriotic, a small minority opposed the Confederacy, and this group of Unionist dissenters is also discussed. Chapters 9 and 10 return to the chronological continuum. Chapter 9 analyzes the situation in Montgomery, set against a disintegrating Confederacy. Chapter 10 describes the city's surrender.

Montgomery was a young city when the Civil War began. Alabama had been admitted to the Union in 1819, and Montgomery, designated the county seat of Montgomery County, came into being during the same year. The village was situated near the headwaters of the Alabama River, a tributary that wound 325 miles south to Mobile and the Gulf of Mexico. Montgomery also formed part of the Black Belt, the alluvial prairie lands stretching west across central Alabama. As the southwestern cotton kingdom opened up, geography contributed to Montgomery's evolution from a village to a large town. Whites settled there voluntarily. Slaves, who could not choose their place of residence, also contributed to steady growth. Montgomery's designation as the state capital in 1846 portended greater prosperity. The city had slightly over 8,000 residents at the time of the Compromise of 1850. As the 1860s began, white Montgomerians were reasonably optimistic about the future. Black Montgomerians, accustomed to bondage but not resigned to it, surely felt differently. Neither race foresaw that the increasing tensions between North and South would culminate in war, and neither one could possibly have imagined the effect that such a conflict might have on their city.

Acknowledgments

I would like to express my gratitude to various people who have helped me with this book. John Marszalek, Mary Ann Neeley, and Robert David Ward read the book in manuscript form and provided insight and direction. A debt is also owed to the readers who examined the text for The University of Alabama Press. Both caught errors and made suggestions that significantly improved the book. I thank you very much.

Most of the research was completed at the Alabama Department of Archives and History at Montgomery. The entire staff was extremely supportive. I especially thank Rickie Brunner, Diane Jackson, Keeta Kendall, Norwood Kerr, and Mark Palmer. Robert Gamble, at the Alabama Historical Commission, also facilitated the research. The Special Collections staff at the Amelia Gayle Gorgas Library in Tuscaloosa was very helpful. At Florida State University, the librarians in the Documents, Maps, and Micromaterial Department in the Ralph Strozier Library have aided me. At Florida State, Peter Krafft is a fine cartographer, and the two maps in this book are his creations. At the National Archives, Michael Musick and Michael Meier familiarized me with various record groups.

Various archivists sent me records. I thank Judith Sibley (United States Military Academy), Janie C. Morris (Special Collections, Duke University), Sharon DeFibaugh (Special Collections, University of Virginia Library), and Harry McKown (North Carolina Collection, University of North Carolina Library). From Austin, Texas, Sandra Garrett forwarded me material from a collection I could not have seen otherwise. James P. Jones, who teaches the Civil War at Florida State, provided access to microfilmed diaries. At Rice University, Lynda Crist is directing the compilation of the Jefferson Davis Papers. I consulted her on several occasions, and she always generously provided her knowledge and records from the papers.

Gainesville College has helped fund several research trips. I thank Cathy

Fuller, Steve Gurr, and Amy Reeder for their generous assistance in this regard. Julie Davies, our department secretary, has typed much of this manuscript, and I appreciate her efforts greatly. Priscilla Rankin and Valerie Wood have gone far beyond the call of duty at the Interlibrary Loan Department.

Various scholars have expressed an interest and offered me sound advise. For doing so I thank William C. Davis, Mike Denham, Richard Greaves, Sally Hadden, John Inscoe, John Moore, Paul Pruitt, Bawa Singh, and Ben Wall.

The staff at The University of Alabama Press has made the publication process a smooth one. Director Nicole Mitchell has been very supportive and encouraging. So has everyone else at the Press. I extend a special note of appreciation to Suzette Griffith, Assistant Managing Editor.

Outside of the Archives community in Montgomery, I appreciate the kindness of various people. Nimrod and Lee Frazer have a real interest in Montgomery's past and, during several of my research trips, allowed me to stay at their home. Will Hill Tankersley is very active in the local historical scene, and he also has helped me. At Oakwood Cemetery, I have called constantly on Ellis Doss and Phillip Taunton II. As the sextons, both Ellis and Phillip have provided me more information than I could ever repay them for.

Mary Ann Neeley is the director of Landmarks Foundation and the authority on Montgomery history. As a preservationist and a historian, Mary Ann has contributed incredibly to the city. She has expressed an unfailing faith in this book. I have drawn greatly on her encyclopedic knowledge. Mary Ann's help—from finding photographs to checking the manuscript for accuracy—has been of inestimable value. Her upbeat and consistent enthusiasm has been equally as important. I am only one of many who have profited from Mary Ann's professional advise and enjoyed her personal friendship. Montgomery is fortunate to have such a treasure. For these reasons this book is dedicated to Mary Ann Neeley.

My wife, Lee, has enjoyed her introduction to Montgomery and has gained an appreciation for the city and its history. My mother, Miriam Rogers, is an Alabamian and has a much longer acquaintanceship with the city. I am thankful and better off for her suggestions, encouragement, and interest. More than any other single person, I thank my father. William Warren Rogers is a historian, and he suggested the subject to me. He has advised, corrected, read, and reread the manuscript. As always, his editing and stylistic changes add a great deal to this study.

Montgomery on
the Eve of War

MONTGOMERY BUSTLED WITH EN-
ergy, vitality, and prospects in 1860. Connected by railroad and water, Alabama's capital was the final destination for some, and a natural stopover for
others. Travelers disembarked from a steamboat on the winding, bluff-lined
Alabama River or arrived from the east on the Montgomery and West Point
Railroad. It did not take long for visitors to gain a feel and geographic sense
of Montgomery. Many visitors glimpsed the city first from the wharf. Market
Street, the central artery, ran west from the state capitol on its commanding
hill. The neoclassical building, with a facade of plastered brick scored to look
like stone, had six Corinthianesque columns and a rust-colored dome. The
capitol grounds in 1860, defined by an iron fence, looked bare and untidy, an
anomaly in a city of trees, kept lawns, and gardens.

Half a mile away, down sloping Market Street and toward the river, lay
Court Square. There Market, Court, and Commerce Streets intersected,
forming the heart of the business district. An artesian basin, enclosed by an
iron fence, provided water for fighting fires and served as the backdrop for
various auctions, including sales of slaves. After dark, gas lamps bathed the
streets in a faint, uncertain light.

Market Street scene looking toward the capitol from the Artesian Basin, c. 1861. Lithograph from *Harper's Weekly Magazine,* February 9, 1861, *courtesy of Fouts Commercial Photography, Montgomery, Alabama.*

In the nearby residential neighborhoods, whites and blacks lived alongside each other. Many of the homes were spacious and fine. Charles and Virginia Pollard had a Greek Revival residence on Jefferson Street. The red brick columned home of Tennent and Caroline Lomax on Court Street attested to its owners' social standing. Most Montgomerians lived in more modest cottages that were sometimes brick but were more often clapboard. On the city's periphery, the free black population resided. There was a wide cross section of domiciles—impressive, commonplace, and the frankly disreputable—that dotted a hilly and undulating landscape.

Visitors inquiring about lodging were generally referred to the Exchange Hotel, located just off Court Square. The four-story brick structure was the largest and best-appointed hotel; less demanding travelers could choose between the Madison House and Montgomery Hall, both of which were four-story brick structures. There were several restaurants. Italian-born Joseph Pizalla owned the oddly named Rio Grande restaurant. The Rialto restaurant featured oysters, fish, and game. Alcoholic beverages were available at a hotel bar or at one of several emporiums located on Court or Commerce Streets down by the river. Like other Americans in the nineteenth century, Montgomerians consumed alcohol frequently and often in large quantities. Although local citizens were not overly discriminating in their preferences, George Lyman at the Arcade Saloon advertised brandies and wines to "please the tastes of the most fastidious."[1]

Montgomery in 1860 was a place of wealth, architectural taste, and obvious commercial vigor. Buildings of brick were beginning to replace clapboard structures in the city. On the eve of the Civil War, 8,843 people lived in Alabama's capital, with whites almost equal in number to blacks (4,341 to 4,502). In the state as a whole, Montgomery ranked behind Mobile in size and was only the twenty-fourth largest city in the slave states. Fewer goods and services were available in Montgomery, but the smaller scale, and not generally inferior quality, distinguished Alabama's capital from larger Southern cities.

Most of Montgomery's residents had been born in the South, but some had moved from Northern states, and others had recently come from Europe. George Goldthwaite, practicing law, traced his descendants to Montgomery's earliest period. Samuel Seelye, who had arrived from Maine in 1859, was just beginning a lengthy practice as a physician. Samuel Dreyfus, an immigrant from Germany, ran a dry goods store.

William Anderson, a wagon maker, was one of about a hundred free blacks. The vast majority of blacks were slaves who labored for doctors, merchants, railroad owners, one of two iron founders in the city, and even ministers. Henry, Anderson, Bachus, Stephen, Blunt, and Thomas—slaves typically lacked surnames—worked as carpenters for Jefferson Franklin Jackson, a lawyer. The many mulattoes were evidence of racial mixing and prompted at least one outsider to question assurances that "the planters affect the character of parent in their moral relations merely with the Negro race." As matters stood, one of every two Montgomery residents lived in bondage.[2]

A person's name and financial standing generally determined status. In Montgomery, individual differences in wealth, often wide, generally reflected the antebellum class order throughout the South. Planters, the more successful lawyers, doctors, and various entrepreneurs often had money, slaves, and social standing. Below them on the social scale was a much larger group of modest means. Individuals at this level might own a small retail business. Clerks, the lowest tradesmen, and unskilled workers earned the least. These Montgomerians usually rented lodging and were often debtors.

As the capital and the hub of trade in the southern and central Alabama

hinterland, Montgomery took on a certain vibrancy. Central Bank, run by
William Knox, and the Bank of Montgomery, under the direction of Elliot
Hannon, had busy Market Street locations. Citizens also conducted their af-
fairs at the Greek Revival courthouse a couple of blocks to the north on
Lawrence Street. Concert and Estelle Halls on Market Street were the sites
of balls, lectures, and other social gatherings.

Haberdashers included Ethelbert Halfmann's clothing store on Court
Square, where the motto was "small profits and quick returns." J. E. Churchill
and Company on Commerce Street offered hats of every description. Other
merchants provided casual and formal dresses, milliners stocked stylish hats
and accessories, and there were at least a half dozen cobblers. Jacob Kohn, a
German, and his son, Alexander, made and sold shoes in their shop under the
Exchange Hotel. The eagle gracing a drugstore at the corner of Market and
Perry Streets belonged to partners Felix Glackmeyer and Camillus Hilliard,
and there were five other druggists answering to the public needs.

There was no shortage of dry goods stores. Tools, nails, brooms, and other
household items were available at George Cowles's Market Street store, which
became a clandestine meeting place for local Unionists after the war began.
G. Giovanni and Company sold confectionery across from the Exchange Hotel. Giovanni was Corsican. Nick Becker, a German gunsmith, had a shop on
Commerce Street. H. Lewy, also German, repaired watches in Court Square,
where he competed with at least half a dozen jewelers. Archibald McIntyre
had an ambrotype and photograph gallery on Market Street.[3]

Local attorneys—Sanford, Goldthwaite, Elmore, Semple, and Rice—carried some of the city's best-known names. As with William Lowndes Yancey,
a local lawyer, involvement in politics often followed admission to legal practice. Yancey was hardly the best counselor, but John Elmore, his onetime part-
ner, may have been. William Baldwin, in practice since 1837, exemplified
excellence for two dozen doctors. The hospital might have been better described as a glorified clinic, but it accommodated patients. Physicians Job
Weatherly and Joseph Hannon were opening an infirmary for blacks on
Perry Street in 1860. Stephen Blaum, who had learned dentistry at the University of Heidelberg in his native Germany, claimed to know of "modern
improvements."[4]

The patriarchal order of society afforded women few occupational op-
portunities. Lucy Hancock, a widow, supported four daughters as a seamstress.
There were over a dozen seamstresses and half as many milliners. Catherine
Graham, one of several female schoolteachers, provided elementary instruc-

tion at the Select School. Several other women ran boardinghouses. Women planters, of whom there were at least ten, often commanded considerable resources. Martha Conyers, who grew cotton, owned property valued at $35,000 and would have been regarded as wealthy. The list of women who engaged in enterprise is short, however. Females accounted for half of the Caucasian population but exerted minimal economic influence.[5]

In July 1860, disgruntled residents complained to the city council about the black smoke that poured forth from John Holt's blinds/sashes manufactory. Emissions enveloped homes, and "the occupants of said houses at times can scarcely breathe." The affected area, the northeastern section of the city down by the Alabama River, was the period equivalent of an industrial zone. John Janney operated a steam-powered foundry at the corner of Court and Randolph Streets. Machinists in the Montgomery and West Point Railroad shops of Charles Pollard built cars (including the special car that carried Jefferson Davis into Montgomery for his inauguration). Despite such activities, manufacturing interests were limited. Only about 200 individuals (approximately 2 percent of the population) engaged in industrial pursuits.[6]

Montgomery was typical of Southern cities not only in its general indifference to manufacturing but also in its obsession with cotton. Black teamsters directing cotton-laden wagons were a familiar sight each fall. Stevedores, also usually black, handled over 1 million cotton bales at the wharf in 1860. Commission merchants crowded onto Commerce Street near the warehouses and the wharf in the river area. Frank and William Gilmer, who were brothers, were among the most successful. Meyer and Emanuel Lehman had prospered in their shop in Court Square since their arrival from Germany. Although the brothers' diction was less than perfect, none doubted their abilities. Their recent establishment of a cotton office in New York was further evidence of their success.

Montgomery's growth followed the rise and fall in cotton prices. In 1860 the cotton market was extremely solid. An immense fireproof cotton warehouse on Court Street, completed in August, bespoke confidence in the future. Contractor George Figh and his laborers were constructing a three-story brick office building (named for Figh's contractor father) on Bibb Street. It would eventually house the first Confederate post office. Workers under Figh's direction were also laboring steadily on a synagogue at the corner of Church and Catoma Streets. Mason Harwell was spending the profits from his auctioneering house to erect an impressive brick home on Lawrence Street. Hardware merchant John Garrett was financing the "finest frame building" in Montgomery. The impressive Perry Street residence of William Baldwin was also finished at this time. From the observatory on top of his three-story masonry home, the physician enjoyed a panoramic view of the city and the winding river.[7]

Although Montgomery claimed no institution of higher learning, the city was home to a well-educated intelligentsia. Henry Hilliard, soon to raise a strong voice against secession, had been a classics professor at the University of Alabama before moving to Montgomery and opening a law practice. Thomas Hill Watts, who had graduated from the University of Virginia, would be elected governor in 1863. Albert Pickett, the author of the first history of Alabama, had recently died. Johnson Jones Hooper was alive and well and writing. The author of *Some Adventures of Simon Suggs* and other fiction set on the Southern frontier helped edit the *Montgomery Mail,* one of four newspapers read by the populace of fewer than 10,000 citizens. The other papers—the *Advertiser,* the *Confederation,* and the *Post*—also had loyal readers. In newspaper columns signed with pseudonyms such as "Zenophon" and "Cato," Montgomerians were defiant, outrageous, and occasionally brilliant. Avid readers ensured the commercial success of Pfister and White's bookstore, which was appreciatively described as a "temple to Minerva" and carried works ranging from *Revolutions in English History* to *Passing Thoughts on Religion.*[8]

Montgomerians could hear lectures, enjoy professional and amateur musicians, and sample a wide variety of other attractions. Hundreds turned out to hear Italian soprano Theresa Parodi in April. She caused such a sensation that one observer remarked, "Politics have been thrown aside by the men, town gossip and literature by our female friends."[9] The social graces were important. Allen Robinson, a "dancing master," instructed at Concert Hall.[10] Anna Octavia Lewis Knox was as prominent as her name might suggest. One visitor described Montgomery as "far above the average of Southern cities."[11]

The annual Alabama State Agricultural Fair took place in October. Prize produce, livestock, cotton gins, and carnival-like displays of freaks drew Montgomerians and thousands from surrounding counties to the fairgrounds north of town. At the nearby Montgomery Association Race Course, blacks and whites bet on thoroughbreds. The sporting classes appreciated Richard III and a filly named Sherrod that had gained special renown.

No event was more keenly anticipated than the opening of the Montgomery Theater. Over the spring and summer the vaguely Italianate brick structure rose steadily at the corner of Perry and Monroe Streets. On

October 14, opening night, an audience of over 400 enjoyed *The School for Scandal*, Richard Brinsley Sheridan's comedy of manners. Troupes found a loyal following. In the new playhouse, Montgomerians came to see Margaret (Maggie) Mitchell, a versatile and extremely popular performer. Late in the year, when John Wilkes Booth appeared, the *Post* described him as a "young and promising tragedian."[12]

Recreation and commerce abruptly ceased on Sunday. All the houses of worship were within a fairly close radius. Whites and blacks attended church together. George Petrie, one of the South's most erudite Presbyterian ministers, tended to the spiritual needs of local Calvinists at the Adams Street church. Two Methodist churches, the Episcopal Methodist on Court Street and the Protestant Methodist on Bibb Street, were crowded on Sunday. Strict city ordinances regulated secular activities on the Lord's day. Baptists claimed standing, prominence, and a handsome masonry edifice on North Court Street. Isaac Tichenor, who later served as a Confederate army chaplain, presided at the First Baptist Church.

The Episcopalians attended St. John's Church on Madison Avenue, a striking Gothic Revival structure with a seventy-five-foot spire. The sixty-six-year-old Nicholas Hamner Cobbs, who was the Episcopal bishop of Alabama

Slaves and the view across the Alabama River to Montgomery, c. 1861. *Frank Leslie's Illustrated Magazine, courtesy of Fouts Commercial Photography, Montgomery, Alabama.*

until 1860, was preaching during the last year of his life. At St. Peter's Catholic Church, Father A.D. Pellicer conducted mass. Awaiting the completion of their synagogue, the substantial Jewish population was temporarily meeting (without the services of a rabbi) above O'Dwyer and Doolittle's grocery on Court Square. Noting the closing of stores on Rosh Hashanah in September, an onlooker expressed surprise at the size of the Jewish population.[13]

Black Montgomerians toiled in a variety of trades. Bondsmen worked as brickmasons, painters, servants, common laborers, and field hands. Black women served mainly as domestics. In its restrictions on slaves, Montgomery differed little from other cities across the South. Servants usually lived in their owners' homes or nearby. Chattel could not own a mule, a hog, a horse, or even a dog within the city limits. Slaves could not buy liquor, sleep outside their registered residence, or carry a weapon. Councilmen would not permit William Rives to let one of his slaves sleep in a stable and tend a stallion.

In a city where blacks outnumbered whites, control was considered essential. Bondsmen traveling from one place to another might be asked to produce a pass. The ringing of a bell at 9:00 P.M. ordered slaves to their quarters. For those breaching city ordinances, punishment, which often took the form of whippings, was swift and harsh. Lashes were usually administered in lots of twenty-five, thirty-nine, or fifty. Private owners set the figure arbitrarily.[14]

Custom, reason, and individual circumstances militated against universal application of strictures against slaves. Across the South, those who lived in urban areas enjoyed a better life than their counterparts on country plantations. In Montgomery, blacks often dressed well and sometimes owned finery, broadcloth suits, patent shoes, jewelry, and various other accoutrements. Some hired out their free time and earned money. Slaves ranged throughout the city fairly freely, at least during daylight hours, and enjoyed a measure of autonomy.

The eight slaves who helped proprietor Abram Watt attend to boarders at the Exchange Hotel, or the ten bondsmen who labored for Caroline Bird, may well have longed for their freedom. In Montgomery, as throughout the South, there was an undercurrent of resentment. Blacks were not docile laborers who marched in lockstep. City influences broadened awareness, raised aspirations, and had a liberalizing effect. Some slaves heeded the written and unwritten codes of behavior, but others did not. Defiance might take the form of theft, sabotage, or even flight. It was rare, and usually futile, for a slave

to run away. W. L. Staggers and his bloodhounds were available to help appre-
hend fugitives.[15]

Members of the free black community endured various constraints.
Often resented by whites, free blacks composed 1 percent of the population.
Isaac and Rachel Meritt had five children. Isaac, a wagoner, had $3,000 in
assets, a notable sum at the time. Josephine Hassell, a mulatto seamstress,
owned over $5,000 in real estate and was raising four children by herself. The
oldest was six. Other free blacks were teamsters, dressmakers, carpenters, and
a butcher. Freedom did not entitle these individuals to all of the liberties
enjoyed by whites, however. There were enforced curfews, and free blacks
paid special taxes. Nathan Ellis, a carpenter, and his wife Nancy, a washer-
woman, supported their two children. The Ellises might gain economic security, but achieving respected standing locally was something different.[16]

Men and women of both races committed crimes. City marshal Isaac
Maxwell and a police force numbering between twelve and fourteen made
arrests for public drunkenness, fighting, petty theft, and other misdemean-
ors. Most offenders stayed overnight in the Monroe Street jail and appeared
the next day in mayor's court. On a typical day in August, Mayor Andrew
Noble ordered two vagrants to leave town within twenty-four hours. A black
boy who had stolen seventy-five dollars and a gold pen was sentenced to
fifty lashes "in the most approved style."[17] An "intimate acquaintance of John
Barleycorn" appeared before the mayor late that summer. Having passed out
on a sidewalk and been carried to jail by police, the defendant protested that
authorities had "interfered" with his "rights." His threat to leave the city did
not deter Noble from levying a fine of five dollars.[18]

When two boisterous Irishwomen appeared before a magistrate, an observer compared them to the fierce and independent citizens of ancient Gaul.
The defendants and their neighbors, it was said, "paid regular homage to the
gods of Mars, Apollo, and Bachus."[19] Ordinances outlawing gambling were
frequently violated. Similarly little attention was paid to four different ordinances concerning "lewd women or persons of bad reputation as to chastity."[20] Prostitutes, but not the men visiting them, were considered to be vio-
lating the law. Eliza Coppinger was one of the best-known madams, though
she was listed in the 1860 census merely as the proprietor of a boardinghouse.
Montgomerians liked to regard themselves as cultivated, but elements of the
frontier were sometimes obvious. As the year ended, the city council passed a
statute forcing saloon proprietors to restrain patrons who threatened to dis-
turb others by "cries, noise, songs, or otherwise."[21]

On the eve of the Civil War, Alabama's capital was a place of contrasts. Fields of cotton and corn stood at the ill-defined city limits. The streets leading through town were dirt roads rather than the macadam found in some other cities, and they gave rise to clouds of dust. At the close of 1860, loose cows and hogs became a public nuisance, and Marshal Isaac Maxwell ordered citizens to keep them locked up. Slave depots provided another aesthetic distraction. These places where blacks were confined in pens before auctions, troubled some citizens because they subjected the city "to the remarks of visitors as wanting in good taste."[22]

Some Montgomerians lived in palatial homes attended by servants. Others lived in hovels and eked out a livelihood as best they could. A few were extremely well educated; many others could neither read nor write. Class lines were clearly drawn and took race into account. Slaves such as Sam, a waiter and carriage driver for the Jefferson Franklin Jackson family, had little opportunity to rise in society. If Sam was judged of "good moral character," he might receive a badge that allowed him to hire out his time, but few avenues to prosperity awaited him as a free black. Restrictions were not harsher in Montgomery than in any other municipality with large numbers of blacks. That fact provided little comfort to slaves chaffing under a mind-set of subservience and the lash.

In 1860 Montgomery's future depended in part on initiatives being taken by wealthy businessmen who were often intellectually inclined. Charles Pollard, president of the Montgomery and West Point Railroad, anticipated the completion of the Alabama and Florida Railroad that would connect Montgomery to the Gulf Coast. William and Frank Gilmer's plans to connect Montgomery by rail to north Alabama were also well advanced.[23]

In another sense, even more determinative of the future for Montgomery, was the 1860 presidential election. The contest, sectional in emphasis, would be the bitterest in the nation's history. Geography, labor, and culture had combined to create two distinct societies, one slave and the other free. Southerners regarded themselves as having less and less in common with citizens in the North. The free and slave states had never been alike, but never before had they seemed as different as they did in 1860. Southern whites considered the North a hostile land populated by crass, money-driven businessmen. Fanatical leaders sought to level society and, having gained the ascendancy, appeared to be setting a radical agenda in the North. One vision had manifested itself in the recently created Republican Party. Public opinion exaggerated not only the differences between Southern and Northern society but also the intentions of Republican politicians. Growing numbers of Southerners were convinced that "Black Republicans" intended to destroy slavery.

Montgomerians resembled other Southerners in their fears, prejudices, and simplistic assumptions. Republican control, white Montgomerians were collectively certain, would imperil slavery and time-honored custom. It was immaterial that most citizens did not own slaves. For people at all levels of society, the peculiar institution provided controls, structure, and order. Without this ordering principle, society would plunge into chaos. Few questioned the conventional wisdom: blacks were indisputably inferior. For their own welfare, no less than that of everyone else, slaves must remain subordinate to whites.

Writing his brother in Germany, Jacob Weil, a clothing merchant, denounced the hypocritical Northern slave traders. "One man has no right to sell property to another . . . and claim that the buyer is evil and should divest himself of his property." More publicly, William Lowndes Yancey for years declared that abolitionists posed a long list of dangers. Yancey had become a preeminent advocate of secession. Increasing numbers of Montgomerians agreed with his views.[24]

Alabama's status as a southern state with some 400,000 slaves made it impossible for Montgomerians to escape the sectional tensions attending the 1860 presidential election. Troubling signs were discernible when Governor Andrew Moore delivered his second inaugural address in December 1859. He dwelled on states' rights—a topic that Moore had not even mentioned four years earlier. Moore did not use the word "secession," but the idea lurked in public awareness. Like most white Southerners, Montgomerians worried about what a Republican president might do. The city's residents were acutely conscious that they lived in a city where slaves and whites were roughly equal in number. Thoughts of a Republican victory conjured up visions of Northern critics remaking the Southern world in the image of rabid abolitionists.

The intensity of public feeling was evident in conversation and from the most casual perusal of local editorials. Basil Manly fully understood the prevailing sentiment. Having recently replaced the Reverend Isaac Tichenor, Manly presided at the First Baptist Church. Speaking of an acquaintance who had mentioned coming to Montgomery and speaking on behalf of abolition, Manly wrote to family relatives, "I shall advise him that he would better not make the experiment."[25] In February 1860, Benjamin Davis, a bookstore owner, burned the works of the well-known Baptist sermonizer Charles Haddon Spurgeon. The *Montgomery Confederation* maintained that Spurgeon's work "smacks too much of Abolitionism."[26] Local citizens were more in philosophical agreement with John Van Evrie's *Negroes and Negro Slavery*. According to this treatise, available at Davis's Market Street bookstore, "the Negro is not a black man, or a man merely with black skin, but a different and inferior species of man."[27]

The subjects of race and slavery gave rise to the most controversial questions of the presidential contest. Divisions in the ranks of the Democrats had increased significantly since the last national election. Events in the four-year interim—for example, more strident attacks by abolitionists and particularly John Brown's raid—had given secessionists renewed vigor. The sectional question of slavery was framed by the debate over the institution's expansion into the territories.

There were variations, but the general lines of the argument were clear in Alabama and the South. One faction, citing the Supreme Court's decision in *Dred Scott,* insisted that slavery must be unequivocally recognized in the territories. Although equally committed to slavery and opposed to Republicanism, other Southern Democrats accepted more readily the concept of popular sovereignty, identified with Senator Stephen Douglas of Illinois and most Northern Democrats, which was interpreted as meaning that citizens in a territory should be allowed to decide the question by popular vote.

Opinion was divided in Montgomery, and feelings were sometimes heated. Still, most residents claimed a philosophical kinship with either William Lowndes Yancey or Henry Hilliard. An accomplished speaker and a man of unquestioned conviction, Yancey had practiced law in Montgomery since the 1840s. The hot-tempered forty-seven-year-old Democrat had spent some years editing a newspaper and had served several terms in Congress. He supported secession and was known for his compelling, passionate, fierce, and always well delivered oratory. His following in Montgomery grew larger and became increasingly uncritical.

Other observers made a more detached survey of events and alternatives and advocated a more cautious approach than Yancey. The fifty-three-year-old Henry Hilliard, a man of keen intellectual and oratorical powers, was one such public figure. Hilliard during his political career, which included three congressional terms, had been variously a Whig, a Know-Nothing, and a

William Lowndes Yancey, a local lawyer and the best-known Southern fire-eater, c. 1855. *Courtesy of the Alabama Department of Archives and History, Montgomery, Alabama.*

Democrat. He and others were skeptical about the value and practicality of secession.[28]

Secession advanced like a drama in acts, and the curtain rose in Alabama at a meeting that took place on January 11, 1860. Convening at the capitol, state Democrats elected delegates to the national convention to be held in Charleston, South Carolina, in April. Differences between the more militant elements and the opposition were pronounced. After prolonged debate,

Henry Hilliard, a local lawyer who recommended caution as Alabamians considered secession, c. 1860. *Courtesy of the Alabama Department of Archives and History, Montgomery, Alabama.*

the so-called Alabama, or Yancey, platform was adopted. It demanded that the Democrats write into the national platform an absolute guarantee of slavery in the territories. Otherwise the delegation would walk out of the convention. Anticipating the election of a Republican president, the legislature called on Governor Moore to schedule an election so that delegates to a state convention could be selected. Following the national election, if a Republican won, the delegates would determine what was in the "rights, interests, and honor" of Alabama. The answer might be secession.[29]

John Seibels, who was connected with the *Montgomery Confederation,* accurately gauged the temper of the times. Writing Stephen Douglas, the forty-three-year-old lawyer observed, "We are here in the midst almost of a revolution." [30] He did not exaggerate. Military companies were forming throughout the slave states. In Montgomery, martial activity was evident everywhere. The Montgomery True Blues, more visible than ever before, included planters and lawyers, clerks, carpenters, machinists, and even an artist. The True Blues' captain, Tennent Lomax, was a lawyer, a planter, and a civic leader. Another established company, the Mounted Rifles, also intensified its activities. James Clanton, an attorney, served as the captain.

Still another company, the Metropolitan Guards, had been formed late in 1859 and was captained by Joseph Winter. Flamboyant displays of arms accompanied inflamed rhetoric. Reason gave way to intense emotion. In early April, when the Metropolitan Guards received a flag sewn by local women, a large crowd gathered before the capitol. The company appeared in full uniform for the first time. Samuel Arrington made it clear that the troops' duties might well extend beyond the ceremonial. The lawyer spoke of the "imperilled condition of this Southern country" and the threat to "our most cherished institutions." He declared, "You may be called on to take the field." The prospect did not faze Virgil Murphey, who thanked the ladies and predicted conflict "if the hand of fanaticism cannot be stayed." Everyone agreed: honor must be served and a lifestyle defended. Under the circumstances, war did not seem so unthinkable. As the Union teetered, impassioned citizens gathered in towns across the South to protest the perceived threat to all that they held sacred. [31]

On April 23, the Democratic convention opened. Although Stephen Douglas claimed the most delegates, debate focused less on a candidate than on a platform. Douglas's advocacy of popular sovereignty represented a compromise that Northern Democrats and some Southern Democrats accepted. Yet a majority of Southern delegates, resentful of abolitionists, demanded a more positive affirmation of *Dred Scott.* On April 27, Yancey urged the convention to incorporate the "Alabama Platform." His speech was eloquent but futile. Three days later he and Alabama's entire twenty-seven-member delegation withdrew. Most Southern delegates followed. The remaining Democrats made no nomination and adjourned after agreeing to meet in Baltimore in June.

In early May, former members of the defunct American and Whig Parties established the Constitutional Union Party. John Bell, a moderate Tennessean

opposed to secession, headed a ticket that included Edward Everett of Massachusetts. Constitutional Union men condemned the major parties' sectional
nature and vowed to abide by the Constitution. No informed sources regarded the Bell-Everett ticket as having any chance. Republican prospects
seemed much brighter. In mid-May, the Republicans convened in Chicago
and nominated Abraham Lincoln and Hannibal Hamlin. Although Lincoln
was not an abolitionist, he firmly supported the Republican position that
opposed the expansion of slavery. His political prospects, unlike those of Bell,
were promising.

All hopes of forging a united Democratic coalition ended when the
fragmented party met in Baltimore in June. The slavery question led to dis-
putes about how to seat competing delegations. Anti-Douglas Democrats (including every Alabamian) bolted again. On June 23, in Baltimore, Stephen
Douglas was nominated. Several days later, in the same city, dissident Democrats nominated John Breckinridge, a Kentucky slaveholder. Joseph Lane,
an Oregon senator, became his running mate. Given the divisions in Democratic ranks, most observers predicted a Republican victory. By the same
token, some assumed that secession would follow, although the Lincoln administration would plainly resist division. After secession carried, blows
would be struck in defense of states' right to secede and the indivisibility of
the Union.[32]

Montgomerians had always embraced politics, but never before had the
stakes been so high. In various forums—the lobby of the Exchange Hotel,
Henry Lee's Court Square bakery and grocery store, and other gathering
points—the presidential campaign moved to center stage. Southern opinion
expressed itself in all of its manifestations in the *Advertiser,* the *Mail,* the *Confederation,* and the *Post.* Samuel Reid of the *Advertiser* endorsed Breckinridge,
vilified Douglas as a covert abolitionist, and quoted the *Dred Scott* decision.
The paper referred to the "utter hopelessness" that Southern whites would
feel if Lincoln was elected. At the *Mail* office, located on Court Square, similar views prevailed. A troika composed of Johnson Jones Hooper, Henry
Coyne, and John Whitfield handled the writing duties. Secession was not de-
sirable, but it would become necessary, the *Mail* contended, if a Republican
became the next president. Other observers took a more cautious position.
Editors John Seibels and Edwin Banks at the *Confederation* championed the
cause of Douglas and faulted others for extremism. Editor John Gaines of the
Post made the case for John Bell.[33]

Whether they consulted one or a combination of local newspapers, citizens were transfixed by the election. John Breckinridge claimed the allegiance of the majority. Meeting at Estelle Hall on July 11, supporters formed a Breckinridge and Lane Club. Tristam Bethea, Gabriel DuVal, and James Holtzclaw, men of property and repute, were some of the most prominent members. Convening in front of the Exchange Hotel in early August, Breckinridge's advocates listened to oratory "until night had nearly become morning." Rallies were frequent, long, and emotional. On the night of Saturday, September 29, Henry Hilliard raised cheers among Bell and Everett supporters at Estelle Hall. Proponents of Douglas were much scarcer. The pace intensified as November 6 approached. On the evening of October 25, Robert Toombs, who endorsed Breckinridge, reached the Montgomery and West Point depot. Hundreds greeted the Georgia senator, a band played, and a torchlight procession escorted Toombs to his hotel. His defiant message galvanized a capacity crowd at the theater the next night.[34]

There was a corresponding lack of enthusiasm for Douglas. In a letter to Stephen Douglas, John Seibels urged him to make a campaign swing through Alabama. He promised political benefits and declared, "We will take no refusal. Come you must." Douglas accepted the summons. Montgomery was one of the final stops of his campaign. He spoke in Atlanta on October 30 and then addressed Macon and Columbus audiences. He reached Montgomery on the first day of November.[35]

In Alabama's capital, where most considered Douglas too equivocal on the slavery question, the large crowd at midday on November 2 exhibited more curiosity than enthusiasm. After Seibels's introduction, Douglas began a conciliatory speech from the capitol steps. Regarding slavery, he commended the signers of the Constitution for having realized that the laws and institutions that would "suit the granite hills of New England, would be unsuited to the rice, cotton and sugar plantations of the South." Douglas faulted those who had broken up the Charleston convention. They had, he declared, aimed to split the Democratic Party, to assure Lincoln's election, and, according to Douglas, to compel secession. Douglas identified the enemy: Northern abolitionists and Southern disunionists. Concerned about a Republican victory, he argued that Lincoln's election was not a valid excuse for leaving the Union. Most in the audience believed otherwise.

A reception at the Seibelses' residence gave Montgomerians a chance to meet the candidate that afternoon. Later in the day, preparing to move on to Mobile, Douglas and his wife, Adele, boarded the *Virginia*. While Douglas was addressing some final remarks to a riverfront crowd, the deck collapsed. Adele was hurt badly enough to remain at the Seibelses' home for several days. Her husband, assisted by a crutch, and possibly reflecting that the crashing deck reflected his political fortunes, continued down the Alabama River to Mobile.[36]

Lincoln carried every free state and won the election. Breckinridge won ten slave states. His strong showing in the South further highlighted the sectional schism. As had been presumed, the election placed the Union in jeopardy. No argument—for example, that the Democrats still controlled Congress and the Supreme Court or that a compromise could be reached—could halt the rush toward secession. Because Lincoln was identified with the North, his election lent cogency to secessionist arguments. Conventions to consider secession were soon scheduled in South Carolina, Florida, Mississippi, and other Southern states. The position of fire-eaters such as Yancey, once considered extreme, became the new orthodoxy.

A majority of capital city residents had cast their ballots for the most militantly Southern candidate. Breckinridge received 818 votes, John Bell 577, and the city's recent visitor, Stephen Douglas, only 112. Throughout the South a determination to oppose Republicanism persuaded many former advocates of Douglas and Bell to embrace secession. John Phelan articulated the thoughts of many. Writing an antisecessionist acquaintance the day after the Republican victory, the fifty-three-year-old clerk of the supreme court suggested that the state would need to leave the Union in order to protect slavery. It did not matter that Lincoln had promised not to destroy the institution, Phelan maintained; other Republicans would control the president.[37]

Within seventy-two hours of the election, some Montgomerians had gone on record in favor of secession. The sentiments expressed at a meeting held at Estelle Hall on the night of Saturday, November 10, reflected a growing consensus. Charles Pollard, speaking first, urged his fellow citizens to put aside past differences in the interest of a Southern Confederacy. Thomas Hill Watts and James Clanton, both former Bell supporters, indicated their willingness to do so in rousing speeches. The audience, representing a wide cross section of individuals who counted "their wealth by hundreds of thousands and men who earn an honest living by hard labor," shouted its approval.[38] A week later, on November 17, citizens met at the capitol and named Watts and Yancey as delegates to a convention that Governor Andrew Moore had called for January 7 to consider secession. A resolution carried, stating that Alabama would not "remain a member of the government of Abraham Lincoln."[39]

Amid the loud cries for separation came a few voices counseling moderation and caution. Henry Hilliard was certainly one of them. On December 10, at Estelle Hall, the bright and articulate Hilliard was brutally realistic. Secession would probably precipitate war, he noted. Furthermore, the South had no navy, and success was far from certain. Hilliard mentioned the common traditions binding Americans. The man who viewed Lincoln's election as a "calamity" demanded "the abandonment of the crusade entered upon by our enemies." His position—he advocated defending states' rights within the Union—seemed attractive to a dwindling minority.[40]

Hilliard understood the futility of his cause. Visitors to the South in the interregnum between Lincoln's election and the meeting of secession conventions noticed an all-pervasive nationalism. Few events or occasions escaped politicization in Montgomery. When the St. Andrews Society met in late November, the first toast was to the newly formed Confederacy. Members of the True Blues, the Metropolitan Guards, the Mounted Rifles, and a new company, the Independent Rifles, continued their preparations. Several days after Lincoln's election, Captain Joseph Winter spoke of "the present political crisis" and assembled a special meeting of the Metropolitan Guards.[41]

Militant words and resolutions reflected the prevailing passions. At least as revealing were the actions of men who armed themselves and began drilling. The Montgomery Greys formed in December, and the Alabama Fusiliers, clad in bluish gray shirts and black pants trimmed in red, composed yet another company. After Captain Stephen Schuessler, a German-born butcher, had begun training the recruits, an observer remarked, "The company is rapidly advancing in knowledge of the drill and will equal some of the older companies."[42]

Then came the news from South Carolina. On December 20, some 169 delegates unanimously adopted an ordinance of secession. Opinion was much more divided in other states. The so-called cooperationists favored meeting in convention and acting in concert with the other Southern states. Everything short of secession should be tried, but if the decision was made to secede, cooperationists advocated leaving the Union together. Some cooperationists were Unionists who frankly opposed secession under almost any circumstances. More militant "straight-outs" recommended unilateral withdrawal or separate state action. Several states soon joined South Carolina outside the Union. On January 9, secession carried in Mississippi, and Florida left the Union the next day. Few doubted the course that Alabama would take.

Alabamians had gone to the polls on Christmas Eve. Cooperationist candidates ran well in the northern hill counties, where there were comparatively few slaves and there was less enthusiasm for secession. The straight-outs claimed strength in the Black Belt and south Alabama. The 100 delegates who were elected met in the capitol's house chamber on Monday, January 7. Basil Manly, opening with prayer, asked for divine help and declared, "Our conscience doth not accuse us of having failed to sustain our part in the civil compact." This compact was the subject of several days of secret debate. Only the margin remained in doubt when a final vote took place on January 11. At 2:25 in the afternoon, delegates severed Alabama's forty-one-year connection to the Union by a vote of sixty-one to thirty-nine.[43]

In a city enthralled by secession, the reaction was predictable but still somewhat startling. Hundreds of citizens who had gathered at the capitol stormed into the house chamber moments after the vote. Deafening cheers followed when a huge state flag made by local women was raised on the capitol roof. It was fitting that Montgomerians, who represented easily the highest concentration of secessionists in the state, learned of the decision first. A cannon, positioned near the entrance to the capitol grounds, announced the news across the city. Pealing church bells, firecrackers, and general commotion prevailed for the rest of the day and night. An hour after secession, E. Lewis wrote a Kentucky friend, "We here in Alabama are now in a new Republic a foreign country from you Kentuckians." Noting that a lady had fired the first cannon salutation, he added, "So you see not only the men here are for secession but the Ladies." The celebration continued until daybreak.[44]

Several days earlier, on January 8, the convention had taken more definitive action. Delegates voted (along straight-out and cooperationist lines) to honor a request from Governor Madison Perry of Florida. Perry had telegraphed Governor Moore to ask for volunteers to help capture Fort Pickens and other federal military installments at Pensacola. Montgomerians belonging to the True Blues, the Metropolitan Guards, and the Independent Rifles were quick to respond. Several companies from surrounding counties joined the force commanded by Tennent Lomax, who had been promoted to colonel. The forty-year-old Lomax, a veteran of the Mexican War and a man of commanding presence, was a natural officer. On the evening of Wednesday, January 9, approximately 225 men climbed aboard freight cars at the Alabama and Florida Railroad depot. Some wore uniforms and others did not. Most carried a rifle or musket and many had a navy Colt pistol. All seemed enthusiastic. Hundreds of Montgomerians gathered to bid the newly formed Second Alabama Volunteers goodbye.

An extremely volatile situation had developed in Pensacola, where United States troops controlled a naval yard and three forts—McRee, Barrancas, and Pickens. Following the trip south, Colonel Lomax led the Alabamians and some Florida troops to the navy yard and accepted its surrender on January 12. Within hours, Forts McRee and Barrancas had also been occupied without incident. Fort Pickens sat on the western extremity of Santa Rosa Island and commanded Pensacola Bay. Major William Chase, the ranking officer and commander of Florida troops in the area, ruled out assaulting Fort Pickens. As it was, a stalemate developed, and Montgomerians joined others in an indefinite vigil.[45]

In the meantime, another potentially dangerous situation had developed at Fort Sumter in Charleston Harbor. South Carolina authorities demanded that United States forces evacuate the fort, but President James Buchanan refused. As with Fort Pickens at Pensacola, differences remained. War threatened to break out in both South Carolina and Florida.

Montgomery's citizens were proud that local resident Tennent Lomax had presided over the lowering of the American flag at the Pensacola Naval Yard. White Montgomerians also believed that the situation at Fort Sumter called for action. A story in the *Mail* described how rifled cannon could force the "reduction of Fort Sumter."[46] A Home Guard was formed on January 19 at the courthouse. Over a hundred citizens volunteered, representatives from each of the six wards and suburbs were appointed, and a board of protection and officers were designated. Chairman Robert Ware declared, "We are in a revolution. . . . our Northern enemies are threatening us with the sword."[47] The Montgomery Greys and the Alabama Fusiliers, who had not gone to Pensacola, guarded a newly constructed gunpowder magazine near the Alabama River. Women brought the sentinels food on cold nights. When Calvin Sayre returned home, having resigned from the United States Marine Corps, he was congratulated for having abandoned the "old hulk."[48]

In some respects, however, life went on as normal. Some recalled a local man who died in the county jail, "a hapless victim to intemperance." A brass-knuckling thief knocked down and robbed one local resident in late January. Someone shot himself in the foot at a house of prostitution several days later.[49] On January 30 a chimney fire broke out at the capitol, and fire companies rushed to the scene. According to one observer, the firemen were "ready to do what service they could, which could not be much, as there is not a cistern of any consequence nearby."[50] Hundreds enjoyed the English husband-and-wife team of James and Ann Waring Wallack in several Shakespearean productions, including *Macbeth* and *Richard III.* In *Hamlet,* the *Mail* praised Wallack's "masterly personation."[51] It would have been virtually impossible to miss the University of Alabama cadets. President Landon Garland of the recently designated military school hoped that the legislature might appropriate funds for his institution if visiting cadets made a favorable impression. Although one officer worried about "the many temptations that Montgomery would afford," possible benefits overshadowed the potential embarrassment.[52] For the first week of February, the cadets slept on the Concert Hall floor, enjoyed meals at Madison Hotel, and "took Montgomery by storm—convention, legislature, women & all."[53]

The commonplace remained, but dramatic events driven by irrepressible forces soon earned Montgomery a place of transcending importance. By February 1, Georgia, Louisiana, and Texas had left the Union, and the first phase of secession was over. The Lower South—South Carolina, Mississippi, Florida, Alabama, Georgia, Louisiana, and Texas—had become separate republics poised in a temporary limbo of independence and danger. Some kind of union was necessary and had already been envisioned. It remained for the disengaged states to form a provisional government and to anticipate the creation of a permanent government. Doing so involved selecting a time and a place to meet.

Montgomery claimed the honor of hosting the convention. Anticipating the withdrawal of other Southern states, secessionist delegates in South Carolina had taken steps in December to organize a government. Robert Barnwell Rhett, a fire-eater, had proposed on December 26 that slaveholding states (including those that had seceded and those that were preparing to do so) meet at Montgomery on February 13 and establish a government. In early January, nine South Carolina interstate commissioners met in Charleston and devised a procedure for establishing the Confederacy. On January 5, twelve senators in the Lower South released a declaration from Washington, called for secession, and recommended holding a convention at Montgomery no later than mid-February. When the secession ordinance carried in Montgomery on January 11, the convention invited the slave states to a meeting there on February 4.[54]

Montgomery was chosen to become the new nation's provisional capital for a number of reasons. The city offered adequate accommodations, was centrally located, and could be reached by river and rail. Residents had completely embraced secession, so that organizers could anticipate a warm welcome. Gabriel DuVal, an attorney, echoed prevailing sentiments when he wrote a local soldier at Pensacola advocating an assault on Fort Pickens and added, "I wish I was with you to share the perils and honor of the enterprise." Jefferson Franklin Jackson, another prominent attorney, reasoned that because the forts did not defend New York or Massachusetts, the South had a clear right to them. According to Jackson, who had studied history at Yale and had written a paper endorsing the French Revolution, the citizens of the slave states had grievances that differed from those of their seventeenth- and eighteenth-century counterparts but were equally burdensome. Action had been justified in the seventeenth and eighteenth centuries, and strong recourse was a valid choice in the nineteenth century South.[55]

The political turmoil left some Montgomerians feeling bewildered. Lucretia Davidson wrote her daughter, "I just feel it would be a treat if I could be off in some lone country place away from the noise and excitement." Davidson knew that Montgomery, as the provisional capital, would become more exciting and more important, but it could only become noisier in the process.[56]

The Capital of
the Confederacy

As JANUARY ENDED AND THE OPEN-
ing of the Provisional Congress on February 4 neared, Montgomery took on
new life. Hundreds of visitors—politicians, office seekers, soldiers, and adven-
turers—flocked to the Southern capital. Arriving from the east, many newcomers unloaded their bags at the Montgomery and West Point depot. Others
took a steamboat up the Alabama River. Basil Manly wrote his son about
"the army of reporters that have swarmed down this way." Correspondents
from the *Richmond Dispatch,* the *Savannah Morning News,* the *New Orleans
Delta,* and other newspapers were soon crowding into the telegraph office on
Court Square.[1]

The most ubiquitous were people looking for jobs. Many were less interested in the Confederacy than in their own livelihood. The government
needed secretaries (male only) and clerical staff. Army appointments were
no less attractive. People bearing letters of recommendation jockeyed for
position overtly, unapologetically, and incessantly. One observer wryly commented that the applicants' numbers could "put to flight any opposing squadron that an enemy could place in the field."[2] One of a few Northern observers, a reporter for the *New York Herald,* concluded that Montgomery had

"become a focal point of interest to the whole nation." The city basked in the attention.[3]

The bright sunlight on February 4 contrasted sharply with the overcast, rainy days of recent weeks, and conditions seemed to augur well for the new nation. Thirty-seven delegates representing six states took their seats in the senate chamber that Monday; thirteen congressmen from Texas had not arrived. The curved second floor gallery was packed with onlookers. At noon, Congressman William Chilton of Montgomery called for order, and the new government was inaugurated.

For the next three and a half months Congress met at the capitol. A pattern developed. Delegates began business at ten o'clock each day and worked through most of the afternoon. Sometimes they reconvened later and labored into the evening. Deliberations took place behind closed doors, and debate remained secret. President Howell Cobb daily called the convention to order, one of Montgomery's ministers offered a prayer, and shortly afterward the galleries emptied. The arrangement led one correspondent to label the hall the "Temple of Mystery and Birthplace of Liberty." Sunday was a day of rest, and a recess was declared between March 17 and April 28.[4]

The government took shape quickly. On February 8, delegates framed and adopted a provisional constitution. Jefferson Davis was elected president and Alexander Stephens vice president. Davis was soon to arrive from Mississippi. Alexander Stephens, a Georgia congressman who was already present, was inaugurated on February 11. Samuel Rice, a local lawyer, introduced the vice president to a large audience in the senate chamber. No stirring, defiant address marked the occasion. Stephens, who turned forty-nine that day, humbly thanked the assembly for electing him and, anticipating Davis, deferred to him.

Railroad connections between Mississippi and the Alabama capital were incomplete. Davis therefore took a roundabout route through Chattanooga, Atlanta, and Columbus. Some of Montgomery's leading citizens—James Clanton, Samuel Reid, Samuel Arrington, and others—met him at West Point, Georgia, on the evening of Saturday, February 16. Eighty-eight miles to the west, and several hours later, the train came to a halt at the Montgomery and West Point depot. It was about 10:00 P.M., but a large crowd had gathered. The thin and dignified man who stepped from the train spoke briefly. Davis warned that there would be military reprisals if the Lincoln administration interfered with the formation of the Confederacy. Davis flatly stated that the time for compromise had passed.

Jefferson Davis, president of the Confederate States of America,
as he appeared in 1861. This portrait may have been made in
Montgomery. *Courtesy of the Alabama Department of Archives and History,*
Montgomery, Alabama.

A carriage conveyed Davis the short distance to his lodgings at the Exchange Hotel near Court Square. At the Exchange, Davis made short remarks
from a balcony. He drew a by now familiar analogy between the Southern
cause and that of the Revolutionary War forefathers. The Mississippian did
not have to convince the enthusiastic audience. Yancey, Montgomery's best-
known proponent of secession, then spoke briefly and made the comment for
which he is most remembered: "The man and the hour have met." The scene
became legendary.[5]

The inauguration was set for February 18. Plans for the occasion called

An artist's depiction of William Lowndes Yancey introducing Jefferson Davis at the Exchange Hotel. This was the occasion of Yancey's famous remark "The man and the hour have met." *Courtesy of Fouts Commercial Photography, Montgomery, Alabama.*

for a processional beginning at the Exchange, continuing half a mile up Market Street, and ending at the western end of the capitol. There Davis would take the oath of office. There was an unmistakable local flavor to the proceedings. The Independent Rifles, recently returned from Pensacola, and the Alabama Fusiliers, who had never left the state, accepted invitations to march in the parade. Colonel Tennent Lomax, still in Pensacola, provided a carriage and six handsome gray horses for the presidential party. William Snow, a veterinary surgeon, agreed to drive. Hugh Watson, manager of Montgomery Hall, was chosen grand marshal, and Frank Arnold, a German musician, agreed to direct the recently formed brass band. Basil Manly would deliver the invocation.

The ceremonies in Montgomery preceded the Washington inauguration of Abraham Lincoln by several weeks, caught the attention of the nation, and drew comment in London and European capitals. Indeed, the inauguration of Jefferson Davis was an event without precedent in Montgomery. Men, women, and children took to the streets early on February 18. Several thousand visitors had come to town for the occasion. More than any other single event the inauguration gave focus and a sense of being to the Confederacy.

On a Monday that was anything but ordinary, dignitaries, soldiers, and band members took their places in the parade line forming on Montgomery Street. The pace quickened at noon, when Davis emerged from the hotel and stepped into the elegant presidential carriage with its saffron and white lining. Alexander Stephens, Basil Manly, and Captain George Jones, who acted as a military escort, rode with Davis in the open carriage. At the cue of Marshal Watson, who carried a baton bound in red, white, and blue, the slight climb up Market Street began. Frank Arnold's band and several military companies formed the vanguard. The presidential party followed, and carriages conveying various officials, including the Montgomery City Council, trailed behind. Mounted assistant marshals, one from each of the seven states, escorted the procession. Between 6,000 and 8,000 cheering people watched as "Dixie" and martial music filled the air. Some were perched on rooftops, others in windows, and more moved forward toward the capitol grounds. Cannon were fired periodically. One observer called the scene "grand beyond description."[6]

At about 12:30, William Snow stopped the presidential carriage at the capitol. As the band struck up the "Marseillaise," William Chilton and Robert Barnwell Rhett escorted Davis through the crowd and into the building. Within the hour, the assembled Congress had signed the provisional constitution. The president-elect spoke briefly, congressmen filed out to their seats, and Davis took his place on the raised portico between Howell Cobb and Alexander Stephens.

In the meantime, the spectators, many of whom had walked up from Market Street, maneuvered for position. Manly offered a prayer and then made way for Howell Cobb, who introduced Davis. The president-elect en-

The only surviving photograph of the inauguration of Jefferson Davis, c. 1861. *Courtesy of Fouts Commercial Photography, Montgomery, Alabama.*

gaged in no arcane philosophizing, but neither did he deliver a fiery oration. In what one observer called a "calm but forcible" manner, Davis began reading a brief speech justifying secession. At various points, those who could hear him, and even those who could not, responded loudly.[7] According to one well-positioned witness, latecomers stood little chance of hearing Davis. Ellen Noyes Jackson, the Boston-bred wife of the lawyer Jefferson Franklin Jackson, was present with her children. She later wrote, "The crowd about used them up." William Culver, an employee of Archibald McIntyre, the local photographer and ambrotypist, took the only surviving picture of the inauguration. Davis concluded his remarks within twenty minutes, and moments later Cobb administered the oath of office. The executive carefully recited the oath and, after repeating, "so help me God," kissed a large Bible. Jubilation followed. The proud citizens of the Confederate States of America celebrated well into the night. That evening, at Estelle Hall, Davis and others attended a reception.[8]

Several days later, in a letter, Davis told his wife, Varina Howell, about the "large and brilliant" inauguration.[9] He had by then settled into room 101 of the Exchange Hotel. Until offices were complete elsewhere, Davis conducted governmental business in a parlor connected to his room. The executive insisted on informality and prided himself on rustic simplicity. Raphael Semmes soon met with him. The future privateer was amazed to see Davis himself write out an order and described his style as "unpretending." Davis often took his meals casually in the hotel dining room.[10] Varina did not join him until early March, but the president told her that the Alabama capital was "a gay and handsome town" and one likely to prove "not an unpleasant residence."[11]

The new chief executive immediately settled into a grinding routine. Partly because it was the largest and best hotel, and partly because it housed Davis's office, the Exchange became the unofficial center of the new nation. No less than the Willard Hotel in Washington, it served as a sort of political clearing house and mecca. Various shops occupied the first floor, and three floors of rooms accommodating about 300 guests were above. The guileless, the scheming, and anybody else who wanted information climbed a flight of stairs to the second floor bar and reading room, or lobby. One observer described the lobby as a "pretty respectable conversational Parliament." Another felt it "smacked no little of pandemonium."[12] At night, the crowd and noise intensified. Army and cabinet appointments, pronouncements about the border states, and the work of Congress dominated conversation. One participant

The Exchange Hotel, c. 1874. This photograph, made after the war, shows the building as it looked when Montgomery was the capital of the Confederacy. *Courtesy of Fouts Commercial Photography, Montgomery, Alabama.*

decided that the subjects were discussed "with heat" that was "equaled only by ignorance."[13]

More business was conducted at the Government Building, a recently constructed brick structure, located at the corner of Bibb and Commerce Streets and within a block of the Exchange, that became the Confederacy's headquarters. It was neither the city's most aesthetically appealing public structure nor the least. One observer compared the Government Building to "a great red brick pile."[14] Another likened it to "a handsome first-class warehouse."[15] The unadorned two-story edifice was utilitarian. A plain sign identified Davis's office on the second floor. Modest signs pointed the way to other individuals who wielded immense power. One observer, desperate to excuse a certain bleakness in appearance, ascribed "old Republican" virtue to the government.[16] All too aware of what was lacking, Henry Capers, a clerk in the Treasury Department, arranged with John Powell, who ran a furniture store, for delivery of a desk, chairs, and a table. Nothing could be taken for

The Government Building, headquarters for the Confederate States of America, as it looked c. 1905. *Courtesy of Fouts Commercial Photography, Montgomery, Alabama.*

granted, and Capers found it necessary to train his "green office boy" in "the proper mode of receiving a visitor at the front door."[17]

Activity was at its most frenetic at the War Department. Early in March, Congress began the work of setting up an army and a navy. Hundreds sought appointments. Future Southern military heroes arrived, including P. G. T. Beauregard, Joseph Johnston, and Kirby Smith. The acclaimed Indian fighter Earl Van Dorn of Mississippi traveled to Montgomery. Ben McCullouch of Texas, another established foe of Indians, registered at the Exchange. Charles Henningsen knew more about political revolutions than about Indians. Henningsen had followed the Hungarian revolutionary Louis Kossuth and had more recently taken part in William Walker's ill-fated Nicaraguan fili-bustering expedition. William Hardee, the author of the much-consulted *Light Infantry Tactics,* advised Secretary of War Leroy Pope Walker regarding army organization. Finding himself constantly besieged, Walker took out-of-the-way routes back to his hotel. Stephen Mallory, secretary of the navy, spent much of his time conducting interviews.[18]

Some soldiers arrived on foot or on horseback; others came by rail or took a steamboat on the Alabama River. Hundreds moved on to Pensacola, where the military situation remained tense, but some stayed in Montgomery indefinitely, awaiting orders and camping on the edge of town. From neighboring Georgia came the Macon Independent Guards and the Ringold Guards. Montgomerians welcomed the soldiers with hams, breads, and desserts. From nearby Greenville, the Greenville Guards, wearing new gray uniforms trimmed in red and marching in step behind a flag bearer, presented a handsome appearance. In more casual moments, thanks to local citizens, they enjoyed "liquors in abundance."[19]

Montgomery had been a quiet place significant chiefly as Alabama's main place of government. Virtually overnight, however, it became a booming city and the capital of a nation. In saloons pianists pounded out the "Marseillaise" incessantly as boisterous and intoxicated patriots confused the words. James Morgan, later famous as a commerce raider, witnessed an odd scene. At one hotel he watched and listened as a German piano player repeatedly struck up the French anthem while a drunken Southern clientele butchered the melody and lyrics. On a rare break Morgan heard the German mutter, "Dom the Marseillaise."[20] Visitors occupied themselves differently. For a week following the presidential inauguration, Dr. David Grieve of Louisville nightly delivered a lecture at Estelle Hall entitled "Mental Philosophy," during which a hot air balloon was launched "for the amusement of the audience." Some local residents flocked to theatrical productions such as *Katy O'Sheal, The Young Prince,* and the comedy *Still Waters Run Deep.*[21]

Montgomerians welcomed some of the Confederate elite into their homes. The unofficial hosts were the same people who habitually entertained lavishly and who generally moved in higher social circles: the Pollards, the Gilmers, the Goldthwaites, the Bibbs, the Seibelses, the Semples, the Wares, the Hilliards, the Elmores, the Judges, the Wattses, the Betheas, and others. Cards carried formal invitations to dinner parties and teas. In early February, Georgia congressman Thomas Cobb wrote his wife, Marion, of an upcoming party at John Seibels's, "where the town promises to exhibit."[22] On February 9 several hundred people attended the "grand affair" at the Seibelses' Italianate home on Adams Street. Such elegant dinners might start with a first course of oyster soup, followed by fish salad and oysters, with ham, turkey, mutton, or beef—often in combination—as the entrée. Waffles and coffee or tea followed, and a choice of cakes, jellies, charlotte russe, and ambrosia frequently completed the fare. Cobb reported that ambrosia "is considered a great delicacy here," though it "is nothing but sliced oranges and grated coconut." Each course included libations, from wine to brandies and liquor.[23] Charles and Virginia Pollard hosted a party in February that Mary Boykin

Chesnut described as "brilliant."[24] As the month ended, over 300 guests attended a ball given by Benajah and Sophia Bibb. Tables of meat were rivaled by cakes arranged in pyramids. "I never saw so ample a repast," Thomas Cobb exclaimed.[25]

In the social whirligig, Alexander Stephens received numerous invitations. Few evenings could have been as demanding as that of February 28. At five o'clock Stephens arrived at John Seibels's home for dinner and excused himself at seven o'clock to keep an appointment. At eight he was due at the home of Henry and Mary Hilliard, and at ten, before dinner had been served, the vice president left for another meeting. He wrote in frustration of the late meal at the Seibelses' and his premature exit from the Hilliards', where his host seemed "quite surprised" by Stephens's departure.[26]

Varina Howell Davis also became heavily involved in the social scene. After concluding her affairs, the First Lady finally arrived by steamboat on March 1. Acquaintances described the thirty-four-year-old brunette as an attractive woman but not a beautiful one. Accustomed as she was to Washington society, Varina was unfailingly gracious and polished and was popular from the outset. She held her first formal reception, appropriately and without delay, at the Exchange on March 6. At the gathering, according to Mary Chesnut, wife of South Carolina delegate James Chesnut, there were "too many people of note to attempt to name them."[27]

At dinner parties, on the streets, in rollicking saloons, among patricians and the proletariat, talk concentrated on the prospect of war. On February 4, as the Provisional Congress convened at Montgomery, the Peace Conference met in Washington. Answering the call of the Virginia legislature, twenty-one states had sent delegates in a desperate attempt to avert conflict. States outside the Union were not represented. Some Southern observers placed their hopes in the three commissioners whom Davis had selected to negotiate with the Lincoln administration. The priorities of the Southern commissioners included persuading federal authorities to relinquish control of remaining Southern forts. Congress rejected proposals by the Peace Conference in March, however, and Lincoln refused to meet with the commissioners. The president directed much of his March 4 inaugural address to the South. Attempting to allay fears, Lincoln assured Southerners that he would not interfere with the institution of slavery and called secession both illegal and impossible. Lincoln pronounced the Union "perpetual" and steadfastly promised to defend the Southern forts. It seemed clear that he would protect the Union

Varina Davis, First Lady of the Confederacy, c. 1860. *Courtesy of the Alabama Department of Archives and History, Montgomery, Alabama.*

at any cost. Nevertheless, the Confederate Congress unanimously adopted a permanent constitution a week later, on March 11.[28]

As momentous events transpired at the Southern capital, the pedestrian commanded attention as well. Local businesses fired some employees who were members of the True Blues and Independent Rifles and had left their clerking positions for duty at Pensacola. In the ensuing controversy, both companies passed resolutions agreeing to boycott the guilty businesses and firms. A magic show and a traveling animal trainer—with a Brazilian tiger and an 1,800-pound Australian bear—arrived in town during the first week of April and were greeted so enthusiastically that the engagement was extended. Ringleader Lovell was described as a man of "unflinching intre-

pidity" who had "spent most of his life capturing and taming wild animals." [29]
The Reverend A. B. Cabiness, a missionary to China, spoke at the Baptist
church on his recent experiences in the East. His topics included tea growing,
cotton culture, and "the religious condition of the Chinese."[30] Other speak-
ers, according to a reporter for the *New Orleans Picayune,* "favor us with feats
of reason." Also in April, the pugilist Aaron Jones, variously known as "the
bruiser" and "Young Hercules," defeated two Irish opponents.[31]

As might be expected, officials at the Government Building had little
time for the frivolous. Davis, Secretary of War Walker, and others believed
that the situation at Fort Sumter or Fort Pickens would precipitate war.
Montgomerians had focused on Pickens more than on Sumter because Pensacola was nearer and because more local residents were there. Even so,
Montgomerians became better informed about events in Charleston. As
March ended, the *Mail* noted Major Robert Anderson's obstinacy and indeli-
cately suggested that a few "iron pills" might provide the solution.[32] Ellen
Noyes Jackson, who had attended the inauguration, declared, "We will not
trouble him [Lincoln] to take care of our defenses or collect our revenue."[33]

P. G. T. Beauregard, who had met with Davis late in February and had
then assumed command at Charleston, decided with policymakers to keep
the fort from receiving reinforcements. In early April it became apparent that
Federal troops would not evacuate Sumter. Instead, on April 8, the Lincoln
administration announced that an expedition was setting sail to resupply the
fort. In a hastily called meeting that extended into the night, Davis and the
cabinet determined to prevent reinforcement even if doing so meant firing
the first shots of war. Word of the expedition's departure from New York
circulated quickly. Meanwhile, Davis, Walker, and others decided to attack the
fort before the expedition arrived. From the telegraph office on Court Square
orders were tapped to Beauregard on April 10. The general was instructed to
demand immediate surrender. If Anderson refused, Beauregard should "reduce the fort." On April 11, the following day, Major Anderson rejected the
ultimatum. Continuing negotiations failed, and at 4:30 A.M. on April 12, harbor batteries opened fire. The bombardment that began early Friday morning
continued intermittently for the next thirty-three hours.[34]

Montgomerians were among the first to learn of developments. At about
9:00 A.M., a flag went up over the Government Building and the telegraph
office, a signal that shots had been fired. The attack had seemed imminent for
some time. As Basil Manly had written to his son on the previous day, "we
are in hourly expectation of hearing that a collision has occurred at Fort

Sumter." Citizens anxious for details gathered at the Government Building and the telegraph office, where encouraging bulletins were posted all day. That night a crowd went to the Exchange and called for Davis. The president did not emerge, but Walker appeared near midnight. He predicted that the fort would capitulate within twenty-four hours, because a cannonade barrage had damaged Sumter's walls, and the garrison was running low on ammunition. At 12:00 on Saturday, April 14, Anderson surrendered. The Civil War had begun.[35]

In Washington, Lincoln called immediately for 75,000 volunteers to put down the "rebellion." The president gave its supporters twenty days to desist. With conflict seemingly inevitable, the upper South and border states were forced to make a decision. Opponents of secession had prevailed earlier in the spring at Virginia and were also in the majority in North Carolina, Tennessee, and Arkansas. Nonetheless, all of these states would soon leave the Union. On April 29, less than two weeks later, a special extra session of Congress convened at Montgomery. The clerk read a lengthy address by President Jefferson Davis to the assembled representatives of the eleven states that composed the Confederate States of America.

In his speech, Davis reviewed the events leading up to secession. Northern manufacturing interests had enriched themselves at the expense of the agricultural South. More recently "fanatical organizations" had conspired to end slavery. For Davis the Union was a compact of the states, and ultimately the states remained sovereign. The Northern conspiracy had driven Southern states to form a new compact. Davis reviewed the events of the past few months: the Lincoln administration had ignored the peace commissioners and had attempted to resupply Fort Sumter. The president had effectively declared war by calling for volunteer troops. Davis reiterated that the Confederate government desired peace.[36]

Montgomerians agreed with Davis's presentation of circumstances. As the government formed, they had watched, contributed to, and expedited the move toward independence. Women were no less patriotic than men who anxiously volunteered for military service. One local woman, writing of Lincoln, passionately declared, "I blush to think that you and your Abolition crew are quartered, where our illustrious and immortal Washington once presided." Writing anonymously, she pledged resistance, claimed to speak for a united South, including the slaves, and expressed regret that the capital at Washington had become "an asylum for Northern Puritanical, Abolition lunatics."[37] Her words met with the approval of a large majority. Davis had observed in his address that the South wanted only "to be left alone," but few observers thought this outcome very likely.[38]

Although Montgomerians had played little part in the designation of their city as the Southern capital, most enthusiastically approved of its change in status. An exhilarating sense of Confederate nationalism was everywhere apparent together with vanity and local pride. Donated pictures hung in the capitol, where ladies prepared tables of food for congressmen. Amenities and acts of courtesy abounded. Dignitaries at the Exchange found stationery in their rooms. "Of the manners of the citizens," one visitor wrote, "it is unnecessary for me to speak." The wife of Thomas Cobb, finding herself with no place to go while her husband was occupied, could choose from four different invitations.[39]

During the past decade, since its designation as the state capital in 1846, Montgomery had become a small city. Montgomerians, finding themselves at the center of a new nation, contemplated infinitely greater possibilities. Residents launched a campaign to make their city the Confederate capital permanently. A week after Congress opened on February 11, the Montgomery Insurance Building on Commerce Street was offered to the government. This became the Government Building. Another part of the campaign was concerned with locating a home for the Davises. The *Montgomery Confederation* forthrightly declared, "It would be folly and ridiculous to presume that we are not interested in the welfare and expansion of our city."[40]

The first family moved out of the Exchange. For the sum of $5,000 a year, the government rented a two-story Federal home from Edmund Harrison, a local planter and lawyer. In mid-April the Davises moved in. The frame structure, described as a "modest villa" located on the corner of Bibb and Washington Streets, was within walking distance of the Government Building and the capitol. An iron fence enclosed the residence and its well-kept gardens. In these comfortable surroundings, Varina Davis hosted receptions, reaffirmed acquaintances initiated in Washington, and made new friends.[41]

William Howard Russell attended a reception at the home. A correspondent for the London *Times,* Russell had gained renown reporting on the Crimean War. After a visit to Washington in March, where he met President Lincoln, Russell headed south, with the Confederate capital as his destination. The visit began inauspiciously when he arrived at the Montgomery and West Point depot on the night of May 4. A broken-down omnibus transported him to the Exchange, where he found himself obliged to share a poorly kept room with five other men and various insects. "Had it not been for the fleas," the disgruntled visitor commented wryly, "the flies would have been intolerable." Allowed a bed, Russell was thankful that he was not among "the mattress men." His situation improved the next day. Russell met Howell Cobb in the Exchange dining room and was introduced to various dignitaries. Walking up Market Street, Russell noted with some surprise that there were a number of foreign-owned shops and that some stores sold books and music. Later, as he made his way down Market, he witnessed a slave auction. He saw on the block a girl wearing a plain bonnet and leather patches for shoes. As she gazed "at the buyers from a pair of large sad eyes," she reminded him of a typical servant girl back home in London. Slow bidding caused the auctioneer to give up. Russell retired to the Exchange, with its "noise, dirt, drinking and wrangling."

Highlights of the journalist's stay included a visit with Jefferson Davis and a reception at the presidential home. The president's wife impressed Russell as conversational, well mannered, and a "great favorite." Russell was less taken with Alabama's capital during his five-day stay. He compared Montgomery to "a small Russian town in the interior" and doubted that it would remain the Confederacy's permanent capital.[42]

Many agreed with Russell's assessment. In its role as the center of government, the city struggled with various fundamental problems. The several boardinghouses and hotels could not handle the demand for lodging. One incredulous visitor compared accommodations in Montgomery to "camping out." He wrote that "hotels, boarding houses, private apartments, stables, and hen-houses" all "have their occupants in the form of men." Samuel Cooper, Abraham Myers, and David DeLeon (respectively the adjutant general, quartermaster, and surgeon general) quickly wearied of their quarters and moved to what they called the "Ranche." The Louisiana delegation took a cottage. Most newcomers were less fortunate. Unaccountably, the Madison Hotel, recently closed, remained unavailable. Under normal circumstances the Exchange was little more than adequate, and circumstances were anything but normal in the spring of 1861.[43]

Visitors complained about high prices in a city where opportunism was now rampant. Many Montgomerians were no less mercenary than they were patriotic. One critic observed that "fabulous sums" were being asked for house lots and "enormous" rent for dwellings. The price of living was generally high. A public appeal admonished landlords to ask lower rent or to expect the capital to move elsewhere. Accommodations were not alone in being expensive. Retailers arbitrarily raised prices. Alexander Stephens grudgingly paid twice the normal price for an umbrella.[44]

Another problem was the mediocre and limited fare available at restaurants. A patron called the dining room at Montgomery Hall a "den of horrors." On Sunday, given Sabbath restrictions, visitors might find it difficult, if not impossible, to purchase a newspaper or tobacco, much less a glass of beer. At least some observers found Montgomery a backwater, far too provincial a setting to be the national capital.[45]

In late April, when the special session of Congress met, delegates from the most recent additions to the Confederacy—Arkansas, Tennessee, North Carolina, and Virginia—took their seats. The question of removal, not considered during the first congressional session between early February and mid-March, moved onto the agenda now that the war had begun and the Confederacy had expanded.

Some observers had early speculated that, if Virginia joined the Confederacy, Richmond would become the new capital. Acting on instructions from the president, Alexander Stephens left for Richmond when Virginia seceded, soon after the firing on Fort Sumter. The state's convention had voted for leaving the Union, but actual secession depended on the outcome of a May 17 referendum by Virginia voters. Although ratification was not in doubt, the Montgomery government moved quickly in the interim to forge a temporary military alliance. Stephens appeared before the secession convention on April 23. The vice president did not propose relocating the capital, but he used the possibility to persuade Virginia to align itself with the Confederacy. Montgomery had not been designated the permanent seat of government, the vice president noted. Virginia would likely be the main theater of war, and relocation was "quite within the range of probability."[46]

Stephens had returned by the time Congress reconvened late in April. In a different forum—its members had moved across the hall and into the more spacious and better-ventilated house chamber—the question of removal was to receive considerable attention. Of the five Virginia representatives, Robert Mercer Talliaferro (R. M. T.) Hunter was the most influential. Hunter, whose family was one of the state's oldest, had recently resigned from the United States Senate and had been considered for the Democratic presidential nomination in 1860.

Hunter was quintessentially a Virginian. Although his loyalties lay with the South, he was a late convert to secession, having joined the secessionist camp only after the firing on Fort Sumter. His allegiance to the Confederacy, however, was unquestioned, if belated, and so was his interest in having the capital transferred to Richmond. After registering on May 9 at the Exchange, Hunter quickly went to work, arguing, as Thomas Cobb wrote his wife, that the government should move "at once."[47] Hunter, whom Mary Chesnut described as the "sanest, if not the wisest man in Montgomery," made converts, and his cause gained momentum.[48]

Even so, relocation was first officially proposed to Congress not by a Virginian but by William Boyce, a congressman from South Carolina. When the Provisional Congress had opened in early February, Boyce had written Hunter, urging him to push for secession. "Come in," advised Boyce, "& Virginia shall have things exactly as she wants them capitol included." Honoring his promise, Boyce introduced a bill on May 1, authorizing the government's transfer to Richmond. The measure was placed on the calendar. Divisive debate lay ahead.[49]

Opponents contended that relocation would increase the capital's risk of being captured. Just over 100 miles separated Richmond from Washington. The *Montgomery Post,* hardly an impartial commentator, declared that men such as Hunter threatened nothing less than "the great cause of Southern Independence." Some observers framed the argument in terms of justice. They perceived the Virginians as opportunistic latecomers who had hesitated before leaving the Union and did not deserve to have the capital. After all, John Breckinridge, the presidential candidate identified with forging a new nation, had easily carried Montgomery but had finished last among Democrats in Richmond.

One scenario seemed possible to some observers versed in Machiavellian tactics. Richmond would stake its claim as capital, the war would end quickly, and Virginia would remain the seat of government, although it had contributed nothing to achieving independence. If so, Montgomerians complained that citizens of the Old Dominion would undeservedly reap the benefits of government position and patronage.[50]

In the Lower South there was resentment of Southerners who had originally balked at secession. Alexander Stephens privately recorded his fears that the original secessionists might give the Virginia delegates "the cold shoulder." John Beauchamp Jones, the observant war clerk, expressed a similar concern. If some politicians in the Lower South could be sure that there would be no war, Jones believed, they would oppose any affiliation with the border slave states.[51]

Those favoring Virginia as a site for the capital cited its stature and its size.

Richmond was four times larger than Montgomery. With a trace of condescension, the reporter for the *Richmond Dispatch* wrote from Alabama's capital, claiming "hundreds of extraneous advantages possessed by 'Big Richmond' over the agreeably little city of Montgomery." Other observers maintained that relocation might entice several wavering border states to join the Confederacy. Maryland offered the best example.[52]

Most important, proponents assumed that some of the most critical fighting would take place in Virginia. To them logic dictated that the government should be nearby. Some individuals in this camp argued that Davis should lead the Southern forces. Writing from the Executive Mansion on May 10, the First Lady noted the possibility, adding, "I hope it may be done for to him military command is a perfect system of hygiene."[53]

Thomas Cobb remained undecided, but early in May he remarked that support for removal "is growing stronger every day."[54] R. M. T. Hunter marshaled his forces. Watching, John Beauchamp Jones commented that the Virginian "has a way of moving large bodies" and predicted that Hunter would make the critical difference.[55] On May 10, within hours of arriving, Hunter presented a resolution passed by the Virginia secession convention inviting the government to Richmond. The resolution's language gave the Confederate administration considerable latitude. It stated that Congress could designate Richmond as the capital if "the public interest or convenience may require it." In Hunter's opinion, both "interest" and "convenience" would be served by doing so.[56]

Convenience was indeed a consideration. Government officials had been finding Montgomery less convenient since the last session. Increasingly hot temperatures in May caused complaints. Varina Davis remarked to a friend, "This is a very pretty place" and would be ideal "were not the climate as warm as is the enthusiasm of the people."[57] Mary Chesnut had predicted that uncomfortable hotels would sway Congress. Arriving in early May, war clerk Jones's first observations concerned the prevalence of mosquitoes. Thomas Cobb complained of high temperatures, worried about sickness, and informed his wife as the session opened that conditions at the Exchange were "decidedly worse . . . than when we were here last." He added, "There is a good deal of talk about going to Richmond."[58] As an outspoken secessionist, Cobb had wanted to help establish a new nation in the Alabama capital. He was much less certain that Montgomery should continue to be the seat of government. He noted that Davis and all members of the cabinet except Secretary of the Treasury Christopher Memminger favored heading north. Consequently, Cobb assured his wife, "it will be done."[59]

R. M. T. Hunter, the future Confederate secretary of state, had on May 10 offered the resolution relating to removal. That same day Frank Bartow of Georgia introduced a similar resolution. Bartow contended that Virginia's safety, and by implication the security of all the Southern states, depended upon having Jefferson Davis and the Confederate government in Richmond. The vote against tabling the measure was close; the question would be controversial. One observer described opponents of relocation as "the most terrified set of mortals you ever saw" but mentioned the "great vehemence" demonstrated by those who were arguing Richmond's case. On May 11, the next day, a compromise was reached that allowed Congress to meet next in Richmond while the Executive Department remained in Montgomery. The resolution passed, but within the week Davis had vetoed the bill. He declared it unfeasible for Congress and the government to be separated by over 500 miles.[60]

The general public had difficulty determining exactly what was happening, since the congressional sessions were closed to the public. The more discerning observers realized that bold predictions about Montgomery's solid position were premature. Even so, rumors that Richmond would necessarily be selected seemed exaggerated. Confusing matters further was the possibility that Congress might move without the departments. "Confusion" indeed seemed to be the operative word. "One day we have it from sources that a removal has been decided upon," wrote a frustrated journalist, "and the next day a flat contradiction is given." In the meantime the temperature had risen to more than eighty degrees on several days earlier in May.[61]

Most Montgomerians wanted their city to remain the capital. Residents could passionately disagree about the choice of the next mayor, the relative merits of education for women, or the definition of proper public deportment. But a sense of patriotism and an interest in Montgomery's advancement created like minds for the most part when it came to the capital question. It was easy to find a consensus at Jacob Sutter's saloon on Court Street or in any other forum. Not quite everyone agreed. Some observers admitted that removal was in the interest of the Confederacy. Still others, like an unnamed woman who expressed her opinion to Mary Chesnut, favored removal from a fear that Montgomery would otherwise become another Washington, complete with intrigue and dissipation.[62]

The views of assorted Montgomerians, however, had no bearing on the decision. By mid-May, with Congress preparing to adjourn, the capital question, the most outstanding piece of unfinished business, became the special order for Monday, May 20. On the morning of that day, Basil Manly opened the session with a prayer. A recommendation from the Committee of Finance concerned the purchase of army books for tactical instruction. Other routine business came up, but in the afternoon a vote establishing Richmond as the capital, departments and all, drew lines of commitment. It became clear that a majority of delegates from Alabama, Florida, Mississippi, and South Carolina opposed the move and that most members from Arkansas, Georgia, Texas, and Virginia favored it. When representatives from Louisiana split, the resolution failed. The faction encompassing the states of the Lower South had temporarily prevailed, but within the hour the question was reconsidered. The lines shifted slightly but crucially. George Ward, a Florida delegate, and Alexandre DeClouet of Louisiana swung their states into Hunter's column. Twenty-four delegates voted for removal, and twenty voted against it. Most important, six of the nine states approved of the move. William Chilton, the Montgomery lawyer who sat in Congress, tried one last time to save the capital. His motion to postpone the question failed. It remained only to secure the approval of Jefferson Davis. The next day, presumably at the Government Building, the executive provided his signature.

Some matters were certain. Congress had strongly disagreed on various issues, including the capital question. Cajoling and deal making took place off the floor. Debate was not recorded, and so it is impossible to summarize the remarks made on the floor. Yet as one knowledgeable observer declared, "no other action of Congress (past or anticipated) has been so harshly criticized." [63] The day after Davis signed the bill, Alexander Stephens wrote his brother, "There are great & rather strong objections" to leaving; "whether it was wise to do so or not the future must prove." [64] Treasury clerk Henry Capers recalled the "respectable minority" that opposed the move and the "regrets sincerely felt and warmly expressed." [65]

Various arguments ranging from the philosophical (Richmond's tardiness in embracing secession) to the practical (the expense of moving) to the strategic (the threat to the capital's security) were invoked in vain. Some members on both sides of the question were motivated by considerations of personal gain. Neither group was blameless in this respect. Yet Congress was generally guided by sincere and legitimate differences rather than by self-serving considerations. As Emory Thomas has noted in his study of Richmond during the Civil War, military considerations were paramount and calculations relating to strategy most compelling. Jefferson Davis and others accepted the argument that the government should be near the front lines. It was clear that Virginia was soon to be invaded. And on May 24, just days after the definitive vote had been taken, Federal troops occupied Alexandria.[66]

Richmond offered important advantages. Montgomery had significant shortcomings. No single inherent drawback—high prices, the mosquitoes, the heat, or constraints of space—fully accounted for removal. Even so, in combination, they paved the way by creating considerable dissatisfaction. William Howard Russell, learning the news while visiting New Orleans, was not surprised. The *Times* correspondent observed that Montgomery's accommodations suited the "modest wants of a state legislature" but "vanished or were transmitted into barbarous inconveniences by the pressure of a central government."[67] Thomas DeLeon noted that the city's population was hospitable and that it might legitimately claim to be sophisticated and cultured. Even so, he concluded, "there was still much lacking of what the world expects of a city."[68] Henry Capers, who served with the Treasury Department, expressed his high regard for Montgomery's wealthy, socially polished, and well-educated population but concluded that Richmond was better equipped to be the capital. The ultimate decision was also attributable in part to the persuasive qualities of R. M. T. Hunter, though Hunter had not been obliged to persuade Jefferson Davis. Davis, Thomas R. R. Cobb noted, had favored the move "decidedly."[69]

Congressmen took their seats at the capitol for the last time on Tuesday, May 21. Two and a half months had passed since the brisk and clear February morning when the Provisional Congress had convened. The last day began in the same way as the others. John Mitchell, the Episcopalian rector at St. John's, delivered the invocation. There were few observers on hand. With the passage of time, fewer visitors came to the galleries, just to be ushered out as the session convened.

Congress had appropriated $40,000 for removal. The government contracted immediately with a local furniture store to do much of the packing. Laborers loaded most of the archives on cars at the West Point Railroad depot. Appropriately, the weather was hot and sultry. "Recall to mind the last time you moved your household from one tenement to another," a journalist wrote, "and you can form a tolerably good idea of the condition of Montgomery." Jefferson Davis's departure contrasted starkly with his arrival. He and Varina attended St. John's Church on the morning of Sunday, May 26, as usual. Without attracting much notice, the couple boarded a Montgomery and West Point train in the evening and began the journey north. The president, taking a seat in a rear car, was suffering from chills and exhaustion. The departing train left silence in its wake. Behind it stood the suddenly empty and silent capitol where a nation had been born.[70]

A resident had recently written of designating Montgomery as the permanent capital and "the many advantages [it] would afford our city." Montgomerians accepted that logic. Civic pride, a sense of Southern nationalism, and not insignificantly, an eye for financial profit, shaped public opinion. Each of the four newspapers editorially opposed removal. As the switch to Richmond became more probable that spring, Montgomerians dissented, sometimes vigorously. The collage of arguments they offered, whether selfless or not, made no difference. The ultimate decision was disappointing, but there were other considerations. The goal of independence was paramount. What the attempt to achieve it would involve, few Montgomerians could imagine.[71]

3

A Military Post

THE WAR WOULD BE WON OR LOST
on the battlefield, but failure was certain if soldiers lacked equipment and
supplies. At the outset, Congress established the Quartermaster, Commissary
General, Medical, and Ordnance Departments. Subsistence, or Commissary,
was ultimately responsible for feeding Confederate troops. Quartermaster
functionaries collected supplies, oversaw the manufacture of clothing and
shoes, coordinated transportation, and performed a multitude of other duties. The Ordnance Department, headed by Josiah Gorgas, was responsible for
arming the soldiers properly. Surgeon General Samuel Preston Moore presided over a growing number of government hospitals. Administration and
efficiency required order, and the Confederacy was divided into territorial
departments, districts, and subdistricts. Posts were designated within the military organizational framework.

In short, a huge bureaucratic network emanating from Richmond took
shape. Department representatives were stationed throughout the South.
Some were vigilant and competent, and others less so. All labored under less
than ideal circumstances. That was certainly true in Montgomery.[1]

The capital initially formed a military post within the Division of Alabama and West Florida. Major Walter Jones served as the post commandant.

He coordinated activities, handed down orders, and generally made policy. Jones took office early in 1863 on the second floor of an office on Commerce Street and remained throughout the war. His tasks were as varied as they were numerous. One of Jones's first orders confirmed the appointment of Captain John Echols as the local provost marshal, to "be obeyed and respected accordingly." A year later, in a typical pronouncement, Jones ordered all citizens to provide the names of soldiers convalescing in their homes. By spring 1864, advancing Union troops under General William Sherman were pressing forces commanded by General Joseph Johnston in Georgia. In Montgomery, Jones fulfilled his limited but essential role by overseeing efforts to send vegetables to Confederate troops stationed there.[2]

Major J. L. Calhoun, the chief purchasing agent and quartermaster for Alabama, also became a familiar figure to local residents. Montgomery was quickly designated as a major quartermaster depot. Shirts, jackets, pants, tents, all camp equipage, and other standard issues were stored there. Calhoun kept steady hours at his office at the corner of Bibb and Commerce Streets. He was in charge of providing raiment for at least 75,000 troops in the field. Isolated orders reveal the pattern of his responsibilities. Calhoun provided a regiment in Atlanta with tents and camp equipage in September 1861. In March 1863, Calhoun received a directive to provide for a legion that was organizing to defend the Gulf Coast. Quartermaster General Abraham Myers specified tents, wagons, and any available stores.

By 1864 Captain William Gillaspie, chief clothing quartermaster for Alabama, was also in Montgomery. There clothes were made as well as stored. An order filled in the spring indicated the scale of operations: 1,000 suits of clothing were provided to General Dabney Maury's command at Mobile. Soldiers on the move were constantly in need of shoes. A shoe manufactory was set up in 1864, and production began in the Winter Iron Works Building on Tallapoosa Street. By late 1864 Captain Gillaspie was employing over sixty shoemakers and about a dozen tailors.[3]

Quartermaster agents also handled the transportation of soldiers and supplies over the two railroad lines leading to and from the city. Edwin Harris, a local cotton broker, received and forwarded goods and generally coordinated government traffic. The Alabama and Florida Railroad line, completed as the war began, greatly facilitated transportation between Montgomery and Mobile. The Montgomery and West Point line, connecting Alabama's capital with Georgia and areas beyond, was even more important. It was a key link in the Confederate railroad trunk line that bisected central Mississippi,

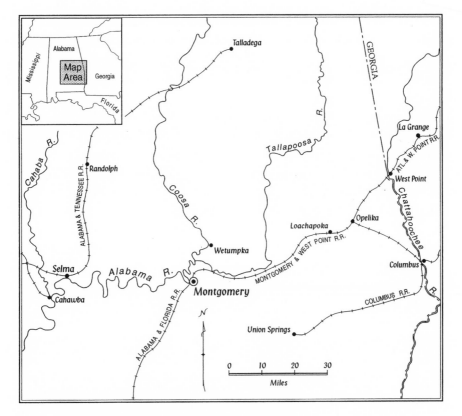

Railroad lines entering and exiting Montgomery, c. 1860.

Alabama, and Georgia before angling north through the Carolinas into Virginia. The vital line connected the western and eastern Confederacy. The Montgomery and West Point depot anchored the north end of Court Street. Several blocks away, at the western end of Bell Street, also near the river, cars arrived and departed from the Alabama and Florida depot. Troops, boxes of rifles, raiment, flour, and other essentials passed through both depots.

Edwin Harris and other officials found their jobs fraught with difficulty. First, the lack of a railroad between Alabama's capital and Selma, forty-five miles to the west, caused extreme inconvenience. All traffic coming from or going to Mississippi had to be forwarded overland or carried on the Alabama River. Another problem was the distance of a mile and a half that separated the Montgomery and West Point depot from the Alabama and Florida depot. Freight had to be unloaded at one depot, conveyed to the other depot or the river, and then reloaded. It took an average of five hours to move a regiment with its baggage and camp equipage from one point to another. The time required meant that huge drayage bills accumulated. As early as December 1861, Charles Pollard, the railroad developer, identified the problem to Quartermaster General Abraham Myers. Pollard proposed linking the lines through the town but lacked the funds to carry out this plan. As it was, Pollard noted, "we are very *poor.*"

Transportation facilities were of critical importance in the summer of 1862, when the largest single movement of Confederate troops by rail was accomplished. The Army of Tennessee under General Braxton Bragg had to be moved from Tupelo, Mississippi, to Chattanooga. Soldiers were taken down to Mobile, up the Alabama and Florida Railroad to Montgomery, over the Montgomery and West Point track into Georgia, and eventually to their destination in Tennessee. Over a period of two weeks, the combined efforts of railroad president Charles Pollard and quartermaster officials made it possible for over 40,000 troops to be conveyed to and through Montgomery.[4]

The river, wharf facilities, warehouses, and location in the fertile Black Belt made Montgomery the prewar hub of the market economy in central Alabama. These circumstances also accounted for the city's establishment as an important subsistence depot. Meat, corn, and other provender were stockpiled in warehouses. An observer commented that government corn was "just pouring into our city," as "if some modern Joseph [had] been inspired to collect and store up provision against the time of famine."[5] W. W. Guy, district commissary for thirteen south Alabama counties, ran the district from his office in Montgomery. His task primarily involved procuring food and supplies for the Confederacy. Writing early in 1863, Guy mentioned that hogs were suffering from cholera and that cattle had been reduced by the demands of the army and the civilian population. Despite the problems, he had high hopes for the corn, pea, and potato crops. An official praised Guy's concern for the "public interest" and approved the work habits of a man who "transacts business at all hours of the day."[6]

Commissary officials also purchased and slaughtered cattle. Hospital patients consumed some of the beef locally, and thousands of pounds went out to troops elsewhere. Quartermaster officials used the dried hides as leather for shoes, saddles, and other equipment. T. J. Ambrage, a Texas infantryman wounded at Gettysburg, acted as herdsman for a time. Commissary employees at the government bakery on Court Square produced 2,000 pounds of bread daily and "good hard tack." When the Army of Tennessee passed through in 1862, Commissary officials provided fresh supplies of bread. An official in late 1864 called Montgomery "one of the largest distributing depots."[7] By then there was so much Confederate beef in warehouses that there was fear the meat would spoil.

Efforts to manufacture weapons were more modest. Direction of the arsenal fell to Major Charles Wagner. Work began haltingly near the Montgomery and West Point depot early in 1862. Machinists, blacksmiths, gunsmiths, and harness makers labored there. Small arms were repaired, and percussion caps were manufactured. Horse harnesses, infantry accoutrements, haversacks, and canteens were produced. Even so, a lack of adequate machinery and competent machinists hindered the operation. After a visit in July 1862, Governor John Gill Shorter wrote Secretary of War George Randolph with praise for Wagner's "energy and skill" and to recommend that he be promoted. Shorter informed Randolph that Wagner labored "amidst difficulties almost insurmountable."[8]

John Mallet, a chemist at the University of Alabama, visited Montgomery at about the same time to inspect munitions facilities. Mallet had recently been placed in charge of Confederate ordnance laboratories. Mallet was profoundly unimpressed. He reported that there was "no laboratory work doing here" and that Wagner was not optimistic about the future.[9] The potential loss of J. W. Cory, the machinist, could only make the situation worse. When Cory was threatened with field service early in 1863, Major Wagner protested to ordnance chief Josiah Gorgas. Wagner called Cory "indispensable to me."[10] By the spring of 1864, Wagner issued a call for mechanics, tinners, carpenters, and other craftsmen with the words "none need apply but competent workmen." The pool of qualified workers was severely limited in a city that, like the South as a whole, was decidedly nonindustrial.[11]

Alabama's capital made a better medical center than a place of arms manufacture. Montgomery, located in the Deep South, was seemingly safe from Union advances and was well served by railroads. In time, six Confederate hospitals were established. The city became the destination for thousands of wounded, sick, and dying troops traveling by steamboat or by rail. Hospital representatives frequently met the wounded at the depots and the wharf. Some soldiers made their way to a hospital under their own power; others were carried in on litters. Whatever the circumstances, it was necessary to register patients, to prepare statements of their condition, and to assign beds. The patient census fluctuated. Soldiers filled less than half the beds at times, but during periods of intense military activity elsewhere, the hospitals quickly became overcrowded.

As in other Southern locales, various buildings in Montgomery that had served other purposes were requisitioned as sanctuaries for soldiers. A large three-story brick building at the corner of Bibb and Commerce Streets was the first to be converted. Treatment began at General Hospital in late 1861 or early 1862. Just across the street, on another corner of Bibb and Commerce, Ladies Hospital began receiving patients later in 1862. The building's role seemed appropriate, given that the structure had housed the Confederate government earlier, when Montgomery was the Southern capital.

In General and Ladies Hospitals, as at similar government hospitals, medical officers handled administrative tasks. There were surgeons of various ranks, nurses (often male), druggists, matrons, laundresses, and general servants. Surgeon Henry Green, a Georgia physician, was in charge by late 1862 at General Hospital. George McDade of New Orleans and J. G. Scott, who had been stationed at Pensacola, performed surgery. Other surgeons came and went. Some men, such as Francis Hereford, who had been wounded at Shiloh, had served in the field. As the war continued, more hospitals were established, and the number of individuals involved in providing medical care increased. H. Dohrmir, a native of Germany, had been a steward on a Mississippi River steamboat before coming to work at a local government hospital.[12]

The situation at General and Ladies Hospitals differed from that at government hospitals in only minor respects. The odor of sulfur, chloroform, and alcohol greeted the visitor. The wards held over 300 patients when they were filled to capacity. Some were ambulatory; others lay prone or were propped up on straw-filled mattresses. Soldiers suffered from intestinal disorders such as dysentery, typhoid and various fevers, pneumonia, and scurvy. Some soldiers had been superficially wounded; others were horribly disfigured. The surgeons removed bullets and shrapnel, amputating when necessary. Almost all surgery was conducted while the patient was anesthetized. As Julian Chisolm wrote in his widely circulated *Surgery Manual,* "the effects of chloroform are wonderful in mitigating the suffering of the wounded."[13] Each day ended at 9:00 P.M. with lights out. As General Hospital's chief surgeon explained, "sleep is essential to a sick man."[14]

In these settings, uniformed surgeons labored on behalf of humanity and the Confederacy. Some patients survived despite a dire prognosis. Many did not. Edward Moren, a doctor, legislator, and resident of Bibb County, watched a young man die over a period of days in November 1861. Moren speculated that the soldier meeting death instantly on the battlefield was better off than "he who dies of a lingering disease." In May 1862, twenty-two soldiers died at General Hospital. Six months later, in December, there were seventeen recorded deaths. During August and September of 1863, roughly one patient was lost every three days.[15] Most were buried unceremoniously in the cemetery northeast of town. As the *Advertiser* gloomily observed, "the funerals of soldiers are becoming such common things in these days as hardly to attract attention."[16]

General and Ladies Hospitals came within the jurisdiction of Samuel Stout, who served as the medical director of the Army of Tennessee. In October 1863, Stout placed Watson Gentry in charge of Montgomery hospitals. No local Confederate official shouldered more responsibility than Gentry. A veteran of the battlefields at Corinth, Shiloh, Perryville, and Murfreesboro, he was a thirty-two-year-old Tennessean with vast experience. When asked to take charge of the hospitals, Gentry assured Director Stout, "The ship will neither strand or be lost, from the want of a captain."[17]

Since the early 1850s the Madison House at the corner of Market and Perry Streets had provided lodging. The four-story brick building was converted into a hospital in 1863. The honeycombed structure accommodated almost 300 patients. Gentry declared that "any poor soldier from the front" billeted there "may think himself fortunate." Courtney Clark, who had considerable field experience in Virginia, soon became chief surgeon. Throughout the network of Southern hospitals, the food ranged from miserable to acceptable, but at Madison Hospital, patients enjoyed beef, chicken, bacon, and plentiful vegetables. Surgeon Clark offered Stout convincing testimony of the quality: the staff ate the food.[18]

Madison Hospital was located across the street from Concert Hall, which had been converted into a hospital by 1864. About 250 patients were housed in two large halls and other smaller rooms. William Holt eventually became the most important surgeon. Other soldiers recovered at Watts and Stonewall Hospitals on the edge of town near the Alabama and Florida Railroad depot. These hospitals were established adjacent to each other in 1863–1864 and were little more than clusters of tents. Such hospitals proliferated throughout the South as a means of providing quick and cheap care for soldiers. At Stonewall Hospital, which consisted of canvas gathered around brick chimneys, two patients shared a tent. Watts also had a temporary appearance, and Surgeon Gentry wrote of the hospital's "elastic capacity." Patients sent there were deemed to need less care.[19]

Dr. Watson Gentry, who supervised Montgomery hospitals through much of the war, c. 1875. *Courtesy of the Susie Gentry Collection, Tennessee State Library and Archives, Nashville, Tennessee.*

Watson Gentry supplied both order and discipline. Within weeks of arriving, Gentry had written Director Samuel Stout that the hospitals "are not popular Institutions with the citizens on account of their mismanagement." Besides, "they have neither system or the proper concern for the well doing of their patients."[20] Administrative problems were common in all hospitals and did not cease when Gentry arrived. Professional deportment was sometimes sorely lacking. Heavy drinking threatened to end the tenure of Assistant Surgeon Robert Campbell at Stonewall Hospital. When Gentry was

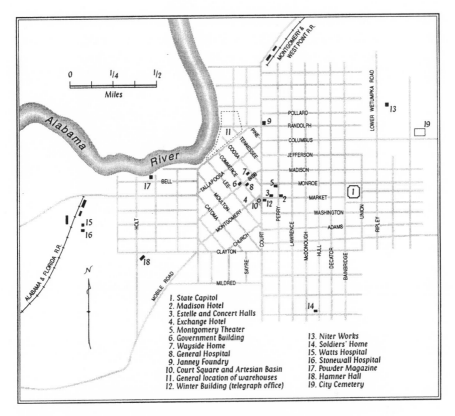

Montgomery streets and wartime landmarks as they appeared in 1860.

unforgiving, Campbell appealed to Samuel Stout. The surgeon claimed to have taken "a solemn mental vow . . . that I will never indulge in intoxicating liquors of any shape or form."[21] Gentry praised a steward as "one of the best druggists I think I ever saw" but lamented that "women is the trouble." When Samuel Bemiss, assistant medical director of the Army of Tennessee, inspected conditions in January 1864, he found matters in general compliance with guidelines. In some wards, however, Bemiss observed patients eating nuts, smoking, and even cooking potatoes in fireplaces and stoves. According to Bemiss's report, two surgeons specifically had "no appreciation of the importance of a Surgeon's duties," and one of the men "would be greatly benefitted by a little field service."[22]

Gentry had promised to place local hospitals in "Tennessee Department order."[23] It was important to achieve this goal, given the events of the spring and summer of 1864. As expected, the Army of the Potomac under General Ulysses Grant advanced on Richmond. Developments in Georgia, however, had more immediate consequences for medical officials in Montgomery. Forces under General William Sherman left the Chattanooga area that spring and headed south toward Atlanta. Various engagements followed between May and July as the Army of Tennessee attempted to check the move. Thousands were injured and killed at Reseca, Kennesaw Mountain, Peachtree Creek, and elsewhere. The wounded were carried in unprecedented numbers over the Montgomery and West Point Railroad line to Alabama's capital. As early as May an observer predicted that the "hospitals will soon have their quota."[24] Patients were jammed into General, Ladies, Madison, and Concert Hall and also Stonewall and Watts on the periphery. Gentry soon informed Stout that all six "are full to their utmost capacity."[25]

Space was not all that gave out. So did medicine, soap, bandages, and manpower. From Concert Hall, Surgeon William Holt appealed to the "patriotic and charitable people of Montgomery" for material to dress wounds.[26] Courtney Clark begged in June for milk, butter, eggs, and "green vegetables of all kinds" to combat scurvy at Madison Hospital. Clark could call on only one surgeon for assistance. In extreme need of medical expertise, Surgeon Gentry pressed into service a half dozen local doctors.[27]

As the fighting wore on, the procession of mangled, feverish, and often dying men continued unabated from Georgia. Jehu Mabry, a Louisiana soldier, had been wounded at the Battle of Reseca. Mabry correctly assumed the worst about his future. On his deathbed he was penitent and admitted to having been "very wicked."[28] Knowing that the end was near, M. M. Saunders, an Arkansan, confided to a chaplain that he wished but to see his mother and to know his "country free and independent."[29]

Despite the problems, conditions at Concert Hall were stable, if crowded, during the summer months. The staffs at General and Ladies hospitals were coping satisfactorily. Surgeon William Cole lacked sufficient help at Stonewall Hospital, but Gentry had pressed into service an assistant surgeon who ironically had come to Montgomery for treatment. The upbeat Gentry promised Stout that "we will get along" but reserved the right "to call on you when I get in the mire and can't get out."[30] He did appeal to Stout in August when a surgeon at Stonewall became incapacitated and Gentry needed more personnel. As matters stood, "we have plenty of Gangrene & are doing everything to stop its spread." The medical staff had little rest for the remainder of the war.[31]

At the post, Montgomerians played an important role. Some held places of extreme responsibility. Mack Copeland, a local cotton broker, was the depot commissary, and Edwin Harris coordinated transportation, a formidable task indeed. Various "citizen doctors" worked at the hospitals. And there were other, faceless laborers. A significant number were slaves. Given the heavy concentration of blacks in Montgomery and the work requirements in the departments, it was logical that slaves would fill the labor void. As a consequence, blacks necessarily performed a wide variety of tasks. Mack Copeland depended on over twenty black workers. The slave work force slaughtered the cattle for the Commissary Department. At the Commissary Department there was a black cooper, and another slave worked at the government bakery. Edwin Harris depended upon at least fifteen slaves to load and unload supplies at the railroad depots. Sometimes slaves were impressed by government officials, and after the fact, their owners notified. "There is a right way and a wrong way of doing a thing," the *Mail* protested in 1864, "and impressing a negro on the streets . . . is certainly not the right way."

Slave labor became more essential as whites were conscripted to fill undermanned Southern armies. When the shoe factory opened in 1864, quartermaster representative A. P. Calhoun promised slave owners fifty dollars per month for the services of capable black shoemakers. Black women acted as laundresses and nurses, and slaves carried out other important functions in the hospitals as well. In 1864, Surgeon John Watters at General Hospital advertised for eight black women and men because of the crowded conditions.[32]

Richmond, Chattanooga, Vicksburg, and other points were of crucial military importance for the Confederate command. Montgomery was not, but Alabama's capital fulfilled a critical role as a depot and transportation nexus. The Alabama River and railroad lines made the city an important conduit. Edward Moren, the doctor and legislator, decided that Montgomery was a "sort of funnel through."[33] On one day in June 1864, some 10,000 sacks of corn were deposited. An observer reacted with disbelief when he read a circular stating that soldiers lacked meat rations. He doubted the shortage given the "huge pile of bacon in the Commissary Department here." Warehouses held enough uniforms to outfit a division. A quartermaster log listed 385 ovens, 900 tin cups, 1,024 iron camp kettles, 4,321 water buckets, 5,189 skillets, and 6,637 mess pans. Six hospitals with over 30 surgeons and 200 staff members could accommodate more 1,300 patients.[34]

Very little functioned smoothly in the Confederacy, and the post at Montgomery was no exception. The size and scope of operations made problems inevitable. At the armory, undermanned and poorly trained mechanics worked with inadequate equipment. Late in the war the armory was pronounced "idle."[35] Unprecedented traffic also wore down the railroad track. Locomotives were overworked and began moving more slowly. The situation had greatly deteriorated by the spring of 1863. "If the war continues," President Charles Pollard predicted to Congressman William Chilton, "the road will be completely run down." Recalling the transportation of the Army of Tennessee over the rails in 1862, the normally undaunted entrepreneurs admitted, "if it had to be done now I should begin the work with a degree of apprehension." Supplies continued to be transported slowly and awkwardly across town between the Montgomery and West Point and Alabama and Florida depots. Not until 1864 were the depots connected by rail. Confederate inefficiency caused great expense, loss of time, and enormous choking clouds of dust.[36]

As previously noted, it was often difficult to find competent workers. Provost Marshal John Echols petitioned post commandant Walter Jones for aid early in 1864. Two disabled soldiers were working for him, and he wanted T. B. Stubbs to provide clerical help. A gunshot wound at Chickamauga had ended Stubbs's active service. Invalid soldiers were increasingly called upon to carry out various duties, since able-bodied men were needed in the army. Captain William Gillaspie of the Quartermaster Department identified a pattern of labor problems. By late 1864 he needed tailors and shoemakers. Appealing to higher authorities, Gillaspie explained that he was unable to keep trained workers; by the time he had trained a man, the army had claimed him for field duty. An invalid soldier often replaced the employee, and this untrained individual spent "one half the time in the Hospital & the other half not able to do much work." At the hospitals, conditions remained uneven. The account of a Mississippi soldier who checked into General Hospital in May 1864 after being wounded during the Atlanta campaign is representative. Writing from "Room No. 6," he complained of substitute coffee, poor food, and general neglect.[37]

By early 1864, the military post of Montgomery lay within the broad confines of the Department of Alabama, Mississippi, and East Louisiana. In October, Alabama's capital became part of the Military Division of the West. Major Walter Jones, praised by the *Mail* as "our worthy post commandant," maintained his vigil.[38] Major Charles Wagner struggled at the arsenal, and Major J. L. Calhoun remained committed to his quartermaster responsibilities. District Commissary W. W. Guy was available for consultation at his second floor office on Washington Street. Surgeon Watson Gentry divided his time between the hospitals and his headquarters above Mason Harwell's auction house. A short distance away, near the river, was the commissary warehouse office of Mack Copeland. Copeland reported to work every day at 7:00 A.M. and promised that he would "never close my office until dark." Hundreds of others labored much more inconspicuously. T. J. Ambrage, the herdsman connected to the Commissary Department, was representative. He pursued his unheralded but important small part in the business of the Confederate States of America. What emerged from the welter of departments in Montgomery was the Confederate infrastructure in microcosm.[39]

4

Life and Labor in Wartime

THE SPRING OF 1862 BROUGHT THE
occupation of New Orleans. Union general Benjamin Butler declared martial law, muzzled the press, and required citizens to take an oath of allegiance.
When a Confederate sympathizer hauled down the American flag, Butler
summarily ordered his execution. Sarah Morgan despaired when Union
forces approached Baton Rouge in May. On May 9 she wrote in her diary,
"Last evening came the demand: the town must [be] surrendered. . . . this
is a dreadful war."[1] Other cities fell later. The occupation of Nashville and
Memphis imposed hardships on citizens. Residents of Jackson, Mississippi,
felt the brutality of war when Union troops arrived in May 1863 and, after
doing considerable damage, returned in July to do still more. General William
Sherman called Jackson a "ruined town." Jackson residents commiserated
with their compatriots in Fredericksburg, which had first been occupied by
Union forces in the spring of 1862 and later became a battleground when
the Army of Northern Virginia met the Army of the Potomac. In 1864
Fredericksburg was occupied yet a third time.[2]

Montgomery, by comparison, remained relatively calm. Life changed
quickly when the city ceased to be the Confederate capital. Late in 1861, a
legislator compared the current general lassitude with the frenetic scene of

the previous winter. "I have never been in a city where more quietness and order prevailed," he wrote.[3] W. C. Corsan, who arrived from England in 1862, described Montgomery as "a comfortable quiet country-town." Although volunteering for military service continued, and the Conscription Act forced the less inclined into the army, the city had not been stripped of its military-age males. The Conscription Act exempted hundreds locally. Some of those who were not exempt used guile and influence to avoid service.[4]

One week generally differed little from those that preceded and those that followed. In particular, Sunday was always the same. As before 1861, the churches occupied a special place in the loyalties of many, and the uncertainties of war heightened the devotion of those at home. A visitor in 1861 declared, "There is no city in the world, none even among the puritanical cities of the east, where the Sabbath is more regularly observed than in this capital." Each major Protestant denomination and the Catholic and Jewish faiths had their congregations. If services were not well attended, it was not because of competing activities. Businesses closed, and a strict ordinance halted almost all economic activity.[5] By and large, Montgomerians went to church. A soldier in the Ninth Kentucky Volunteers found himself in Montgomery on Easter Sunday, 1864. "At the usual hour," he wrote, "young and old, rich and poor, were to be seen winding their way to the temple of God."[6]

The churches, pronounced "rather eccentric in their architecture," were all clustered within several blocks of each other. Basil Manly, who had sworn in Jefferson Davis, conducted services at the First Baptist Church on North Court Street until late 1862. When he left, Isaac Tichenor, who had served as chaplain in the Seventeenth Alabama Infantry, took over the pulpit. At that time the Second Baptist Church was rising on Adams Street. Both the fallen and those in good standing received the attention of James Heard, Edwin Baldwin, and Holland McTyeire at the First Methodist Episcopal Church. Johnson Davis worked at his cotton card factory on weekdays and on Sunday often spoke from the pulpit at the Methodist Protestant Church at the corner of Bibb and Moulton Streets. Luther Hill, an intellectual who had originally opposed secession, provided inspiration at the same church. Blacks and whites had always worshiped together, and they continued to do so. The crowd in the pews now also included refugees, soldiers at the post, and ambulatory patients at the hospitals.[7]

Elders screened those who wanted to affiliate with the Presbyterian church. In February 1863, George McDade, a New Orleans surgeon assisting at Madison Hospital, provided "satisfactory evidence of Christian character."

No one could doubt the credentials of Magdelen Wolters, who had been born in Scotland, or her sincerity (she acted as matron at Soldiers Home Hospital). The Presbyterian congregation on Adams Street held the Reverend George Petrie in high esteem. On any given Sunday, several blocks away at the intersection of Madison and Perry Streets, parishioners at St. John's Episcopal Church listened to Rector John Mitchell. Father A.D. Pellicer presided each Sunday (and at Mass) at St. Peter's Catholic Church. The most recently constructed house of worship was the red brick synagogue on the corner of Catoma and Church Streets. Having fled Union-occupied New Orleans, Rabbi James Gutheim led the worship. Members of the Jewish group were principally the Cahns, the Weils, the Strassburgers, and others of German ancestry.[8]

The war did little to disrupt education. Students of grade school age attended private academies. Principal Henry Bacon of the Home School (for girls only) engaged the services of Sarah Follansbee just as the war began. She had recently moved from Philadelphia and found herself almost immediately being called a "Yankee teacher." Follansbee matter-of-factly told the assembled school that she cared about teaching, not politics. She promised to leave if she was not appreciated.[9] Some girls matriculated to Hamner Hall or Cottage Hill Seminary. Hamner Hall, a day and boarding school sponsored by the Episcopalians, opened in 1861. It offered a well-rounded classics curriculum and piano lessons by Victor Kneringer, a "celebrated pianist." Mademoiselle Roche, of French antecedents, also formed part of the cosmopolitan faculty.[10] During the first few months of war, the white-clad students performed the difficult operatic works of Meyerbeer, Bellini, Donizetti, and Rossini. An admirer congratulated Principal Avery Shepherd on "the musical proficiency of his school." In Montgomery as in many other parts of the country, however, most girls received the sparest of educations.[11]

The world demanded more of men. At least three lower schools—the Classical and Mathematical, the Eclectic, and the Select—catered to boys. R. H. Ramsey emphasized composition and declamation at the Select School. Administrators of the Eclectic School claimed to admit only boys of "good moral character." Even so, it may be assumed that some of those attending were less than models of deportment. At the Classical and Mathematical School, students responded to the Irish intonations of Patrick Savage, who had been born in Kirk, Ireland.[12] Franklin Academy was a classics-oriented preparatory school of some repute. The war changed the education given to boys without redefining it. By 1862, Franklin Academy was offering

Dr. William Baldwin, a well-known local physician, c. 1870. *Courtesy of the Alabama Department of Archives and History, Montgomery, Alabama.*

"thorough military training" and had become Franklin Military Academy. Montgomery Military Academy was founded the year the war began. The sons of the genteel, with names such as Bibb, Baldwin, Gilmer, Knox, and Powell, were enrolled there. Boys drilled, wore gray frock coats, slacks, and blue caps, and hewed to military discipline in varying degrees.[13]

Ministers and teachers were exempted from service by the Conscription Acts. So were physicians and a community of doctors who administered to medical needs. William Baldwin was the most prominent. In the summer of 1862, when smallpox threatened, Baldwin wrote Governor Shorter that most people procrastinated until "the disease is brought almost to the door."[14] Others depended upon German-born Gustav Albright, who offered diagnosis and his own homemade and manufactured medicines, including "wine tonics for strengthening persons in a debilitated state." Albright acknowledged that he did not understand the complexities of female disorders, but he insisted that his sister-in-law did. Some child-bearing women called on Sarah Albright for midwifery.[15] Residents also consulted J. A. Clopton, an itinerant physician from Huntsville, who periodically received patients at the Exchange Hotel and who claimed to have attended to dignitaries with "perfect success." Clopton assured that he had "never lost a patient nor had [known] the slightest accident to happen." The physician Samuel Seelye had recently arrived from Maine. His bedside manner did not reveal his secretly held Unionist sympathies.[16]

There was more hardship and suffering in Montgomery during the war years than at any other period in the city's history. Still, citizens did not forfeit all pleasure and entertainment. In the conflict's first year, J. D. Fitz brought his "Panoptician of the South" exhibition to town. Hundreds enjoyed his mechanical portrayal of the bombardment of Fort Sumter and other events connected to "the Revolution of 1861."[17] Edward Moren, the Bibb County legislator and doctor, himself unable to attend the performances in January 1862, observed that an Irish comedian "has had quite a 'run' here."[18] "Blind Tom," a young slave boy, sang, played various instruments, gave imitations, and demonstrated a remarkable musical facility, although he could not read a note of music. He musically recreated the Battle of Manassas. Over time Blind Tom developed quite a following and had a lengthy career. One woman attending a performance decided that his "talent surpasses anything I ever heard or dreamed of."[19] Not everyone agreed. After first performing early in 1863, Blind Tom returned the next year. "Tom has improved in size and in confidence," wrote someone who saw him on both occasions, "but not much in his musical powers."[20]

The recently completed Montgomery Theater was a center of activity. Actors and actresses with varying degrees of talent stayed for runs lasting anywhere from a week to several months, playing before audiences as small as 50 and as large as 450. The spectators included black people as well as whites; blacks were allowed to sit in the alcove of the theater farthest removed from the stage. The plays were often formulaic and maudlin, with endings that were easy to predict. Principle and virtue almost invariably triumphed.

Montgomerians generally enjoyed the first theater season, which ended soon after the capital's removal to Richmond. By late 1862, they were keenly anticipating the resumption of productions. On December 6, opening night, a large house filled the theater for the German play *Ingomar, the Barbarian,* a well-acted and romantic drama. The Allemanni barbarians (exemplified by the menacing Ingomar) invaded and threatened Parthenia's Germanic peoples. The comely maiden ultimately won Ingomar over. As Parthenia, Ida Vernon drew praise and quickly became a favorite. In the next few weeks *The Hunchback,* a comedy involving intrigue and love, and Walter Scott's *Bride of Lammermoor,* a melodrama incorporating the elements of deceit, insanity, and the quicksand death of Edgar, Master of Ravenswood, attracted large crowds. In the meantime, Ida Vernon answered curtain calls, was idolized, and before departing for Richmond accepted the jewelry with which Montgomerians appreciatively presented her. Ida Vernon became one of the Confederacy's most acclaimed actresses.[21]

Montgomerians were less impressed at other times. After a production of *Pocahontas,* a critic for the *Mail* wrote, "We could not divest ourselves of the idea that we were witnessing the rehearsal." The prices of theater tickets rose in 1863, the quality fell, and patrons complained.[22] William Crisp, the well-liked and talented manager-actor, could not restore theatrical standards. Crisp and his family—his wife and their two daughters and sons took part in productions—delivered some acclaimed performances. So did Thomas Hamilton, who had debuted at Burton's Chamber Street Theater in New York. As 1864 opened, Montgomerians warmly applauded Hamilton in the dramas *Lady of Lyons* and *Retribution. Aurora Floyd,* performed later that spring, would surely have benefited from his presence. According to someone in the audience, one of the actors lacked "the faintest idea of what he was doing," and another would have been better off in the Confederate army. If a third continued to perform, the spectator complained, "we can't vouch for the continued forbearance of the audience." Montgomerians continued to attend the theater during the season, but the quality of productions remained erratic.[23]

Although black residents of Montgomery were permitted to attend theatrical productions, such forms of entertainment catered largely to the white citizenry. The black community had its own preferred forms of recreation. Slaves enjoyed their family and friends. For those who earned money, there were ample opportunities to spend it. Bondsmen attended and bet on horse races. Montgomery blacks also purchased fancy clothes and jewelry. As compared with their rural counterpart, the city slave presented a more groomed look. An advertisement in 1862 described a fugitive as having the "appearance of a plantation Negro." Whites did not observe the Fourth of July during the war, but blacks celebrated the occasion. Their observances included food, drink, music, outdoor activities, and respite from labor. An African influence, as throughout the South, was obvious.[24]

Although blacks claimed some autonomy and identity, the institution of slavery made for fundamental oppression. Labor defined their existence, whether slaves worked as stevedores, blacksmiths, domestic servants, or carpenters. It was common to see black men, the property of private citizens, who had been rented out to the city for work on the dirt streets. The use and regulation of bondsmen did not change noticeably during the war. Yet the tasks performed by some blacks did change. Hundreds were impressed by Confederate authorities for various lengths of time. Taken from their masters, they labored to make the Alabama River more defensible and to improve fortifications around Mobile. On a more permanent basis, about seventy blacks helped cultivate niter and labored under the supervision of Charles Clapp. In General, Ladies, Madison, and Concert Hall Hospitals, slaves cleaned, cooked, and ministered to the needs of patients.

Most whites did not own slaves. Those who did own slaves treated them with varying degrees of respect and compassion. The stereotypes of revered mammies and loyal servants have some basis in fact. Even so, slaves above all remained laborers who were sometimes subjected to inhuman working conditions. In the freezing cold of late 1864, the slaves digging defensive trenches around the city lacked shoes and proper clothes during the day and blankets at night. Many suffered severely. Preacher George Petrie of the Presbyterian Church upbraided Lafayette Harris, a woman, for beating a slave with little reason. She was banned from the church for six months. Indeed, most slaves knew little of the benevolent paternalism that white observers later described.

Montgomery blacks and other Southern slaves were dissatisfied with their station but had little recourse. Most slaves simply adapted and strove to fulfill the expectations of the white world while attending to their own interests as best they might. How aware the slaves were of the declining Southern military fortunes is not known. Blacks were certainly more knowledgeable than whites believed. Some could read, and slaves communicated with free blacks.

As the fighting wore on, some 4,500 bondsmen in Montgomery began to think in terms of liberty. Realizing that the war's end might bring emancipation, the black community waited. Thousands of slaves elsewhere deserted their owners when Union troops arrived. By 1862, Federal soldiers had overrun the sea islands off the coast of Georgia, and several thousand slaves had gained their freedom. Black Montgomerians could not do so, because Union forces did not appear until the war was almost over. In the meantime,

Sunday offered a needed day of rest. On the Sabbath, many blacks, dressed in their Sunday best, could be seen on the streets. The attitude and attire of bondsmen impressed Edward Moren. Blacks seemed to "flourish," he wrote his wife. "Sabbath evening is a complete God Send to them and right well do they improve it."[25]

On Sunday local businesses were required by law to close. The other six days of the week saw merchants attempting to carry on as before the war. President William Knox at the Central Bank provided a measure of stability. Central Bank, on Court Square, was located at the physical and financial heart of Montgomery. At his clothing store on Court Square, Ethelbert Halfmann managed to maintain his inventory "despite the blockade."[26] Those looking for stationery, ink, or schoolbooks "in demand in these blockade times" visited Swedish-born Augustus Philander on Perry Street. Philander had added crutches for wounded soldiers to his stock. Joel White kept open the doors of Pfister and White's bookstore. The books he featured included the *Confederate Almanac* and Edward Pollard's popular *The Southern Spy*. There were a few women proprietors. Women searching for dress patterns, hats, and other

Court Square, c. 1874. *Courtesy of Fouts Commercial Photography, Montgomery, Alabama.*

accessories frequented Elizabeth Norton's establishment on Lawrence and Market Street. E. Wolff's millinery and dry goods establishment sold dresses and, ominously, mourning attire. She and other merchants were supplied by steamboats, such as the *Marango, Ross,* and others that regularly arrived at the wharf.[27]

Nothing indicated the health of the business continuum more than the opening of new stores. In 1862, the year that more than 22,000 soldiers fell at Shiloh, Robert Bonner established a variety store where customers purchased vests, coats, brogans, and "ten thousand other useful articles."[28] If cutting back financially indicated uncertain prospects, Lehman, Durr and Company did not fear the future. In 1862 Emanuel and Meyer Lehman, the German-born brothers connected to the cotton trade, pooled their resources with John Durr, and the next year they purchased a large warehouse fronting Court Street. By 1864, Captain G. T. Shaw, an invalid soldier, had begun selling ambrotypes on Market Street at the Gallery of Art, which the *Mail* described as an "attractive place" with "elegant galleries." That year A. Fitzgerald, who had moved from Dalton, Georgia, opened a cigar shop on Market and was soon making more than 2,000 cigars a day.[29]

In 1862 Joseph Pizzala opened the French Restaurant and advertised fare prepared "in a style unsurpassed." During the war citizens continued to enjoy oysters from the Mobile area. Pizzala, a longtime resident, promised oysters by the hundred or the barrel during the season.[30] The proprietor of Montgomery Hall boasted that his establishment had a well-stocked bar and ample food and was "in point of comfort second to no hotel in the South."[31] Kate Cumming, the observant nurse and diarist who traveled extensively from her Mobile base, pronounced a meal that she ate at the Exchange Hotel in 1863 "splendid." She added, "Everything was there, the same as in peacetimes." [32] A widely traveled northern visitor bathed within sight of the *Nashville* (a gunboat under construction). In Montgomery, he observed, "We . . . tasted the first meal and slept on the first bed which had any approach to excellence." By then a patriot had opened the Beauregard Restaurant and offered fish, oysters, and game.[33]

As the names Manassas, Antietam, and Murfreesboro fixed themselves in Southern minds, Montgomerians enjoyed beer, wine, and whiskey at the Exchange Hotel, at various restaurants, and at the grog and whiskey shops. A loyal Confederate pleased customers at the Dixie Saloon and Restaurant on Monroe Street. Another proprietor honored Thomas "Stonewall" Jackson— without deferring to the general's rigid moral code—by opening Stonewall's

Bar and Billiard Saloon on Commerce Street. Joseph Bihler, identified with
the spirits business, provided competition at Lafayette House on Coosa Street,
where patrons could purchase beer day and evening by the "glass or gallon."[34]
Soldiers passing through were some of the most frequent customers. While
nothing in the comprehensive city code prohibited women from entering
these establishments, they seldom did so. Saloons were regarded as male do-
mains. The law of supply and demand was clearly at work. In 1864 one observer estimated that there were "three whisky shops to each election pre-
cinct." [35]

Although war-related problems ultimately shattered the Southern economy, the conflict actually created some new opportunities. Military demands
were insatiable: soldiers wore out gear, expended shot and shell, consumed
supplies, and sought constant replenishment. Merchants, artisans, and a vast
array of civilians contracted with the government to provide commodities
and services. As elsewhere in the South, merchants remade their old businesses
to serve wartime needs or created new ones. By doing so they served the
Confederacy's interests and their own simultaneously.

Prewar visitors to Charles May's saddlery and harness store on Market
Street encountered the distinctive smell of leather. During the war, May expanded his product line to include knapsacks, cavalry valises, saddles, canteen
straps, and bayonet scabbards for the Confederate government. At the factory of A. Burrows, workers largely abandoned the manufacture of sashes and
shades in favor of various types of tents. In October 1861, Burrows billed the
government for over 500 tents. Military needs meshed well with the wares
of druggists. Felix Glackmeyer supplied the Confederates with Epsom salts,
castor oil, quinine pills, and cough medicine. Partners Stephen Hutchings and
Joseph Williams provided items ranging from chloroform to silver nitrate.[36]

The needs of war veterans led Albert Strasser, a native of Saxony, to enter
the prosthetics business. One observer credited him with having created "the
most perfect imitation of the natural limb" and compared his artificial leg
to one that had won a medal at the World's Fair.[37] Strasser and John Callahan,
an undertaker, entered a partnership, advertised widely in the South, and offered special financial arrangements for the destitute. They began developing
an artificial arm "of an utility adequate to the purpose of a pen," and they
prospered.[38] Luke Dickerson, an undertaker, contracted with the government
to bury soldiers who died in local hospitals. He assured authorities that his
rate of ten dollars per corpse was "reasonable and just."[39]

Charles Clapp, who secretly disapproved of the Davis government, began

A Market Street store that sold pianos is flanked by the Bank of Montgomery and Charles May's saddlery and harness shop, c. 1870. *Courtesy of the Alabama Department of Archives and History, Montgomery, Alabama.*

cultivating niter beds on the Lower Wetumpka Road in 1862. Niter was a basic ingredient of gunpowder. John Janney, the city's preeminent iron foundryman, provided the nearby government arsenal with sword handles, various types of shells and canister, and other items. William and Frank Gilmer, commission merchants and railroad promoters, established the Alabama Arms Manufacturing Company, which soon promised "a superior rifle." In the meantime, manufacturing oil from the ground pea, David Hughes provided the Confederate government two hundred gallons of peanut oil each month.[40] Cotton cards had been previously purchased outside the South. The cards—small wooden and wire objects held in the hand—were fundamental to the spinning of cotton, and the poor especially depended on them. Johnson Davis, one of the city's most devout (sometimes minister of the Methodist Protestant Church) and inventive citizens set up a cotton-card factory. He and machinist James H. Carkett's efforts were rewarded by a contract with the state. By the fall of October 1864, employees were turning out thirty to fifty cotton and wool cards daily and the *Advertiser* claimed Davis "makes as beautiful card as was ever imported from Europe or Yankeedom."[41]

Despite such initiatives, the war ultimately devastated Montgomery's economy and that of the South as a whole. Merchants and consumers soon felt the effects of a Federal blockade that stretched from Virginia to Texas. As the blockade tightened, acute shortages occurred. Unscrupulous speculators in every city purchased large quantities of essential commodities and withheld them from market. Impressing agents for the Quartermaster or Commissary Departments compounded the problem by seizing goods in the name of the Confederate government, often without compensating the rightful owners adequately. Shopkeepers and farmers alike were victimized.

The economy's collapse, however, was chiefly due to the misguided currency policy. When taxation and various loans raised insufficient revenues, Secretary of the Treasury Christopher Memminger chose to increase the circulating medium. The government began issuing treasury notes early in the war. Confederate currency appeared in denominations of fives, tens, twenties, and more. Unfortunately, as treasury notes proliferated, prices soared, and the value of money plummeted.[42]

As early as 1862 a visitor to Montgomery mentioned the "crippling" repercussions of the blockade. The observer noted that many businesses had shut down, producing a "calm and stillness." He likened Montgomery to Oliver Goldsmith's "Deserted Village." The same visitor spoke of commercial "vultures" with "beaks and talons of the carrion crow."[43] Edward Moren deplored the self-serving who "enrich themselves at the expense of cause and country." [44]

Impressment agents drew the ire of many. John Seibels, former editor of the *Montgomery Confederation,* took grave exception in 1862 as officials claimed private property. He and others developed a quick dislike for the uniformed (and often imperious) agents who summarily deprived merchants of commodities and citizens of their horses. Seibels wrote the assistant secretary of war that local residents were seething with anger. According to Seibels, the comprehensive impressment that had been intended to help the Confederate cause was actually hurting the South. The reason was that resentful citizens, knowing that they would not be paid a fair price, concealed articles that they would otherwise have sold to the Confederacy. Anger grew, tolerance diminished, and the situation reached a breaking point late in May 1864, when citizens were found to be hiding stock outside the city to keep it from impressment authorities. Commandant Walter Jones posted guards and confiscated wagons and horses for two days. Even a hearse was turned back. Irate Montgomerians took exception to what the *Advertiser* labeled a "siege."[45]

The presses in Richmond continued to produce currency and thereby fueled inflation in local places of business. One Montgomery observer noted "huge piles of Confederate notes in the hands of Tom, Dick and Harry."[46] The public lost confidence in fiscal policy. Berry Tatum, a Court Square grocer, and other merchants refused old issue (treasury notes) in anticipation of new issues. "If you ask a man now if he has corn, or meat, or anything for sale," one observer commented in the spring of 1864, "the answer almost invariably will be that he has, but prefers new money."[47]

Merchants scaled back, lost money, and in some cases shut down. Montgomery Hall, where patrons had engaged rooms since the 1830s, was a model of managerial propriety. The hotel closed its doors in 1864. Store owners faced an insoluble dilemma with products in short supply and prices high. What took place in Montgomery reflected the state of affairs throughout the Confederacy. Fort Hargrove and P. C. Smith reacted to market conditions by raising prices at their Commerce Street grocery store. H. B. Metcalf, a druggist, admitted to problems. Even so, he filled prescriptions by importing goods from Evans' Sons in Liverpool. Beef, poultry, vegetables, sugar, flour, molasses, and anything else purchased by the pound, bushel, sack, or gallon quickly grew more expensive. Prices climbed steadily, predictably, almost weekly. Edward Moren wrote his wife that he could not find the waffle irons she had requested and doubted that he could afford them if he did find them.

Both buyer and seller made painful adaptations as patterns of commerce were interrupted. Montgomerians had before the war circulated in the early morning hours at the City Market. Fish, beef, and vegetables, the traditional basics, continued to be sold at that institution. Yet vendors now also provided hats, cloth, and other items. One patron was reminded of a European bazaar.

Edward Moren, a legislator, physician, and veteran observer of
Civil War Montgomery, c. 1870. *Courtesy of the Alabama Department of
Archives and History, Montgomery, Alabama.*

After listing some of the prices at the City Market, Moren wrote, "and
whisky! . . . You have no idea how high it is."[48]

Some commodities were prohibitively expensive; others were impossible
to find at any price. Tobacco, coffee, sugar, and salt were among the products
most missed. It was not exclusively poor women who conserved by turning dresses inside out. Governor Thomas Watts, projecting an image of shared
sacrifice, wore a homespun suit at his inauguration in December 1863. Many
other people wore the coarse cloth on that day because they had nothing else.
When Christmas arrived, comparatively few dressed fashionably. In the eyes

of one visitor, blacks were paradoxically among those who did. The situation Anna Kreutner confronted was symptomatic. The wife of the local gunsmith searched exhaustively before finding—at thirty dollars a yard—the white Swiss cloth that her daughter wanted for a wedding dress. Shoppers grew accustomed to shortages, lack of stock, and high prices.[49]

An observer for *Harpers Magazine* in the summer of 1864 painted a bleak picture. For the "Montgomery of today," he wrote, "imagine all stores not closed entirely employed as cotton warehouses."[50] Citizens frustrated by empty shelves on Market, Perry, and other streets looked elsewhere. Mason Harwell, the owner of one of the biggest auction houses, provided some hard-to-find items. Late in 1864, when far fewer commodities could be purchased at local stores, a large and boisterous crowd bid at a Harwell auction where "everything of course brought high figures." As the year closed, there was one exception to the rule of rising prices. Bids at the Artesian Basin slave auctions fell. The future of the peculiar institution was in doubt.[51]

What had always translated into business success—tenacity, skill, timing, shrewdness, and good fortune—continued to earn rewards. William Mount, a free black, had learned wagon-making skills from Joseph Mount, a white man. He continued in the trade during the war. Establishing some continuity was his and other Montgomerians task. With men off at war, some women assumed new responsibilities at businesses and stores. Changes do not, however, seem to have been dramatic. Mary Hinton was the exception. She opened an ambrotype studio. In halting fashion, capitalism went forward, or at least survived. Local merchants, acting on favorable circumstances created by the war, or overcoming obstacles despite it, adapted with varying degrees of success. The situation for merchants and consumers was no worse than it was in Danville, Raleigh, Lynchburg, or other cities. That provided no consolation to Montgomerians trapped in the tailspinning malaise. A journey through Southern cities by 1864 might prompt a visitor to wonder what would collapse first, the economy or the army. If a visitor entered the Montgomery stores still open, engaged a room at the Exchange (the only hotel open), or simply observed the general deterioration, the question was a debatable one.

Through it all slaves waited, daily resorting to devices of accommodation in a white world but increasingly mindful of a better future. In the present, the black population may have suffered comparatively less simply because blacks were accustomed to adversity. While slaves did not become noticeably more aggressive or defiant during the war, when Federal troops rode into Montgomery in April 1865, blacks treated them as liberators.

Distance from the battlefront shielded citizens from the rawest ravages of war. Establishing some continuity was the task of the population. Surely the presentation of the Rev. Dr. Leyburn at the Presbyterian Church in March 1863 had some appeal. As a recent visitor to China, Leyburn promised no academic discourse but rather "the impressions and observations of a traveler fresh from the scenes."[52] The *Mail,* recognizing the escape value provided by the theater, urged attendance during "hot and angry times like these." Until the final weeks of the conflict, Montgomerians carried on a rarely interrupted routine. Church and school remained institutions. Parishioners at St. John's Church took the Holy Eucharist at Christmas in 1864. By then the Franklin Military Academy had closed, but Professor J. F. O'Neal proposed opening a writing school at the same location.[53] Rabbi James Gutheim presided at the synagogue on November 2, 1864, when Herman Strassburger and Fanny Lope married. Jews and gentiles mixed, the traditional wine glass was broken, and the groom "appeared as happy as a fellow should be under such circumstances." Louise Kreutner, the daughter of Anna Kreutner, married two weeks later on November 19. Her mother had found the cloth for a wedding dress, and if a pair of $150 calfskin shoes was not exactly what the bride wanted, they were adequate. The Rev. George Petrie officiated at the Kreutner home on Monroe Street. Dinner followed, and in honor of the festive occasion, coffee was served. Maintaining a semblance of normality was possible in wartime Montgomery. Carrying on as before was not.[54]

5

The Administration of a Confederate City

DURING THE WAR, MONTGOMERY'S
mayor and city councilmen continued to address the city's various practical needs. Efforts to dig a new artesian well had begun earlier at a site near
Montgomery Hall on Market Street. By July 1860 the well had reached a
depth of 487 feet with no results. By February 1861, critics were ridiculing
the project; the well had gone still deeper without finding water. Finally the
auger hit rock and broke. The work was abandoned, according to the *Mail,*
after the city had spent $13,000 for a "hole in the ground."[1] A new powder
magazine near the river on the northwest edge of town replaced a smaller
magazine and proved less controversial. The timing seemed appropriate given
the state of national affairs. As one individual noted a month before the war
began, the magazine "might be needed in certain contingencies."[2]

Such municipal affairs fell under the purview of the mayor and twelve
councilmen, two from each of the six wards. Thomas Glascock (land office
register), William Farley (banker), and Adolph Strassburger (merchant) were
representative councilmen. Three men served as mayor during the war: Andrew Noble, a banker; John Johnson, a wealthy cotton broker, who succeeded
Noble late in 1861; and Walter Coleman, who took office in 1863.

76

Some Montgomerians could not name the mayor, and only a minority voted in the city elections that were held each December. Women, of course, could not vote. The disenfranchised also included over 4,000 slaves. Landslide mandates swept some politicians into office; others prevailed by the thinnest of margins. Councilman John Figh fell only twelve votes short of replacing incumbent mayor John Johnson. William Crusis, returning after being wounded in Virginia, made the mistake of challenging city clerk Augustus Underwood in 1864. Crusis received forty-seven votes, or 9 percent of those cast. Benjamin Keiser sought a seat on the city council that same year. His credentials included action at the Battles of Seven Pines and Fredericksburg. "Surely these sacrifices and his qualifications otherwise," the *Advertiser* stated, "entitle him to a favorable consideration." A large majority of voters in ward one disagreed.[3] Although a record of Confederate service had not appreciably helped Crusis and Keiser, the slightest appearance of indifference to the cause might doom a candidacy. John Abercrombie assured the public that only an affliction had kept him from "serving my country." Abercrombie promised half of his salary to indigent soldier families if he was elected tax assessor.[4]

The mayor and aldermen who ran Montgomery usually met twice a month at the courthouse. Councilmen considered budget questions, allocated or withheld funds for projects, heard various appeals, and generally conducted municipal business. Part of a supporting cast included the city clerk, who issued warrants on the treasury and oversaw tax collection. The city treasurer safeguarded municipal funds and handled tax assessment. A city physician, also appointed by the aldermen, admitted patients to the local hospital and monitored health conditions in the city. The clerk of the market presided during market hours, from before light to early morning and all day Saturday. Anyone possessing more than a keg of gunpowder surrendered the surplus to the clerk of the magazine and paid a storage fee. The wharfinger inventoried commodities that traded via the river. All items—flour barrels, cotton bales, and timber—were taxed. A grimmer task confronted the city sexton. He kept records of the deceased and arranged their interment. There was also a captain of police and a city marshal.

The council's most important responsibilities included funding and assigning priorities to projects. Past aldermen had been by turns extravagant and penurious. At the war's outset, there was unanimous agreement that basic improvements were overdue. In April 1861, a special committee pronounced the wharf in "wretched condition" and proposed extensive changes.[5] At about the same time, the Street Committee issued a discouraging appraisal of city thoroughfares, singling out Washington, where committee members found abandoned carriages, wagons, and buggies "totally unfit for any other purpose than as fuel."[6]

Inevitably, the war forced officials to make cuts across the board. Ten days after Fort Sumter fell, Alderman John Dickinson introduced a resolution calling for retrenchment. The local grocer cited the likelihood of a "protracted" civil war and the consequent strain on city resources. According to Dickinson, the high stakes—"placing our peculiar institution upon an enduring foundation and our Government beyond the power of designing Abolition demagogues"—required extreme fiscal prudence. Given the cautious mood, aldermen agreed to defer large projects and to fund only what was absolutely necessary. The Committee on the Wharf was subsequently disbanded. Euphoric council members had unanimously waived the wharfage fees for Confederate arms and supplies as the war began. More realistically, they rescinded the order in June.[7]

Councilmen depended upon a steady source of revenues. Citizens paid taxes on their real and personal property. Fines and wharfage fees provided operating capital, and retailers were required to purchase licenses. The owners of carriages and hacks paid twenty-five dollars annually for the right to operate. A commission merchant surrendered fifty dollars in exchange for the privilege of conducting his business. In a city that considered itself upright and God-fearing, proprietors of beer saloons paid $250 and those who sold liquor twice that amount. Yet the disbursement column in the city council minutes was always lengthy. Salaries of officials had to be funded, as did the City Hospital. Countless warrants had to be drawn on the municipal account for various services (for example, blacksmithing and street laborers). The cost of lighting the city with gas furnished by the Montgomery Gas Company was a large item. And there were inevitably unexpected expenses. Returns exceeded financial outlays by less than fifty dollars in the first year of the war. A combination of frugality, wharfage fees, and sound management had resulted in the accumulation of a healthy surplus by the end of 1862. As the next year concluded, the Committee on Finances congratulated the city "on the prosperous state of the finances."[8]

As in any municipality, councilmen made some decisions with important consequences for the citizenry. One of the most fundamental responsibilities involved public health. Diseases and epidemics—smallpox, yellow fever, and other afflictions—could wipe out a concentrated urban population. Councilmen had recently purchased a building to serve as a pest house on the city's outskirts. The establishment of this facility proved especially timely, as a smallpox epidemic threatened late in 1862. Women ministered to their children but in doing so sometimes contracted the dangerous disease. Aldermen set up an emergency board of health, called on Thomas Hill, the city physician, and absorbed the costs of mandatory vaccinations. Anyone entering the city by rail or river was required by council fiat to submit to an examination by doctors. The afflicted were quarantined in the pest house to avert disaster.

The aldermen exercised wide discretion in the pursuit of their duties. As the war opened, Jacob Sutter, Joseph Bihler, and several owners of lager beer saloons petitioned city council to reduce their licensing fees. The barkeepers pointed out that some hard-pressed beer establishments might otherwise close, so that Montgomerians would be tempted to desert the "wholesome" beverage of beer for "that bane of all human happiness, ardent spirits." The aldermen remained unmoved by such pleas. Two months later Jacob Sutter applied for a liquor license.[9]

The *Mail* brought the problem of vagrant dogs to the council's attention near the end of 1862. One solution was to kill the dogs and add their carcasses to the niter being produced. "One pound of niter," quipped the *Mail*'s editor, "is worth one thousand curs."

By late 1862 at least several hundred soldiers had died in local hospitals and had been buried in the city cemetery. One individual, appealing to the council's sense of dignity, informed the members that in many cases the name of the deceased had washed off the headboard. The aldermen decreed that hospital officials must provide each soldier's body prior to interment with a marker that bore his name and his company and regiment. Another issue that confronted aldermen in 1862 concerned Catholics and proved more difficult to resolve. Father A.D. Pellicer presented a proposal that permitted the St. Peter's Parish to purchase city cemetery land for a Catholic burial ground. Several councilmen objected from fear that their action might set a bad precedent: other denominations or clubs might request separate plots. The vote carried despite dissenters.[10]

City officials took an oath swearing allegiance to the Confederate States of America. As the conflict began, they also drafted a declaration of loyalty for all residents to take. Eight months into the war, aldermen suspended John Tucker's sentence for an unknown crime, providing that he "go to war." Early in 1862, councilmen appointed a committee to locate church bells and other material that could be cast into cannon. About the same time, aldermen sent $500 to the city of Fredericksburg, where a recent Union bombardment had left many residents homeless.

Councilmen exhibited their Confederate credentials differently. Late in 1863 councilmen considered demolishing a wooden building that violated the city fire code. They made an exception when Surgeon Watson Gentry asked that the building be spared because it was being used for hospital needs. In the summer of 1864, Quartermaster agent Thomas Noble appeared before the council to ask that the city reduce the surcharge it collected from the government for every sack of corn handled at the wharf. Noble reminded the councilmen that the corn was destined for the Army of Tennessee in Georgia. Officials acted favorably on the request.

Early in 1864 councilmen balked when the owner of the Lafayette House applied for a liquor license. Its well-known proprietor, Joseph Bihler, had been connected with the sale of forged substitute papers. In March, aldermen rejected the license application of Augustus Hoefler because he had claimed foreign exemption and had refused to enlist in the army. The council added that anybody invoking foreign protection would be similarly denied a business license.[11]

The council was also obliged to provide for the poor. In all Southern cities an impoverished and growing underclass was appallingly evident. Hundreds of Montgomerians had been in a precarious financial position even before the conflict. Their situation deteriorated when the relatives on whom they had relied for support left for military duty. Circumstances caused the numbers of poor to increase exponentially. Women were the most vulnerable. As the war opened, seamstresses Margaret Booth, Mary Fable, and Nancy Gramby barely made a living. Katherine Webb and Mary Driver fared little better as milliners. Most women had never worked outside the home, but suddenly, with men off at war, it became necessary for them to do so. For the poorest, there was government sewing work provided by quartermaster official John Calhoun.

Less than a year into the war, 142 local women petitioned Jefferson Davis. They wrote of "absolute want." With soldiering husbands absent, the women reasoned, they lacked the "commonest necessaries of life."[12] Neither did employment preclude impoverishment. Significant numbers of women did tailoring for the government. Early in 1863, "Another Soldier's Wife" complained about the salary policy of the Quartermaster Department. She and other women were being paid about six dollars a week to cut out shirts and underclothing for soldiers. "Another Soldier's Wife" noted that although

Sarah Harwell, one of many women on whom the war imposed special burdens, c. 1870. *Courtesy of the Alabama Department of Archives and History, Montgomery, Alabama.*

beef and pork could still be bought, and also eggs, fowl, and vegetables, her salary purchased little. The same situation confronted the author of a public letter from "A Needy Soldiers Wife." Late in 1863 she declared that it was impossible to feed, clothe, and house several children on the sum of twelve dollars weekly that she earned sewing for the government. The beleaguered woman quoted beef prices of one dollar a pound and mentioned the cost of other commodities. The "chilly blasts of winter" were imminent, and she demanded to know how the conscionable could "enjoy their warm houses and comfortable beds."[13]

The situation confronting Amanda Fields was similarly bleak. Her husband was off at war, and she was caring for five children. Fields signed her name to the petition that Montgomery women sent Jefferson Davis. Sarah Moseley, a seamstress who was also in dire straits, also signed. These women and others stated that they were willing to "work to support ourselves and little ones."[14]

The only son of Rosannah Hobson, a widow, had recently been forced into military service. She and her two daughters depended upon him for the "necessaries of life." Anna Knox prevailed in their behalf. The wife of the well-to-do banker explained in 1864 to Governor Thomas Hill Watts that the Hobsons "find it a difficult matter to clothe and feed themselves." The city had many other cases comparable to these. The tradition of female dependency on male providers would have made it difficult under the best of circumstances for women to survive without men. High prices, scarcities, and the pervasive economic disruption caused by the war exacerbated the situation.[15]

The city council faced its greatest challenge in attempting to improve conditions for the poor. As the war opened, the councilmen established a fund of $1,000 for families dependent on absent soldiers. Aldermen also appropriated $100 to each church society aiding families of soldiers and the indigent. As winter approached in 1862, concerned aldermen noted that wood costs were beyond "the scanty means of the poor" and appropriated $500 for the indigent.[16] In the fall of 1863, at the suggestion of Joseph Winter, councilmen purchased a thousand cords of wood for distribution. With conditions worsening, the council set up the Montgomery Relief Market in spring 1864. Money was appropriated from the General Fund for the purchase of slaughtered cattle, and the poor received tickets that they could redeem for beef. As Councilman Joseph Winter argued, the "exigencies of the times" called for action. Funds budgeted for the indigent rose from $300 in 1862 to almost $6,000 in 1864. There was no precedent for the caretaking role, but confronted by the gaunt and the hungry, councilmen dismissed any theoretical objections.[17]

The potential of fire was fully appreciated in a city where residents had watched almost helplessly when the capitol burned in 1849. Aldermen appointed the chief engineer of the Fire Department each year. James Stow, the owner of a local hardware store, was chief engineer throughout the war.

A parade of fire companies at the Artesian Basin, Court Square, c. 1867. Black volunteers are visible here. *Courtesy of Fouts Commercial Photography, Montgomery, Alabama.*

There were three companies comprising approximately 170 firemen, including about 40 blacks: Dexter Fire Engine Company Number One, Alabama
Engine Company Number Two, and the Mechanics Hook and Ladder Company Number One. Blacks formed Alabama Engine Company Number Two.
In early 1862, a rash of fires that seemed to be the work of an arsonist led
the council to post a reward. Whites could collect $500 and blacks $100 for
information leading to an arrest. There were no devastating fires during the
war, although periodic blazes destroyed homes and businesses. On the night
of August 28, 1862, firemen rushed to a burning residence near the capitol.
Three homes were consumed, and a third was pulled down to prevent the
flames from spreading. "From the scarcity of the water," the *Mail* reported,
"the fire engine companies could render but little assistance."[18]

   Chief Stow explained to councilmen that the lack of water was only one
problem. Equally serious was the decreasing number of available firemen. The
Conscription Act of 1862 did not exempt firemen from service. As the war
continued, local firemen were forced into Southern armies. In a city with as
many white citizens as black, slaves partly filled the void. Whites had volun-

teered to combat fires. Blacks were volunteered through a type of civilian conscription. In April 1864, one observer found the blacks' practice drilling "quite credible"; the drill involved throwing water over the theater building.

Several nights later, a kitchen fire spread from one house near the capitol to several others. Citizens and soldiers helped firemen save some possessions, but in the absence of water, their efforts were largely wasted. With the passage of weeks and months, Chief Stow increasingly relied on black firemen. On July 4, 1864, the slave members of Alabama Engine Company Number Two were honored. About ninety black firefighters marched with their engine to a grove just outside the city. Hundreds of slaves congregated, and a black spokesman pledged continued diligence. Captain Edwin Belser (a white man) was given a diamond breast pin in appreciation of the training that he had provided.[19]

It was difficult to keep law and order in peacetime. Wartime conditions increased the challenge. Isaac Maxwell knew more about criminals and crime than anybody else in Montgomery. Maxwell, age thirty-eight in 1861, was active, tough, and wise to the habits and modus operandi of deviant members of society. An appreciative city council elected him city marshal each year during the war. Maxwell more than earned his salary of $1,000, as did Deputy Marshal Thomas Reed. The number of policemen fluctuated between twelve and sixteen. Not all were models of decorum. Soon after the war began, the council reinstated a policeman who had used "improper language in reference to a lady" but had "made full and ample apology."[20]

Violence was probably no more of a problem in Alabama's capital than in other cities of approximately the same size. As in any municipality, residents were safer by day than at night. Crimes ranged from crude knockdown robberies to the subtle passing of counterfeit bills. On the last day of 1862, three men tried to rob E. C. Hubbel, a local citizen, on the Plank Road. Several nights later on Market Street, one individual assaulted another and made off with $500. A stabbing and shooting incident on Commerce Street ended an abnormally eventful week. The vast majority of crimes were petty, and few offenders remained in jail long. A number of felons—including a horse thief, a slave stealer, an embezzler, and a murderer—escaped from the Monroe Street jail by cutting through the ceiling on March 16, 1864.

Councilmen generally left enforcement of the law to Marshal Isaac Maxwell. The aldermen intervened to stop prostitution, however, which continued despite no fewer than four statutes prohibiting it. Ladies of the night also worked during the day. The residence of Eliza Yarborough was a recognized house of ill repute, and several other individuals (including Eliza Coppinger and Jeanne Davis) fit the city code's definition of "persons of bad reputation as to chastity."[21]

Well aware that women entertained men, Alderman Marion Chisholm condemned their houses as places of "fights, quarrels, affrays" and inimical to public order. In the interest of moral rectitude, Chisholm proposed fining madams who sponsored dances or served alcohol on their premises. Considered by councilmen early in 1862, the resolution implicitly acknowledged the impossibility of eliminating prostitution altogether. Alderman George Figh objected to language that identified the brothels. He declared that the council did "not recognize the existence of such houses."[22] Despite the efforts of police and politicians, some women continued to cater to local men, transients, and soldiers. When the legislature met in late 1863, Montgomery remained home to women "of the worst imaginable character."[23]

Blacks, constituting half of Montgomery's population, were bound by far more restrictions than whites, and slaves more than free blacks. It was particularly easy for slaves to break the law because there was so much more of the law to break. John Janney, the iron foundryman, protested to the city council in 1861 when Mayor Noble sentenced one of his slaves to the lash. Late that year, Caroline Hassell, a free black, accused of insolence to a white woman, was charged a fine after aldermen intervened to reduce her penalty. More often, the letter of the law was carried out. Late in 1862, Howard, a slave, was arrested for public drunkenness, and Mayor John Johnson sentenced him to fifty stripes. A group of slaves caught gambling out on the Old Plank Road one night in January 1864 was whipped the next morning. With some exceptions, blacks continued to be charged with trivial offenses and to endure penalties harsher than the transgressions warranted. When the war began, the conduct of blacks was regulated by more than a hundred separate statutes. Councilmen added to the list early in 1864. Noting the increasing number of slaves loitering around shops, aldermen made those doing so subject to thirty-nine lashes.[24]

Police officers A. R. Holton, Abner Griffith, Joseph Duffy, and others routinely dealt with local criminals of both sexes and races. Confederate soldiers represented a new challenge. As one historian has observed, "Johnny Reb was not noted for his acquiescence to military authority." He respected civilian authority even less. Soldiers' definition of relaxation often pushed the limits of accepted behavior, not to mention city ordinances. The thousands of troops who went in and out of Montgomery often behaved in ways that left a great deal to be desired.[25]

Many of the soldiers disembarking from the train or a steamboat went directly to barrooms. In the spring of 1862, Andrew Noble, noting the "drunkenness of soldiers," asked for local cooperation in temporarily restricting the sale of alcohol. "It is hoped," Noble explained, "that all who have the good of the country at heart, will cheerfully cooperate with me."[26] Any benefits of his action were short-lived, however. An Arkansas infantry regiment in transit during August 1862 offered a case in point. Their stay, although brief, was too lengthy for local officials. As private William Bevens related, "We were too many for the police."[27]

By the spring of 1863, the council, the residents, and anybody who spent any time in Alabama's capital knew that alcohol could have a deplorable effect on soldiers. On the morning of May 9, 1863, a crowd of drunken soldiers began breaking up the Oriental Saloon on Commerce Street. Police arrived, a melee followed, and a soldier wielding a bowie knife or a bayonet stabbed officer Edmond Abercrombie.

City officials took action. The next week Mayor John Johnson asked all saloon keepers to close their bars when troops passed through the city. When problems persisted, a special council meeting was called on the last day of August. Mayor Johnson and the aldermen listened as post commandant Walter Jones reminded them that a small number of policemen could not control a large number of troops. Major Jones attributed much disorder to readily available liquor. Even the hospitalized soldiers sometimes caused trouble. So-called "hospital rats"—soldiers who prolonged their recovery to avoid service—convalesced indefinitely. The repeated transgressions of recuperating patients caused Surgeon John Watters at General Hospital to issue a policy statement late in 1864 warning that men who violated city statutes might find themselves dispatched to the front "without an hours delay."[28]

Midway through the war Governor John Gill Shorter reminded citizens that they needed to "yield a ready and hearty obedience to the demands which the country makes upon you."[29] As elsewhere in the South, however, the mayor, councilmen, and citizens often found themselves trying to balance local concerns with the greater good of the Southern government. The two were often at odds. Mayor Johnson and the councilmen argued in July 1863, for example, that policemen should be exempted from the Conscription Act. The officials petitioned President Davis to waive the service duties of Isaac

Maxwell, Thomas Reed, and five policemen from army duty. As city representatives explained, Montgomery was "on the great thoroughfare of travel" and was extremely vulnerable without experienced policemen able to deal both with civilians and with soldiers who broke the law. The fire department was similarly essential, and the councilmen petitioned Jefferson Davis again in 1864, imploring him to exempt firemen from military duty.[30]

Attempts to conscript three workers connected to the Reverend Johnson Davis's cotton card factory raised other questions about priorities. The poor desperately depended on the cotton cards to make clothes. In summer 1863, Governor Shorter argued to Secretary of War James Seddon that the men were more important to the local indigent than they would be to the army. Shorter's successor, Governor Thomas Hill Watts, agreed. Less than six months before the war ended, Watts warned of dire consequences if the cotton card factory work force was disrupted. "To stop this manufactory," he declared, would be "a public calamity." Some appeals had the desired effect; others did not. Confederate operatives in Richmond could be unyielding and unsympathetic. For them, the importance of winning the war overshadowed local concerns.[31]

Four years of war greatly complicated the administration of Montgomery. A correspondent for the *New Orleans Delta,* recording events early in 1861, wrote that the city had "thrown off its dreamy appearance of a country village" and had assumed the mantle of "a fashionable metropolis."[32] While Montgomery never became a metropolis, it was no longer a quaint village, and its governing, especially during the war, required more skill than ever before. The government's effectiveness may be judged in part from the fact that the city ran no deficit either at the outset of the war or at its conclusion, when General Lee surrendered at Appomattox. Another index of success might be public safety. Montgomerians felt reasonably safe during the war, and city fathers were able to maintain an adequate police force despite conscription demands. An official promised in 1862 to suppress "gambling houses, drinking houses or bar rooms, and brothels." That they remained open was less an admission of police ineffectiveness than the inevitable measure of a wartime city alive with transient soldiers.[33] Recognizing the unprecedented burdens that were being placed on the force, Councilman Chisholm in 1862 asked the council to raise the policemen's salaries.

In Augusta, Georgia, the city council established the Augusta Purveying Association for the needy. Similarly placed individuals in Richmond provided wood and sustenance to the poor. Montgomery aldermen were equally responsive to the plight of the indigent. When Private Michael McDonough of the Montgomery Greys was killed at the Seven Days' Battles in Virginia in the summer of 1862, the council was asked to provide for his widow and their two children. In late 1863 wood was commanding prices of forty dollars a cord, and the council had established a wood fund. By 1864 many more women would have signed the petition that had been sent earlier to Jefferson Davis. The city council acted to alleviate the distress. Understanding that the impoverished were also the unhealthiest, officials provided medicine for the indigent and ill. The city was sometimes also called upon to assume the costs of burial. Public assistance, narrowly defined in the nineteenth century, was expansively redefined during the war.

The aldermen struggled to maintain a solvent treasury, to establish a safety net for the poor, and to keep policemen on the beat. Of even more critical importance, however, was the recruitment of more black firemen. Lewis Cahn, the secretary of Dexter Fire Engine Company Number One, had protested the conscription of fellow firefighters in the spring of 1863, which he said would not leave enough men "to work the machine." Richmond authorities overruled him. To guard against catastrophe, the city council authorized the recruitment of more black firemen. As the events of April 1865 revealed, the decision was timely.

The Civil War interrupted and altered plans—short and long range. Conflict generally played havoc with the management of all Southern cities. Providing structure and order in an abnormal and difficult setting was the most elemental function of city government. In Montgomery, officials faced serious challenges, but they did so with some success, and city government served its citizens well.[34]

6

Waging War on the Home Front

Identifying herself as "A Soldier's Wife," one local woman wrote a long public letter to Abraham Lincoln as the war began. "Though I am but a delicate woman," the anonymous Confederate citizen declared, "I feel strong in my resolves." She regarded herself and Montgomerians as "American Independence" patriots and issued a warning to the commander-in-chief of the "Abolition hirelings." She and others would not stand for subjugation and coercion: the conflict was about independence and liberty. "A Soldier's Wife" left victory in the hands of God. At least at the outset of the war, her thoughts and feelings reflected those of citizens at all levels of Montgomery society.[1]

In 1861 Montgomery's preparations for war had many aspects. Pfister and White's bookstore offered seventeen different military books that included *The Artillerist's Manual, Science of War,* and *Manual of the Bayonet.* Clothing merchant Charles Pomroy promised "military headware of every description," and John Johnson advertised half prices to soldiers wanting their flannel shirts dyed. Contractors George and John Figh offered Confederate officials slaves, wagons, horses, and mules for hire. Sick soldiers passing through received free treatment from city physician Thomas Hill. Charles Pollard, president of the West Point and Montgomery and the Alabama and Florida

Railroad Companies, promised to transport without charge all articles donated to Confederate hospitals. Pollard declined to collect fares from wounded or sick soldiers and asked furloughed troops for half fare. Black stevedores were kept busy loading and unloading at the two railroad depots and the wharf. Shipments of mortars, carloads of bombshells, and the large Columbiad cannon were commonplace. A 5,795-pound Morton drew notice. It had been used against Fort Sumter and was being removed to Pensacola. William Boyrer, a music professor, composed the stirring "Montgomery Parade March," which he dedicated to the Montgomery Metropolitan Guards.[2]

Patriotic sentiment abounded in Montgomery as elsewhere in the Confederacy. Meeting on May 16, the "Israelites of Montgomery" promised support for the "cause of Southern Independence." The congregation, which boasted a recently constructed synagogue, faulted the Lincoln administration for directing an "unjust" war at those asking "only to be let alone."[3] A tavern keeper named James Jackson had been shot and killed in Alexandria, Virginia, when he resisted Union soldiers' attempts to remove a Confederate flag. Montgomerians, outraged, treated him as the South's first martyr. Citizens donated over $300 to the family, and the *Advertiser* declared that James Jackson's name would be "honored while men retain the love of noble, patriotic, and manly deeds."[4]

When the District Court of the Confederate States of America convened, grand and petit jurors donated their pay to the Soldiers Fund Committee, which helped the families of poor soldiers. Patriotism transcended age and sex. Small children wore the decorative Zouave uniforms and waved flags. The Montgomery Cadets, a company composed of boys too young to serve, were soon fitted for caps at J. E. Churchill's. In early June, when local girls gave the Cadets a banner, Lieutenant J. C. Alexander in accepting spoke of the "dawn of our Second Revolution."[5]

Montgomerians blamed the Lincoln administration for the war. They also viewed the conflict from a practical framework. Self-preservation was of the essence. Enemy aims were pernicious and transparent. Southern society was under siege, the victim of a war-minded president intent on subjugation. Self-aggrandizing forces threatened to invade, conquer, and reduce the region to territorial status and complete subordination. Readers of the *Montgomery Post* were sure that the enemy fought "not to redress any wrong" or to "defend any right" but aggressively, in order to harm Southern people and their institutions. Northern soldiers sought to "destroy [Southerners'] lives, rob them of their property, [and] lay waste to their homes."[6]

At least as ominous was the vision of fanatical abolitionists who would expose the South to the evils of emancipation. The editors of the *Mail* spoke of a struggle to preserve the "purity and integrity of Saxon blood" in the "war waged to destroy slavery and blend the races into equality." Such emotions, sweeping a jingoistic South as the war began, were conspicuous among men and women in Montgomery. In the spring of 1861, "A Soldier's Wife" assured Lincoln that she herself would shoulder a weapon if necessary.[7]

Jacob Weil, a clothing merchant from Germany, departed in some ways from the prevailing mentality. Unlike the vast majority of whites, he had reservations about slavery. Nevertheless, Weil strongly opposed the Lincoln administration. Weil explained to his brother in Germany that the enemy had provoked war by invading the South. Weil's reasons for loyalty to the South were simple. "This land has been good to us all," he wrote, and "I shall fight to my last breath . . . to defend that in which I believe."[8]

Montgomerians soon found themselves in the field fighting and dying for their principles. Tennent Lomax wrote Governor Moore as soon as the conflict began and pronounced the Montgomery True Blues ready "to march to the seat of war upon a moment's warning." Both the True Blues and the Montgomery Metropolitan Guards became part of the Third Alabama Infantry Regiment (composed of ten companies), which organized at Montgomery on April 28. The Alabama Fusiliers provided more local flavor. Unable to muster enough men to form a separate company, some of the German-dominated company joined the Third Alabama. Tennent Lomax soon became the regiment's colonel.

When orders to depart for Virginia arrived, the Third Alabama Infantry became the first soldiers to leave the state. On April 30, three weeks after Fort Sumter, women, children, family, and friends gathered at the Montgomery and West Point depot to say goodbye to the departing soldiers. The scene at the depot was one destined to become familiar throughout the South.

The Sixth Alabama Infantry Regiment also formed at Montgomery. John Seibels, an officer in the Mexican War and the editor of the *Montgomery Confederation,* had opposed secession and had been responsible for Stephen Douglas's visit to Montgomery. Even so, Seibels was the driving force behind the regiment's creation and became its colonel. Twelve companies, about 1,400 soldiers, formally organized at the capital city on May 6. Two of the companies, the Montgomery Greys and the Independent Rifles, consisted entirely of local men. In late May, the Sixth Alabama left by train for Corinth, Mississippi. Hundreds again provided a send-off.[9]

Tennent Lomax, lieutenant colonel of the Third Alabama Infantry, who was killed at Fair Oaks in 1862, photograph c. 1860. *Courtesy of the Alabama Department of Archives and History, Montgomery, Alabama.*

Concern with "honor" and "duty" obscured the reality of war and its hardships. Like other Southerners, Montgomerians believed that the war would end soon. Victory would be theirs because the Yankees were no match for the Southern men of arms. The events of the First Battle of Bull Run on July 21, 1861, near Manassas Junction, Virginia, strengthened convictions. Confederate soldiers routed Union troops in the war's first major confrontation. No Montgomery soldiers participated, but Montgomerians were nonetheless jubilant. John Phelan, a local magistrate, privately wrote an acquaintance, "Your heart no doubt like mine is filled with gratitude to the Great God for His victory at Manassas."[10]

The reference to the deity was not casual. From the outset residents were convinced that God favored their cause. In April 1861, when Montgomery was the Confederate capital, Jefferson Davis had assured Congress that the Southern cause was "just and holy." His view, shared by the Southern majority, caused many to regard the enemy as ungodly. The Almighty was expected to ensure the Confederacy's triumph and to punish sinning purveyors of death and destruction. The president formally designated days for "fasting and prayer." Sermons about the essential godliness of the Southern position came from pulpits in Charlottesville, Little Rock, Raleigh, and Montgomery. God's will would be done, and according to church spokesmen, God had willed Southern victory. A critical observer might have found it difficult to separate the church and religion from the Confederate state.[11]

Ministers in Montgomery made no attempt to do so. The clerical community included some of the Confederacy's most ardent champions. On July 24, three days after the victory at Bull Run, citizens at the First Baptist Church on Court Street adopted resolutions recently passed by the Confederate Congress thanking God for the triumph. Ministers Luther Hill, George Petrie, and Basil Manly addressed the congregation. Merchants, artisans, lawyers, common laborers, and others heard their words. John Mitchell, rector of St. John's Episcopal Church, offered a resolution further recognizing the deity's hand in Virginia.

Each Sunday clergymen led prayers on behalf of the Confederate States of America. Some ministers cast down God's condemnation on the enemy. Edward Moren described a message delivered by Basil Manly as "the fiercest war sermon I ever heard."[12] Manly's successor, Isaac Tichenor, had served as chaplain of the Seventeenth Alabama Infantry and was on the Shiloh battlefield. On August 21, 1863, proclaimed a fast day, Tichenor spoke at the capitol in condemnation of the "Vandal Hordes." The war had recently turned against the Confederacy in Virginia and Mississippi, but Tichenor predicted ultimate triumph. He reminded his listeners that "the race is not to the swift nor the battle to the strong."[13]

Rabbi James Gutheim had left New Orleans when Union troops occupied the city in April 1862. General Benjamin Butler required residents to swear an oath of loyalty to the Union. Writing a Northern acquaintance, Gutheim said that he refused to recognize "the Dictator in Washington" and vaguely spoke of plans to travel "into Dixie."[14] Acquaintances in the Alabama capital led Gutheim to Montgomery, where he assumed rabbinical duties in the summer of 1863 and quickly felt comfortable. An outspoken Southern nationalist, Gutheim clearly relished the opportunity to voice his opinions. He described the Union's "lust for gain and dominion" and faulted the Lincoln administration for prosecuting the war.[15]

In Montgomery's evangelical society, church organizations institutionalized sacrifice. Throughout the South, women's auxiliary societies organized along parochial lines. In Montgomery, the Methodist Protestant, Methodist Episcopal, and Presbyterian churches established the Ladies Aid Association as the war began. Other societies with Baptist, Episcopalian, and Catholic affiliations operated under its general aegis. Sophia Bibb, a devout Methodist, served as the association's president. The Hebrew Ladies' Sewing and Benevolent Society was affiliated with the Ladies Aid Association. Caroline Hausman, its president, believed that victory was predicated upon "The Being Above."[16]

Hausman and other women also understood the need for secular labor. From the first, women mobilized enthusiastically and thoroughly. Even at the outset, Confederate troops were underclothed and poorly supplied. Montgomery women knitted socks and fashioned uniforms in the basement rooms of the Methodist Episcopal Church on Court Street. In the war's early stages, women worked six days a week, taking orders in shifts. Appropriately enough, the headquarters of the Ladies Aid Association moved in summer 1861 to the former Government Building.

Winter clothes for soldiers were soon being stockpiled. Jews and Gentiles shared an antipathy toward the United States of America that transcended theological differences. Late in 1862, Caroline Hausman donated 114 pairs of socks to the Confederacy on behalf of the Jewish community. The spokeswoman for the Hebrew Ladies' Sewing and Benevolent Society stated that the gift was being made in honor of "this gigantic struggle for liberty and self-government." [17]

As the war lengthened, soldiers increasingly suffered from deprivation. The government found itself less and less able to provide for them. The sewing continued, and women also collected a multitude of items that were forwarded to the soldiers. Writing from Missionary Ridge, Tennessee, in October 1863, Lewellyn Shaver, a Montgomery private, asked Sophia Bibb for several items of clothing and observed that the last month had been "full of toil, privation and danger."[18]

Sophia Bibb, president of the Ladies Aid Association and a devoted friend of soldiers, c. 1870. *Courtesy of the Alabama Department of Archives and History, Montgomery, Alabama.*

The Montgomery Greys, part of the Sixth Alabama Infantry and the Army of Northern Virginia, benefited from donations in the spring of 1864. Acknowledging the much-needed footwear, representatives thanked the women for shoes, which were "a luxury seldom indulged in by an entire company of the Army of Virginia." The Ladies Aid Association remained a conduit for goods that the public donated to promote the cause of Southern victory.[19]

It soon became the responsibility of Montgomery women to care for wounded and sick soldiers. The amateur nurses often had patrician backgrounds. Sarah Bellinger, the wife of Carnot Bellinger, a physician, teacher, and planter, fit the profile well. Early in the war, she called public attention to the lack of facilities for the treatment of soldiers. The Bellingers donated a four-room cottage just south of town as the war began. Located in a field of scattered trees, it became Soldiers Home and predated government hospitals. Women solicited money, beds, sheets, and other supplies to operate the facility. Local druggists provided medicine, and physicians belonging to the Medical Society of Montgomery volunteered their services.

The accommodations at Soldiers Home were pristine, pastoral, and soon thoroughly inadequate. There was not enough space. In 1862 Soldiers Home became Ladies Hospital and relocated downtown. Women remained integral to its administration and comforted thousands of soldiers there. Thomas Hill Watts, who had recently become the Confederate attorney general, understood the women's commitment. Writing Secretary of War George Randolph, Watts declared that no words in the English language could do justice to their sacrifice.[20] Mary Jarrett Bell was particularly prominent in the operation of Ladies Hospital. Early in 1864, when she advised against the transfer of two surgeons, her complaints were answered by the medical director of the Army of Tennessee. "Be assured Madam," Samuel Stout promised, "that I shall exert myself to retain in the Ladies Hospital on duty any medical officers who shall be the choice of your association."[21]

In Ladies Hospital and all the other hospitals, women did their best for patients. Nursing was not recognized as a profession at the time, and no women had any real experience. They quickly gained a great deal. Sarah Herron, Mary Ann Phelan, Eliza Moore, and many others frequently made rounds in the wards. Young men from Arkansas, North Carolina, Florida, and elsewhere lay in hospital beds in varying degrees of distress. Women regularly brought them flowers, newspapers, and books. Women bathed the patients and wrote letters for those who were disabled. Edward Moren, who circulated in the hospitals as a doctor, noted that the women "wait on them and nurse them as if they were their own children." Some women who could not endure the grim scene simply left and did not return.[22]

By the summer of 1863 the hospitals were crowded with veterans of the Battle of Chickamauga. Sophia Bibb appealed to the public for support and noted that hundreds of the wounded waited in hospital beds. Acknowledging that her cause represented a "constant drain" on citizens, she asked for butter, eggs, chickens, and "eatables of every kind."[23]

A private wounded at Reseca, Georgia, was brought to Montgomery in the spring of 1864 and checked into Madison Hospital. A woman immediately examined and dressed his wound. In the following week, women visited daily. Writing from room eleven of the hospital on June 1, the grateful soldier pronounced himself "ready for the front."[24]

Surgeon Watson Gentry, in charge of hospitals, reported that "the soldier finds rest and food" at the Wayside Home. Wayside hospitals (established by the Confederate Congress in 1862) offered food and quarters to sick, disabled, or furloughed soldiers.[25] It became necessary to establish such facilities because thousands of troops passed through on the railroad. The Wayside Home, as Montgomerians called it, stood at the intersection of Bibb and Coosa Streets. Tired, hungry, and often incapacitated soldiers made their way there from the two train depots and the wharf. Three meals were served daily to coincide with the trains' arrival.

The Wayside Home was supported in part by the government but also depended on local charity. Montgomerians donated meats, vegetables, and all types of sustaining fare. William Bell—a successful merchant, an elder in the Presbyterian church, and the husband of Mary Jarrett Bell—directed operations. Adolph Strassburger, the owner of a dry goods store, acted as superintendent. Appealing to the public in May 1864, Strassburger described his clientele as having "received but little or nothing besides their toils and wounds." Several hundred soldiers were fed daily.[26]

As the war came closer to home, Montgomerians took more action. The Montgomery Battlefield Association, composed originally of forty-one men and twenty-eight women, was organized at the First Baptist Church on June 9, 1864. The members collected items for soldiers in the field. The association acted in coordination with the recently established Reserve Relief Committee, which took various articles to the front and performed many services. By the spring of 1864, military affairs were pressing in Georgia, where retreating troops from the Army of Tennessee were falling back toward Atlanta. Surgeon Watson Gentry soon wrote medical director Samuel Stout that surgeons and eighteen "industrious, active and sympathetic gentlemen are in complete readiness." Making known their travel plans toward the Georgia front, Isaac Tichenor, the chairman of the Reserve Relief Committee, called for coffee, sugar, wines, and cotton and linen rags for bandages.[27]

The Reserve Relief Committee moved into Georgia several times during the crucial months of spring and summer. Watching anxiously to the east, Montgomerians learned that the committees planned to "[proceed] to the battlefield."[28] Citizens dropped off provisions at A. P. Watt's store on Commerce Street. William Bell, president of the Montgomery Battlefield Association, soon announced that supplies would be sent "to the front regularly." On the night of July 16, citizens listened attentively for two hours as a chaplain in the Army of Tennessee described the battlefield and told his audience that relief societies made a great difference.[29]

Patriotism was evident in other ways. On April 12, 1861, Confederate batteries had opened fire on Fort Sumter. Two weeks later a group of Montgomerians met on April 26 at Estelle Hall, where they formed the Soldiers Fund Committee to address the needs of soldiers' dependents "whose means are slender." In a city of scarcities and inflation, impoverished families were many and increasing in number.[30]

Samuel Norton, a doctor and a compassionate advocate for the downtrodden, became the chairman. The committee began by setting up a stall for the indigent at the City Market in 1862. The stall later evolved into the Free Market, where the poor received vegetables, meat, meal, molasses, and other donated goods. Charles Linn, a grocer, gave a cask of rice, and others offered what they could. Samuel Norton, placing faith in his fellow residents, optimistically announced, "It is only necessary to announce that a sufficient sum has not been collected."[31] The women on the committee were eventually commended for having dealt "out profusely to the representatives of 430 wanting ones." Other organizations—the Montgomery Supply Association and the Montgomery Indigent Relief Committee—superseded the Soldiers Fund Committee in 1863–1864.

Norton remained central to benevolent efforts. In the spring of 1864, he asked Montgomerians for any surplus vegetables. One of the nine children of Samuel and Julia Norton accepted donations at the family's home on the corner of Jefferson and Perry Streets. A generous population also left provisions at the Supply Store on Tennessee Street.[32]

Concern for fatherless children, who were increasing in number, prompted citizens meeting in April 1864 at the First Baptist Church to take steps to establish a state orphanage. Thomas Hill Watts made a moving appeal to what he called "all the better sentiments of human nature."[33] Joseph Sutherlin, who had moved to Montgomery from Virginia, donated $15,000. "Though physically unable to share the toil, exposure and privations of the tented field," he said, "I readily acknowledge the claims of those patriotic men who have left home, wife, [and] children."[34] Richard Offutt, a grocer, provided $1,000, and Samuel Rambo contributed $500 from his income as a dentist. All told, more than 100 parties contributed. Within several months the Protestant Episcopal Orphans Asylum had opened, a matron had been designated, and "a little household of orphans" had been placed under her care.[35]

In the meantime, Montgomerians attended various benefits for war-related charities or institutions. Southern women raised money for the navy with gunboat societies and raffles. In April 1862 Professor Burton used the theater to exhibit painted scenes depicting the enemy in full retreat at Bull Run, gunboat warfare on the Mississippi, and the arrival at Mobile of captured prisoners from Shiloh. Burton charged admission and gave the proceeds to the local Women's Gunboat Fund. Henry Henderson, a slave, organized black musicians and donated the profits from his "Grand Ethiopian Concert" to the Free Market early in 1863.

As the year ended, a large crowd turned out to hear Sam Bard, a government agent, describe bitterly cold conditions in distant theaters as part of an appeal for clothes and blankets. Judge John Phelan recited the poem "The Soldier in His Blanket." On June 19, 1864, hundreds enjoyed Blind Tom's singing and dancing. It was easy to justify spending money on entertainment when the proceeds were split between the Wayside Home and the Soldiers Home. Montgomerians attended shows that benefited the Montgomery Battlefield Association, the sick and wounded in the Army of Tennessee, and various other causes.[36]

In Louisiana, Virginia, and wherever the Southern flag flew, new weapons were unveiled, ships were launched with fanfare, and bold predictions were made. From the outset, Montgomerians were fascinated with weapons that promised to give the South a tactical edge or just to even up the military odds. As the war began, hundreds examined the "St. James Torpedo" at Montgomery Hall. A witness to the demonstration of the so-called centripetal gun considered it potentially "very destructive."[37] An inspired Thomas Durden, justice of the peace, began developing a miniature breechloading cannon, which was "effective and convenient," a weapon that, according to the *Post,* could "be admirably adapted either to a retreating or advancing army." [38]

Sometimes the enthusiasm for an invention exceeded its practical value. George Pattison, a resident, wrote Secretary of the Navy Stephen Mallory in 1861 about his design for a new type of vessel. The "Fire-Ship" pumped gallons of turpentine spirits onto enemy ships, causing them to explode. According to Pattison, his vessel would "end the war on our terms." Department officials filed his plan (complete with a sketch) without pursuing it.

Pattison, frustrated, again tried to interest officials in his idea after the ironclad *Monitor* made its successful forays in March 1862. "I have not found the man yet that can see where it would fail," he wrote.

The scene at the Montgomery waterfront on May 7, 1863, might have taken place in many Southern settings. Hundreds attended the launching of the *Nashville.* The vessel was one of several ships constructed at a modest local shipyard. Cheers were raised as the *Nashville* slid into the water and, flying a Confederate flag, quickly moved out of port.[39]

Promoting the Confederacy invited the creative if sometimes quixotic impulses of some. Thomas Taylor correctly observed that Southern rivers made the Confederacy extremely vulnerable to Union gunboats. After prolonged observation and at least one boat trip up the Alabama River, he had an idea for minimizing the enemy's advantage. Sinking triangular wooden obstructions in the riverbed occurred to him. "I have turned my attention," Taylor wrote President Davis in the summer of 1863, "to studying not books, for their contents are known to military men . . . , but to nature, whose hidden wisdom man has never yet fathomed." Taylor's idea had been inspired by an oak that he observed in the river. Taylor understood, he related, that military authorities were skeptical of panaceas dreamed up by naive civilians, but he could not resist suggesting this means of "frustrating the Yankee Vandals [which] is the greatest wish of my heart."[40]

The so-called Travis Gun was displayed for several days in front of John Egger's Hull Street jewelry store in October 1864. Captain John Travis, its self-proclaimed inventor, called his creation "one of the most dangerous projectiles known to civilized warfare."[41] David Hughes, a local oil manufacturer who had earlier developed and patented a remarkably similar weapon, was not only interested but outraged. Hughes wrote the *Mail* "to let the public know in whose brain [the gun] was first initiated, and by whose hands it was first constructed."[42]

The *Mail* and the *Advertiser* reported news of the war's progress (the *Post* and the *Confederation* both went out of business during the conflict's first year). The latest accounts were posted at the newspaper and at the Southern Telegraph Office on Court Square and were sometimes hawked on the streets by newsboys in "noon editions." Montgomerians quickly ceased to doubt the enemy's resolve and ability. Basil Manly wrote his son in August 1861 that his fellow residents "admit now, that the Yankees can, & will fight."[43] Edward Moren observed early the next year that the "exploits of the Merrimac in destroying the Yankee blockading fleet is hailed with great joy here."[44] The news was increasingly dismaying, however. William Lowndes Yancey informed Jefferson Davis in May 1862 that the fall of New Orleans had "created a profound impression upon the public mind here."[45] He noted some gloom but enduring optimism. Victories achieved at the Seven Days' Battles and at Fredericksburg in 1862, and again at Chancellorsville by General Robert E. Lee's Army of Northern Virginia, helped sustain the hopes of the population at home. In 1863, the Confederate military position suffered setbacks when the Army of Northern Virginia was defeated at Gettysburg, and the garrison at Vicksburg surrendered in July.

William Lowndes Yancey also died that month of kidney trouble. A large crowd attended his funeral, stores closed, and the Reverend George Petrie officiated. The *Advertiser* offered a eulogy: "His principles will live and flourish in the hearts of the people."[46] Some may have linked Yancey's death with the impending demise of the Confederate States of America, which he had helped create. On every front the Southern military position had become precarious by 1864. A few continued to speak optimistically of future prospects. "Some are foolish enough to believe what they say," Edward Moren wrote. He believed that most "are talking for the same reason that the little boy whistles while passing the graveyard 'to keep his courage up.' "[47]

In June the Army of the Potomac under General Ulysses Grant moved south of Richmond and laid siege to Petersburg. The telegraph office and the newspaper offices, where the latest war news was posted, were crowded by anxious Montgomerians. Developments in Mobile in August shocked residents even more. Union gunboats commanded by Admiral David Farragut successfully passed Forts Morgan and Gaines, which guarded Mobile Bay. Writing from Montgomery, one citizen reported "the almost stunning effect on our community." The fall of Atlanta to William Sherman and Union troops in early September added to the general gloom in 1864.[48]

Military defeat and hopeless economic conditions dimmed residents' will to fight and to make sacrifices. Most white residents continued to believe, however, that the war was worth waging. In their minds, Lincoln's government had begun the war and had invaded the South. Union atrocities—real, exaggerated, and imagined—made it easier for Montgomerians to frame the fight in terms of good and evil. The enemy, no less barbaric than the Huns and the Visigoths, was determined to bring about social revolution. The Emancipation Proclamation dispelled any doubts of Republican intentions toward the slave population. An embattled population felt that Armageddon was at hand.

In the end, as at the outset, the church stood at the center of the Confederate nation. Few Sundays passed without reaffirmation of the South's version of truth and right from local pulpits. Recalling the philanthropic efforts of the recent past, a local woman reflected that "all religion was patriotic, and all patriotism was religious." Montgomerians held daily prayer meetings at alternating churches during the summer of 1864. The congregation consisted largely of women who knelt in prayer, hope, and, increasingly, despair as they sought to reassure themselves that the Confederacy carried God's blessing.[49]

Exercises in nationalism continued long after the war had been lost. Only the trappings of the Confederacy remained by August 1864 when young girls presented the Watts and the Montgomery Cadets with a banner and spectators listened to patriotic oratory. On the night of November 17, Montgomerians attended the comedy *The Honey Moon*. The proceeds went toward the purchase of a battery of Travis Guns for troops commanded by General Nathan Bedford Forrest. At Ladies Hospital, the day after Christmas, philanthropists underwrote a banquet for the patients.

The Civil War produced a disproportionately large number of casualties. Native sons of Montgomery fell at Fredericksburg, Chancellorsville, Murfreesboro, Shiloh, and other battlefields. Few soldiers matched the career of Watkins Phelan for sacrifice and heroism. Phelan, a soldier in the Army of Northern Virginia, had ties throughout the war to the Montgomery Metropolitan Guards. He was shot through the shoulder at Fair Oaks in 1862 and in the leg at Chancellorsville the next year and sustained another wound during the Wilderness campaign in 1864. A week before Lee surrendered to Grant, Captain Phelan died in the trenches at Petersburg. Lewellyn Shaver and Montgomerians belonging to the Sixtieth Alabama Infantry were also in the trenches at Petersburg under the command of Brigadier General Archibald Gracie. Shaver and his fellow soldiers settled in a sector known as "Gracie's Mortar Hell." Incoming mortar shells inspired that designation. Cold, filth, sniper fire, and privations made for misery.

A sense of shared sacrifice was unmistakable among civilians of Montgomery. The view of an unfaltering population prosecuting the war to its fullest is simplistic and false. Even so, Montgomerians generally believed that righteousness, duty, and honor were at stake, and acted accordingly. A visitor to Montgomery walked among the hospitalized soldiers in the spring of 1864. He noted the efforts of local women at Ladies Hospital. At the Wayside

Home, he noticed the accommodations for soldiers in transit. He was also complimentary of the Orphans Asylum. An "appreciation of the soldier," he concluded, "has been nowhere more strikingly manifested than in the little city of Montgomery." It was left to Rabbi James Gutheim to speak "in defense of our sacred cause."[50]

7

Dissenting Voices

"**I** WOULDN'T GIVE THE UNION FOR a thousand of your Confederacies," declared William Bibb, a local planter from one of Montgomery's most respected families.[1] He characterized secession as "criminal and destructive" and steadfastly refused to take a loyalty oath to the Confederate States of America.[2] David Carter, who also lived in Alabama's capital, spoke of the "so-called Confederate States."[3] Israel Roberts traced the progress of Union forces on a map. His prediction of Lee's surrender in Virginia was off by only thirty days. William Hedges, also a Unionist, declared himself "loyal in every throb of my heart to the Union."[4]

These men defied the local consensus but not openly; a visitor entering Montgomery would never have known that an association of Unionists had existed there from the outset of the war. "As a Northern man I naturally drifted into communication with these loyalists," William Hedges stated. He added, "the rebellion was not a month old before I had a perfect understanding with them all, and knew my position exactly." At no time were there more than thirty loyal Unionists. The group remained small.[5]

That Unionists lived in Alabama's capital was not surprising. Unionists were to be found in all Southern towns and cities of any size. Many had been born in the North and remained loyal to the region. Others grounded their allegiance to the United States in politics or philosophy. Some had been Whigs. Unionists considered men such as William Lowndes Yancey self-serving, radical, and fundamentally wrong. They found secession unconstitutional and deplored its effects for all Americans. In the 1860 presidential election, Unionists had supported John Bell or Stephen Douglas; a few had voted for Abraham Lincoln. Theory dictated practice, and differences persisted after the war began.[6]

Unionism transcended class lines. A few Unionists who supported the Lincoln government were wealthy citizens with social status, but most were people of more modest means. Their ranks included several merchants, the owner of a boardinghouse, the registrar of lands, and at least two doctors. William Bibb, who had more than $100,000 in assets, had practiced law until failing eyesight caused him to become a planter. Lewis Owen was president of the Montgomery and Eufaula Railroad Company. In contrast, William Hedges shared a room with four other Unionists; all earned modest salaries as railroad employees. Benjamin Hardy ran a bakery and an oyster cellar. David Carter could not even meet his doctor bills during the war. While the dissenters all opposed secession, not all disapproved of slavery. Some owned slaves and regarded the peculiar institution as advantageous for both races. William Bibb had about fifty slaves on his plantation when the war began and about seventy-five when it ended. Lewis Owen used slave labor to stretch his railroad track. Montgomerians rejecting the Davis government in thought (and sometimes deed) were not abolitionists. They were loyal citizens of the United States.

The Unionists formed a loose coalition resembling an underground network. One local dissenter recalled the "closest fellowship."[7] Adversity and a sense of common identity fostered that relationship. They met in secret, sometimes at Israel Roberts's hardware store on Commerce Street or at the Market Street dry goods establishment of George Cowles. Roberts came from Maine, and Cowles was a native of Connecticut. Lewis Owen, also from Maine, was often present and described himself as "an adherent of the Union cause" although he had lived in Montgomery for over twenty years. Dr. Samuel Seelye, a resident of the city for only a couple of years, would have been even less likely to espouse the Southern cause. Seelye had moved to Alabama's capital in 1859 from Maine. Brothers James and Milton Caldwell, originally from New York, sometimes attended the Unionists' gatherings. Meetings do not seem to have been called; there were no secret handshakes or passwords, but the bond of the Union was a powerful cementing

Samuel Seelye, a Unionist physician from Maine, c. 1870. *Courtesy of the Alabama Department of Archives and History, Montgomery, Alabama.*

force. James Stow—a native of Connecticut who owned a hardware store and was chief of the fire department—listened and joined in sympathetically. At meetings the Unionists shared Northern newspapers, discussed the latest military developments, and damned both the Confederacy and the myopia of Montgomerians.[8]

Although the majority of Unionists had northern backgrounds, William Bibb, the most outspoken, had spent his life in Alabama's capital. Bibb was a forty-one-year-old cotton planter when the war began. His wife, Anne, and their young daughter were central to his life. Bibb held strong political convictions. February 18, 1861, the day when Jefferson Davis was inaugurated, was the occasion of great despair in the Bibb home. Bibb had voted for John Bell and had opposed secession. Like other Unionists, Bibb refused to support the Confederacy when the conflict began. Unlike other Unionists, however,

Bibb did not hide his opinions. He believed secession was treasonous and considered the Union "next as sacred as the Bible."[9] Once the war began, he deplored Southern victories as prolonging the war. Bibb attended the Methodist Episcopal church, and following one irritating sermon laced with Confederate rhetoric, informed the Reverend Johnson Davis he would not return if the theme was repeated. Bibb also visited Northern prisoners being held locally and sold his carriage horses to prevent the government from impressing them. There was no mistaking Bibb's point of view. For Bibb, the Confederacy was a false government, without constitutional validity, established by demagogic extremists.

Bibb eventually testified before the Southern Claims Commission, established by Congress in 1871 to compensate Southerners who had been Unionists and who sought restitution for property seized by Federal troops during the war. The process involved calling upon witnesses to attest to the petitioner's Unionist sympathies. It would have been difficult to doubt Bibb's loyalty. Shephard Darby recalled Bibb's audacity in a statement made before the commissioners of claims. "He did not seem to be afraid to speak openly," Darby remarked. He added that Montgomerians considered Bibb a "traitor to his family and country—the Confederacy."[10] Israel Roberts described Bibb to the commission as an "unquestioned Union man."[11] Mayor Walter Coleman said that Bibb's "own family got down on him"—unsurprisingly, considering that his parents, Benajah and Sophia Bibb, were two of the city's most respected citizens and were avid Confederates. Sophia Bibb was the president of the Ladies Aid Association.[12] Benajah Bibb quoted his son as believing that the "United States government was the best on earth."[13] When a cousin asked William Bibb to subscribe cotton to the Confederacy, the Unionist refused, as he did when approached with other requests for money to support the Confederacy. Bibb replied in no uncertain terms that it was "against his principles to contribute anything to the cause of secession."[14]

David Carter, a kindred spirit, had lived in Montgomery since the 1840s without losing any of his affection for the Union, although he had married a native of Montgomery. Carter, a native of New York, owned a boardinghouse and a stable and lived on Catoma Street with his wife, Martha, and their six children. During the 1840s Carter had a government contract to carry the mails through much of Alabama. In fact, one of his mounted "express couriers" rushed the news of General Zachary Taylor's victory at Palo Alto to Montgomery during the Mexican War. When the Civil War opened, Carter continued the business of running a livery and a boardinghouse. Like William Bibb, Carter voted for John Bell in 1860 and counseled against secession. With the outbreak of war, Carter seriously considered leaving the region, but poor health and his wife's desire to remain prevented him from doing so.

The war confirmed the worst of Carter's expectations. Although Carter as a man in his forties was too old to be drafted for military service, he fought his own private war. The Unionist refused to join the Home Guard and secured a medical deferment from Dr. William Baldwin when he was threatened with jail. Carter courted local animosity by offering to bet Stephen Schuessler, a local butcher, $10 in gold to $1,000 in Confederate currency that the South would be defeated. Carter became the target of considerable local criticism when it was learned that he had secretly given a party commemorating the fall of Vicksburg. Carter had no relations in the Confederate army (two of his nephews had fought for the North), but the bloodshed often made him despondent. Dr. James Berney, who took walks with his patient, often lent a somewhat sympathetic ear. Although somewhat sympathetic, Berney finally gave Carter some stern advice that had nothing to do with medicine but might affect his physical well being: curtail all public talk against the war.[15] That was sound advice that local Unionists generally observed.

Berney's admonition made perfect sense. Unionism was anathema— an untenable and indefensible viewpoint—in the eyes of most Montgomery residents. It was not acceptable to oppose the Confederacy publicly, and those who did so could not expect tolerance. Unionists were constrained to dissent in secret, to leave, or to pay a penalty for holding their views. C. S. Aldrick, a music instructor at Franklin Academy, soon left and commented on "the utter impossibility of living in Montgomery as a Unionist."[16]

Elijah Kerr, a local attorney and a native of Pennsylvania, in June 1861 somehow offended a number of citizens at least some of whom called for his exile. A committee appointed by the mayor judged Kerr guilty but recommended conditional mercy. Kerr repented and remained in the city. Dr. Edmund Fowler also encountered the hostility of some who found him too solicitous in caring for wounded and sick Union prisoners. Captured at the battle of Shiloh, the soldiers had been brought up the Alabama River by steamboat and were by the summer of 1862 incarcerated in Montgomery. A three-story building served as a makeshift prison. Many were sick and suffering. Acting from a sense of concern and professional obligation, Fowler attended to them. His Unionist sympathies also accounted for the physician's actions. These circumstances provided the backdrop for his apparent forced exile from Montgomery. By the fall of 1862 he and his family were living in New York City. Once there, Fowler made contact with George Templeton Strong, the noted New York diarist. Hearing from Fowler of his travails, Strong empathetically recorded his impressions of the "well-mannered" and "intelligent" physician who had been "cast out." Other qualities—a certain compassion and obvious Unionist proclivities—had brought about his departure from Montgomery.[17]

During the war's first summer, city council members drafted a loyalty oath, and citizens adopted it at a courthouse meeting on August 2. The oath pledged fidelity in the "mortal struggle for . . . rights and independence with a reckless and relentless foe." Concerned citizens meeting at Estelle Hall a week later established a twenty-four-person Vigilante Committee. Some of the city's best-known residents—Dr. Robert Ware, Frank Gilmer, James Farley, and Judge Abram Martin—were members. The charter enjoined everyone to monitor "suspicious" persons at the railroad depots, steamboat landings, and other public places. Strangers whose reason for visiting was not clear could be brought before the Vigilante Committee for questioning. Residents of Montgomery with a reputation as subversive elements could expect the same treatment. Concerns about the loyalties of a female hairdresser from Philadelphia led the Vigilante Committee to force her out of the city.[18]

It was no small wonder that men such as Samuel Seelye and James Stow spoke their minds to only a few trusted individuals. Even William Bibb observed certain limits. At one point cavalry officer James Clanton asked Bibb to sell him a two-year-old colt. Acting against his basic instincts, Bibb agreed. When the Southern Claims Commission asked him to explain his action in Washington on May 29, 1877, Bibb replied that "it would be necessary for a man to be there to appreciate [the circumstances] fully" and added that "not to have done something would have subjected me to a certain sort of inconvenience which can be very well understood." Ignominy, insult, and even physical danger awaited the perceived traitor.[19] James Stow, who fully grasped the dangers, recalled having had many conversations with David Carter when "we could get where we could talk." Both men balanced their Unionist convictions against the necessity of discretion.[20]

In some parts of the South, Unionists lived in real peril. In others, they spoke and acted with little fear of reprisal. In the Upper South, where secession had never been universally popular, fidelity to the United States was sometimes pronounced, public, and tolerated despite being unpopular. Unionists were subject to less condemnation in cities occupied by Northern armies. Following the fall of Jacksonville, Florida, in March 1862, Unionists met publicly and denounced the Rebel government. In Memphis later in the year, after the city had been occupied, citizens paraded and cheered when General William Sherman spoke. Over 500 citizens belonged to the Nashville Union Club. In occupied New Orleans, Federal officials appointed Unionists to the public school system, and a loyal newspaper was published. The *Newbern Daily Progress,* a pro-Lincoln newspaper, found a readership in North Carolina.[21]

The situation was vastly different in Montgomery, where secession sentiment had been overpowering. Opposition to the North was deeply entrenched, and local Unionists lacked the support of Federal troops. "It was considered that every person who thought the north would succeed was a traitor," David Carter stated, "and any person heard of as expressing such sentiments was watched and suspected."[22] William Bibb's family connection and a physical infirmity (he was lame) provided him more security and sympathy than other Unionists. As someone remarked, Bibb could "say and do things that other men would not have been allowed to say or do."[23] Even so, there was talk of bringing Bibb before the Vigilante Committee, of forcing him to leave the city, and even of hanging him for treason. Unionists who wanted to carry on daily life, earn a livelihood, and circulate in the community needed to be circumspect. In some quarters, such as Israel Roberts's store, Unionists might be demonstratively anti-Rebel, but the time, place, and audience had to be right. As Samuel Seelye remarked, if townspeople had known what he and others said confidentially, they would "have put our neck in the halter before night."[24]

David Carter believed "that their eyes were all on me." He was afraid of being murdered. Carter's fears appeared more justified after he helped Benjamin Hardy leave Montgomery late in 1863. Hardy had been born in the North but for some time had operated a local bakery and an oyster cellar. He objected to the Confederacy perhaps on philosophical grounds or perhaps because he thought that, because he came from the North, he should not be forced to serve in the Southern army. In any case, Hardy wanted to leave the South, but he could not obtain from the provost office the necessary traveling pass.

Hardy turned to Carter for help. Through a tenant at his boardinghouse, Carter managed to procure the coveted pass. According to a plan formulated by the two men, Hardy made his way south to the squadron in Florida waters that was blockading the east Gulf Coast. He found sanctuary at St. Andrews

Bay, Florida. Unfortunately, Carter's role in assisting Hardy soon became public knowledge in Montgomery. Life thereafter was never the same for him and his family. Carter's complicity with Hardy confirmed what many had suspected: Carter was an enemy of the government and a traitor. Accordingly, he and his family were "discarded socially."

Hatred and danger awaited Carter at every turn. Augustus Underwood, the city clerk, denounced him as an "abolitionist" and was vocally abusive whenever they met. One citizen proposed attaching weights to Carter and dropping him down the artesian well. Another foe, finding him reading a Boston newspaper at the stables one day, threatened to bring him before the Vigilante Committee. Officer James Clanton, a resident, accused Carter of providing the enemy with information and vowed to exact retribution. Carter's Catoma Street home was frequently under surveillance, and he told James Stow that some were "after him."[25] He was neither deluded nor paranoid. As Stow later emphasized when he spoke before the Southern Claims Commission, "he *was* in some danger."[26] Carter's son later recalled, "We were very afraid Pa would be hung." The personal toll was excruciating. Carter considered leaving for Huntsville, then occupied by Union forces, but practical considerations prevented him from doing so.[27]

Daniel Starr, a brickmason who had been born in Connecticut, lived with his wife and their two children south of town on the corner of Mildred Street and the Mobile Road. Starr had lived in Montgomery for over a decade and appeared at least superficially to be an ordinary, unremarkable citizen. He moved homes for people, undertook tough jobs, and, after marrying locally, was apparently well situated. Then came the Civil War. Starr, at fifty-two years of age, did not always hide his disdain for secession or, once the break had been made, for the Confederate States of America. He seems to have had little contact with the Unionists who met covertly, but he nevertheless shared their outlook and spoke as a United States citizen.

On March 10, 1863, a search of Starr's home revealed a journal. One friend speculated that Starr might have mentioned its existence while he was inebriated. He seems to have drunk heavily. Whatever the exact circumstances, Starr did not peacefully surrender. He resisted, and shots were fired before Starr was apprehended and jailed. What the journal proved—apart from his hatred for the Confederacy—is not known for certain, but it was described as an "Abolition manuscript" and caused Starr to be summoned before the Vigilante Committee. Several hours of testimony spread over a couple of days settled nothing conclusively. On the afternoon of Saturday,

March 14, after more hearings, he was returned to the Monroe Street jail to await trial in circuit court. Late that night, unknown parties seized and lynched Starr. On Sunday morning the corpse was discovered hanging from a tree on the edge of town. The *Mail* correctly observed, "How it got there will probably never be made public."

Some local residents condemned the lynching, but most probably did not. In the eyes of most whites, Daniel Starr was a subversive figure deserving of little sympathy. Why would anyone feel remorse for a man whose efforts had contributed to the death of Southern native sons? Popular reasoning was elementary, cold, and definitive. Unionists understandably took a different position. They condemned vigilante justice in the abstract and feared it on a personal level. Samuel Seelye and David Carter considered means of self-defense. Unionists felt sorry for Starr. While some may have considered him a martyr, many regarded him as a fool.[28]

William Hedges, the machinist, took note of Starr's death. Opportunity, or "the logic of high wages," had prompted Hedges to leave his Northern home and had drawn him to Montgomery late in the 1850s. In the short term, he did not regret the move. Hedges secured a position as foreman of the Alabama and Florida Railroad, a job that, initially at least, "afforded me precisely the opportunity I wanted." After Lincoln's election, however, Hedges with increasing misgivings watched as soldiers drilled and his adopted home became virtually an armed camp. The high hopes and pageantry of secession, which exhilarated most of Montgomery's residents, caused him extreme despair. Hedges attended Davis's inaugural, which he described as a "solemn mockery." Like David Carter, he seriously considered leaving but did not do so immediately because "I knew my value to my employers, and I determined to remain and trust to circumstances to deliver me from whatever perils might arise."

The perils proved to be considerable. Hedges roomed with four other Northern men—George Folwell, Peter Martin, James Ward, and John Pierce—who also worked as mechanics on the Alabama and Florida Railroad. Initially, they assumed that the war would end quickly. When it did not, Hedges and his roommates began to worry. Although there were obvious constraints, they found their situation acceptable for a couple of years. The mechanics enjoyed a certain camaraderie, and their residence became something of a refuge, a place where the five men felt able to express themselves freely without fear of reprisal. Those whom Hedges described as the "loyal men of the city" met frequently, read Northern newspapers and periodicals, and followed the war's military developments. Wages collected from the Alabama and Florida Railroad (owned by Charles Pollard, a staunch Confederate) somewhat compensated for the "impalpable oppression" that Hedges described. So did the "superior qualifications" of a black cook that the men hired.

Subtle changes occurred after the start of conscription in the spring of 1862. Even so, because the five men were railroad employees and were therefore important to the war effort, they were exempted from service. Confronted by a provost guard one evening, Hedges needed only to show his pass. As the war continued, however, the men's status was challenged and threatened. Authorities began canceling exemptions in an attempt to fill the depleted ranks of the army. By November 1863, the railroad employees' open-ended passes had been cut to sixty days. Hedges and his friends worried that mandatory service would follow when this period expired.

It was especially disconcerting to see conscription agents seizing, handcuffing, and forcing men into service against their will, as often happened. Under the circumstances, with service seemingly imminent, the men made plans to leave by way of Florida. They arranged for passes and a guide and left by train under false pretenses on November 21. They took with them a ham (bought at the City Market), some crackers, and two shotguns. After joining their guide in the vicinity of Pollard, 100 miles south of Montgomery, the five comrades proceeded to the safety of Pensacola.[29]

Most local Unionists could have left and chose not to do so. They were not helpless in their struggle against the Confederacy, and they sometimes acted defiantly. A collection was taken up so that money could be given to Charles Sheats when he was released from jail. A notorious Unionist in north Alabama, Sheats had been incarcerated after aiding the enemy and helping to raise Federal troops. William Bibb presented him the money. Early in 1863, following the Battle of Shiloh, Carter helped Dr. Edmund Fowler comfort captured Union soldiers. Carter and his wife smuggled food and mosquito nets from their boardinghouse to the prisoners of war and on one occasion managed to provide the prisoners with the meat from five slaughtered sheep. Carter's audacity matched his loathing of the Confederacy. He gave Benjamin Hardy not only a travel pass but also a hand-sketched map. Having operated a mail stage whose lines extended over 1,000 miles, Carter knew the state's geography well. The map, complete with annotative comments, suggested a route that invading forces might follow to reach Montgomery. Carter stressed the importance of destroying train locomotives and the

Montgomery and West Point line, which transported valuable supplies to Alabama's capital and beyond. He included estimates of troop strength and indicated where federal troops could expect to find Confederate materials. Carter instructed Hardy to give the map to Union officials. "I thought that raids by large forces would soon break up the war," he told the Southern Claims Commission, "if striking at the proper points." Facilitating the escape of Benjamin Hardy constituted a crime that Carter could have been imprisoned for committing. Providing a map outlining an avenue of approach to the former capital of the Confederate States of America went well beyond that.

Most individuals who opposed the Confederacy offered the Lincoln administration little more than philosophical support. Carter's contribution was exceptional. Embattled and fearful, he severely curtailed his activities after helping Hardy. Carter later recalled that Unionists "were so weak that we could do no more than to meet and talk and sympathize with each other." Anyone who did much else risked severe retaliation. Carter claimed at least one Confederate ally. Gus McGibboney had formerly worked for him, was a fellow Mason, and appreciated past favors that the boardinghouse owner had done him. Although McGibboney was loyal to the Confederacy, he assured Carter that he would be discreet and would keep their conversations confidential. McGibboney reaffirmed what the Unionist already understood: there "were men in town who would hang me at a moment's notice."

Black Belt Alabama bore no relation to the hill country of the Ozarks or Appalachia, where Unionism was common. Significant numbers of Federal troops were recruited in parts of Virginia, east Tennessee, western North Carolina, and northern Alabama. A majority of the people in these areas had opposed secession. The situation in Montgomery was different. Although the most fervent patriots wearied of the war and the collapsing economy caused severe hardships, Unionists continued to face persecution in Alabama's capital. As the conflict progressed, the increasing certainty of Confederate defeat was a source of satisfaction to men like Samuel Seelye and James Stow, who felt personally vindicated. The decline of the Confederacy did not bring increased tolerance for its critics, however. Unlike cities in the Upper South, where there was significant Unionist sentiment, and various other places occupied by Federal troops, Montgomery offered the Lincoln government negligible support. David Carter somewhat dramatically declared that "it was a perfect terror here." In fact, authorities carried out no purges of Unionists, even those whose allegiance was publicly known.[30]

A number of Montgomerians had opposed secession and faulted William

Lowndes Yancey. Even in Montgomery, the fire-eater had never been without critics. Almost half the population had voted for Stephen Douglas or John Bell. Yet the conflict brought matters into sharper focus, and the enemy had been clearly delineated by the spring of 1861. In Unionist circles, however, men such as William Bibb consistently viewed the situation differently. "If ever the Confederate government had an enemy in the midst of its friends, or the Union a friend in the midst of its enemies," Reverend Johnson Davis declared, "I think Mr. Bibb was that person."[31]

Thousands of Unionists left the South. In Montgomery, Benjamin Hardy fled, as did William Hedges and his friends. So did George Cowles. Cowles had previously made substantial profits at his dry goods store on Market Street. Advertising on the war's eve that 400 sewing machines had been sold locally, he promised to give buyers sewing lessons. It was much more difficult to promote Unionism, however, and Cowles understood the risks of trying to do so. Samuel Seelye also fully appreciated the dangers for those considered "not sound on the Confederate question."[32]

Most Unionists were unable to leave Montgomery for practical reasons. Those who remained behind struggled to escape unwelcome attention. Hedges studiously conformed to an unwritten code for Unionists in Civil War Montgomery that he described: "safety lies only in silence." Theirs was an unspoken and carefully guarded covenant.[33]

8

Military Preparations Deferred

Proponents who favored removing the capital from Montgomery to Richmond had argued that Virginia would be the scene of critical fighting. They were right. In fact, attempts to take the Confederate capital, and efforts to defend it, framed the fight in the east throughout the war. The opponents of removal had argued that Montgomery was a much safer setting, reasoning that was also borne out by the course of the war. Alabama was generally spared the devastation and occupation that other Southern states suffered. Still, Montgomerians were not able to ignore the threat of Federal forces. As the war wore on, and the enemy advanced into the Deep South, Alabama's capital became less secure.

Some concerns were voiced as early as the spring of 1862. The loss of Forts Henry and Donelson in February shocked Alabamians and permitted the Union to infiltrate the Tennessee Valley. Gunboats traveled up the Tennessee River in the same month and temporarily took control of Florence. More significantly, the Army of the Ohio under General Ormsby Mitchell occupied Huntsville in April. Other towns in north Alabama soon fell into enemy hands and most notoriously Athens, where Union troops committed atrocities. Residents of south Alabama also worried. About 10,000 troops were stationed at Pensacola until the spring of 1862. The Davis administration then shifted its priorities, and forces evacuated the port in May. Mobile, where Confederates controlled garrisons at Fort Gaines and Fort Morgan, remained the linchpin of defense in the area.[1]

Montgomerians initially feared an approach from the Gulf. Some observers wondered what could stop Union gunboats from venturing up the Alabama River if Mobile's defenses were overrun. The *Mail* doubted that the enemy was capable of moving past the port city, and even if it were, the invaders would be unable to find a river pilot who could direct their gunboats. As for an approach up the Alabama, the paper declared early in 1862, "We have banished all doubts."[2] More than a few of the 10,000 residents remained unconvinced and far less brazen. One citizen took pen in hand to observe caustically that everybody worried about a gunboat raid but nobody took precautions. The observer suggested putting slaves to work felling trees and building pens to sink in the river. "We may talk till their gunboats are at the wharf," but "vigorous exertion can and will defeat them."[3] The *Mail* favored establishing military posts at strategic points that could repulse passing ships. Forts or stations commanding the Alabama River were recommended. "A boat might pass the 1st, 2nd, 3rd, 4th, and 5th forts" but, it was noted, "be crippled at the 6th and sunk at the 7th." More time and energy were spent on theorizing than on action.[4]

The river represented but one path. Encroachments in north Alabama in April 1862 caused Governor John Gill Shorter to call for the organization of four cavalry companies. On May 3, a summit of representatives from eleven southern counties (including Montgomery) took place at the theater. The leading local citizens who attended included Congressman William Chilton, P. T. Sayre, John Elmore, and William Rives. In a city missing much of its male population, women had the most to lose. Some women were in the crowd, although none seems to have spoken. William Lowndes Yancey and James Clanton provided the patriotic oratory. Yancey had recently returned from diplomatic maneuvering in Europe as a government envoy. The Battle of Shiloh had most recently concerned Colonel Clanton of the First Alabama Cavalry. Judge John Phelan, proposing a worst case scenario, mentioned the real possibility of occupation. Consideration was given to erecting defenses on the Alabama River. Anticipating a Union advance, William Rives read resolutions calling for the destruction of baled cotton in local warehouses before it could fall into the hands of Federal forces. It remained to pledge continued resistance to the "hateful and despotic Government," from which Alabamians had "withdrawn never to return."[5]

As the governor and a resident, John Gill Shorter worried about the city's safety. In the spring he expressed his concern about a possible Union raid to General John Forney, who commanded the District of the Gulf at Mobile. Shorter suggested removing some federal prisoners from Alabama's capital to Columbus or Macon, Georgia. He also worried about the cotton that filled warehouses. If the capital fell to the enemy, so would the cotton. A rapid advance by the enemy might necessitate transferring the cotton quickly to a safer place. If the valuable staple could not be moved, it should be destroyed. It would be difficult to destroy the bales, however. Cotton was highly flammable, Shorter reminded Forney, and a fire would endanger the city. The correspondence between the two men reached no definitive conclusions, and no action was taken, although Shorter's fear about fire was prophetic.

The governor also expressed to Secretary of War James Seddon a concern about the city's lack of readiness. In a letter to Seddon, Shorter listed potential Union plunder. The inventory included the state capitol, government hospitals, quartermaster, commissary, ordnance stores, and the Alabama Arms Manufacturing Works. If Montgomery was worth capturing, the city was worth defending. Shorter anticipated that Federals might move up the Alabama and "come & occupy Montgomery when they get ready."[6]

Indeed, there was no reason to think otherwise. Montgomerians' early enthusiasm for the Confederate cause had not extended to military preparations; there simply had been none. A home guard that had formed early in 1861 was all but defunct. The Firemen's Guard, led by Captain Edwin Belser, which was far from intimidating, had formed more to protect its members from conscription than for any other reason. The Montgomery Foreign Guards, numbering twenty-four men from such diverse countries as Austria and Canada, were cosmopolitan and little else. Basil Manly was quick to observe that the city had special significance because it had been the first Confederate capital. He concluded that Montgomery in the enemy's eyes was "a special object of hatred."

Despite the warnings, no corrective defensive steps were taken. Nashville, New Orleans, Memphis, and other cities were in Union hands by 1862. In Alabama, Huntsville had been occupied and Mobile had been threatened. Even so, Montgomery did not have a single artillery piece in place, had few men able to offer resistance, and had failed to anticipate the enemy's arrival apart from discussing the problems presented by some cotton bales. Such was the state of affairs when 1863 opened.

Events in the Tennessee Valley in the spring alarmed even the most com-

placent Montgomerians. Over 1,000 Union troops under Colonel Abel
Streight crossed north Alabama. The act—bold but futile, since Streight was
captured—inspired alarm and awakened Montgomerians from their lethargy.
Three militia companies formed within weeks. Edmund Harrison, a local
commission merchant, captained the Alabama Light Infantry Rebels, which
consisted of eight officers and over seventy privates. About the same number of men joined the Montgomery Guards, captained by Samuel Marks. A
planter and lawyer, Marks had recently resigned as Alabama's chief of ordnance because of health problems. The Montgomery Mounted Infantry organized under Captain Samuel Hardaway, a cotton broker. Hardaway had
served as an officer during the Mexican War. In a city where substantial numbers of potential recruits had avoided service, there was no lack of able-
bodied men.

The martial stirring represented more an exercise in self-delusion than
serious preparations for an encounter with a formidable foe. Civilian militias
across the South suffered from a lack of military expertise, of leadership, and
often of patriotic zeal. Such was at least partly the case in Montgomery. In
total, no more than 250 men enrolled. Few knew much about soldiering skill,
and some did not exhibit a desire to learn. This was a civilian militia in
the truest sense, comprising physicians, teachers, people who had hired sub-
stitutes, and others exempt from service, all of whom began belatedly practicing military skills. Job Weatherly (physician), Jacob Kohn (shoemaker), and
Joseph Hale (druggist) were privates in the Alabama Rebels. How diligent
they were it is impossible to determine, but when drilling of the civilian
militia began there was an evident lack of will, a failure of participation, and
general disorganization. As the memory of Streight's raid dimmed, attendance at drill flagged embarrassingly.[7]

Montgomerians did not bask for long in the illusion of security. Ulysses
Grant forced Vicksburg to capitulate in July 1863, and two weeks later Union
troops captured Jackson. These events renewed concern in Alabama. Some
Montgomerians assumed that Federal soldiers might move from Mississippi's
capital toward central Alabama. Fearful Montgomerians called a meeting, and
a large turnout indicated an alarmed state of mind. At the courthouse gathering on July 13, William Chilton listed the dangers posed by troops in north
Alabama and Mississippi. The audience supported Chilton's recommendation
that preparations be made "to meet the enemy with hostile arms." A committee considered laying out defensive plans that included overdue fortifications. Subsequent weeks saw the reinvigoration of the Montgomery Guards

and the Alabama Rebels (the Mounted Infantry had broken up). Merchants began closing at four o'clock three times a week to allow drill.[8] Captain Edmund Harrison threatened to court-martial any Alabama Rebels who failed to attend drill.

It was clear that local defenses could benefit from the support of the Confederate government. In July, Governor Shorter, long concerned about the situation, wrote General Dabney Maury at Mobile to ask that an engineer be dispatched to Montgomery to direct the construction of defense works. Shorter reminded Maury that the capital "offers inviting inducement to the roving marauders of the enemy."[9] Help provided by the government was at least as important as the thin security offered by the militia.

As 1864 opened, seventeen well-placed local men expressed the same views in a letter to Secretary of War James Seddon. James Powell, William Gilmer, George Goldthwaite, and the other signatories understandably took little comfort in the volunteer companies. Pointing out that Montgomery was "in easy striking distance of a cavalry raid," they requested troops to protect the city.[10] Hardened soldiers might be effective; the local companies did not inspire even a false sense of security. The petitioners' assessment of the situation proved correct. Despite the earnest recommendations for defenses and the mustering of local companies, Alabama's capital remained extremely vulnerable. As the *Advertiser* noted, "if there is anything in or about Montgomery which could be called a fortification, we have never seen it."[11]

In the meantime, the city had gained the enemy's attention. Lieutenant General Grant, soon to assume command of all Union armies, envisioned what one scholar has termed a policy of "hard war." His strategy called for a series of raids on Southern cities and railroads that would destroy the South's capacity to make war.[12] Montgomery was one of the state's three significant military targets in the state. Mobile and Selma, one a Gulf port and the other an arms manufacturing center, were the other two. Following the Chattanooga–Lookout Mountain campaign, Union troops had concentrated at this key Tennessee position late in 1863. In December, Grant proposed borrowing from the Tennessee force and immediately pushing into Alabama. He envisioned taking 35,000 troops down the Mississippi to New Orleans, quickly moving against Mobile, heading north to Selma, and then proceeding east to Montgomery. At best, the campaign could bring Mississippi, Alabama, and part of Georgia under Union control. At worst, Grant explained, the thrust would prevent Confederate forces from reorganizing before the spring of 1864. Charles Dana, assistant secretary of war, confidently wrote Secretary of War Edwin Stanton, "I can see nothing to con-demn, but everything to approve, in the scheme." Dana mentioned the po-tential prizes of Selma and Montgomery. Even so, the proposal remained just that. General-in-Chief Henry Halleck considered it more important to con-solidate gains elsewhere and ruled out the advance.[13]

Montgomery's security and that of the Confederacy as a whole were in-extricably linked. This fact boded ill for the Alabama capital. Campaigns in the east and west during 1863 had gone badly for the South at Gettysburg, Vicksburg, Lookout Mountain, Missionary Ridge, and elsewhere. The situ-ation deteriorated further in 1864. Held at bay since the war's outset, the Army of the Potomac began an advance on Richmond that eventually led to the capital's fall. In Georgia, enemy forces in the spring and summer moved toward Atlanta. In June, Jefferson Davis had dispatched General Braxton Bragg to Atlanta to assess the Confederate position. Among other conclusions, Bragg noted the vulnerability of transportation and the threat to supplies. "Our railroad communication with Montgomery is now at the mercy of the enemy," Bragg concluded, "and a mere raid may destroy Montgomery. . . . this is no fancy sketch."[14]

Montgomerians were of course not privy to the correspondence be-tween high-level Confederates. The city remained in a defenseless state. Even the city council, composed of responsible public servants, exhibited a studied lack of concern. A revival was in full swing by June, and soldiers (and others) were baptized in the waters of the Alabama River. J. J. Kane, who fought with the Montgomery Greys and the Sixth Alabama Regiment, came home hav-ing lost a leg at Gettysburg and having spent nine months at the Old Capital Prison in Washington. He received many visitors. Local girls sang "The Moon Rose O'er the Battle Plain," "Drummer Boy of Shiloh," and "My Love Is a Soger Boy" during a benefit for wounded soldiers. B. F. Blount and Joseph Hale, next to the Central Bank on Court Square, advertised the arrival of blockade goods, including indigo, quinine, and castor oil, in their drug-stores. Even so, as the *Mail* conceded, the absence of the new issue of money was "severely felt," and "business is dull." Such was the situation when Union raiders suddenly approached the city.[15]

Braxton Bragg had mentioned the possibility of a raid and the likelihood that the railroad line linking Atlanta and Montgomery would be destroyed. His surmise partially anticipated Federal objectives. Montgomery's capitula-tion was not as high on the Union's list of military priorities as was inter-rupting railroad communication between central Alabama and Confederate forces in Georgia. In July 1864, the task fell to General Lovell Rousseau. A veteran of various campaigns, Rousseau had served at Decatur, Alabama. After consulting with General William Sherman (who was then near Kennesaw Mountain and was moving toward Atlanta), Rousseau mounted an offensive into the heart of Alabama.

Rousseau planned to head south from Decatur, cross the Tallapoosa and Coosa Rivers, and fall on the Montgomery and West Point Railroad east of Montgomery. Wiring Rousseau from his Georgia headquarters on July 6, Sherman declared, "If managed with secrecy and rapidity the expedition cannot fail of success and will accomplish much good." The objective— clearly stated and consistent with federal war strategy—was to wreck the Montgomery and West Point Railroad and to inflict structural damage. A neat surgical strike might crucially weaken the Confederate supply line.

On July 10, Rousseau and about 2,500 cavalrymen left Decatur. Moving south, the mounted men reached the Coosa River in three days. Outnumbered cavalry forces under Montgomery's James Clanton unsuccessfully contested the crossing at Ten Islands Ford on July 14. All opposition temporarily disappeared. The Federal horsemen occupied Talladega the next day and on Saturday, July 16, continued south toward Montgomery. Later that day, Rousseau's force was within thirty miles of the city. Having feigned an advance on the city, Rousseau turned east and made for the Montgomery and West Point Railroad.[16]

Notice of the enemy's approach reached Montgomery soon after Rousseau left Decatur. Skeptics initially raised doubts, but confirmation that Union troops were at Talladega and were continuing to approach prompted a general alert. There was growing concern by Friday, July 15, and on Saturday, with the cavalry moving toward the capital, anxiety reached a new level. What had once been unthinkable—the specter of marauding Yankee cavalrymen galloping down city streets—now began to seem inevitable. Knots of citizens traded speculations. Store owners closed their shops. Some of the populace fled the city.

The war, it seemed, had finally reached the birthplace of the Confederacy. A large crowd attended an emergency meeting Saturday evening at the courthouse. General Jones Withers, commanding state reserve troops, and the ranking local officer took charge of defense. Post commandant Walter Jones also figured importantly. Couriers rode to strategic points and ferries where Union troops might cross the Alabama River. The Montgomery Guards and Alabama Rebels, marching down Market Street, ostensibly resolved to offer forceful resistance. Calls for volunteers rang out, makeshift defenses took shape, and Captain Charles Wagner passed out weapons from the government arsenal. Furloughed soldiers and even some hospital patients took up arms, and by 11:00 P.M. civilians and soldiers had formed a line of defense.

Major Jones and other informed observers understood that frantic and belated preparations could not compensate for previous neglect. It was not even remotely possible that the Union cavalry could be repulsed. It could only be hoped that Federal troops would not come to Montgomery. Citizens waited in various stages of anxiety. Women and children remained in their homes. No one could be sure what the enemy intended to do. Late Saturday night some welcome news came. The Federal troops had moved east and away from the city. Although little else was known, the crisis had passed by Sunday morning.[17]

In the meantime, Rousseau's forces reached their objective. On Sunday, July 17, Union cavalrymen arrived at Loachapoka, a small village forty miles east of Alabama's capital, on the Montgomery and West Point line. Sherman had urged Rousseau to tear up the rails by heating and twisting the iron so that the track would be beyond repair. The troops worked through the night and went beyond Sherman's instructions by burning several buildings at Loachapoka. Enemy detachments set off in various directions on Monday morning. Forces under the command of Major Harlon Baird of the Fifth Iowa Cavalry moved several miles southwest to Chehaw Station on the railroad line.

In Montgomery, opposing forces had assembled. Honoring the requests of authorities, General Dabney Maury at Mobile had sent 500 soldiers to the city. Arriving on Sunday, they piled on a freight train that evening and headed east to confront the enemy. Sharp skirmishing resulted when this force encountered Major Baird's soldiers at Chehaw Station on Monday morning, July 18. Although the Union forces were initially at a disadvantage, they routed the Confederates, and the destruction continued there and elsewhere. Rousseau's men repeated similar acts on Tuesday and then moved east and rendezvoused with Sherman's forces.

Montgomery had been spared, but over thirty miles of track between Chehaw Station and Columbus, Georgia, lay in ruins. As Rousseau was to report, the troops had destroyed the rails in a "most thorough manner."[18] Union cavalrymen also pillaged commissary and quartermaster stores, freight cars, and various buildings. For several weeks supplies (mainly stored at Montgomery) and munitions (manufactured at Selma) were delayed in reaching Confederate troops in Georgia. Success cost the Union fewer than fifty casualties. One conclusion was inescapable: given the short notice, the lack of available resources, and the enemy's effective plan, the results could have been worse. Montgomerians could contemplate what might have been. Several captured Union prisoners were armed with repeating rifles, sabers, pistols, and generally the "most approved of deadly weapons."[19] As it was, the price for one family had been high. Lieutenant Theodore Bethea, the twenty-two-year-old son of Tristam and Eugenia Bethea, was at home recovering from a wound received at Spotsylvania, Virginia. He left with the forces from Montgomery and was shot and killed at Chehaw Station.

The task of mending the thirty-mile break and restoring the link with Atlanta assumed high priority. General Maury dispatched Major George Whitfield of the Railroad Bureau to Alabama's capital and urged him to "please press it forward with all your energy." Montgomerians responded when the Quartermaster Department advertised for 200 wagons to haul freight. Frank Gilmer, president of the South and North Alabama Railroad Company, donated a number of wagons, mules, and drivers. Telegraph wires were restrung, and connections with Atlanta were restored. Slaves were vitally involved in the reconstruction work. Black teamsters were soon hauling supplies overland to Columbus to be forwarded to Atlanta by rail. Slaves also helped repair the railroad track, and on August 27, ten days after Rousseau's depredations, the first through train reached Montgomery.[20]

In his memoirs William Sherman minimized the raid's impact, because the railroad was quickly repaired. Still, he thought that the results "must have disturbed the enemy somewhat."[21] He was correct. The incursion destroyed residents' false sense of security and brought home the gravity of warfare. As the *Mail* reported, the city lost its "reputation of being one of the safest places of the Confederacy." The fearful image of the marauding Federal horseman took on a new reality.[22]

In the wake of the threat posed by Rousseau's troops, definitive preparations began at last. Although the war was in its thirty-ninth month, there were no fortifications. Captain John Vinet of the Engineering Bureau soon arrived and began directing construction. Once again the black population was called upon. Within several days of the raid, slaves began digging rifle pits and breastworks at the city's edge. Vinet supervised and drafted an imposing defensive blueprint. It had taken near disaster to provoke action, but progress was rapid. As one living in the Alabama capital wrote, "We might almost imagine someone had found the lamp of Aladdin, and had summoned the genie to his assistance." Eventually, trenchworks four feet deep and six feet wide stretched from the north to the south bank of the Alabama River and circled the city. Ramparts provided further protection. Twelve small field cannon were arranged in an open block on Washington Street. Sixteen larger and more imposing guns waited at the arsenal. The powder magazine out on Bell Street near the river was fully stocked with ammunition.[23]

Citizens remained alarmed by the recent past and were unable to reassure themselves about the future. Rousseau's accomplishments were less important in isolation than in the context of the war as a whole. The fractured Confederacy was now more vulnerable than ever. Two weeks after Rousseau's raid, on August 5, gunboats commanded by Admiral David Farragut moved past Forts Morgan and Gaines and into Mobile Bay. The situation in Mobile stabilized, but Atlanta fell several weeks later in early September.

Once again it became necessary to assess Montgomery's security. Earlier in 1864 the Indian tragedy *Metamora; or, The Last of the Wampanoags* had played at the theater. In it, the wise and noble Chief Metamora died valiantly fighting the white encroachers on Wampanoag tribal lands. The scene increasingly seemed relevant to Montgomerians.

There was an understandable reaction to the removal and publication of the *Memphis Daily Appeal* in Montgomery. Its proprietors had first fled Memphis when Union troops occupied the city in 1862. Federal troops had subsequently forced the peripatetic paper from Grenada and Jackson, Mississippi, and then from Atlanta in August 1864. Issues of the *Appeal* first appeared in Montgomery in mid-September. Worried that the paper represented the "avant courier of the Yankees," one observer admitted that citizens were "by no means delighted at the idea of its domiciliation."[24]

Early in the war the Unionists had settled on a strategy conceived by General Winfield Scott. The Anaconda Plan called for a naval blockade of the southern coast. Land and naval forces were then to move down the Mississippi River toward New Orleans so that they strangled the South economically. As early as October 1862, Edward Moren speculated that "the great Anaconda will surely begin to tighten." The assumption that Montgomery might be taken and burned seemed possible by 1864. Federal policymakers had earlier considered moving on the first Confederate capital but had made no concerted effort to do so. The situation changed, however, as the war wound down.[25]

9

The End Nears

WHAT MONTGOMERIANS READ IN the *Mail* shortly after New Year's Day 1865 came as no surprise. The editor declared that without "Providential interference," which seemed unlikely, the Confederacy could not prevail. "It would be wicked to deceive others," the *Mail* concluded, and "it is unwise to deny the truth to ourselves."[1] From Drewry's Bluff, near Richmond, Corporal Thomas Caffey wrote his relatives on January 15, "I have from the beginning of the war thought there did not exist a doubt of the South's finally achieving its independence." Now the Montgomery soldier felt differently.

As 1865 opened, there were unmistakable signs that the Confederate States of America were in peril. Having left Atlanta in smoldering ruins, Sherman's army had marched eastward across Georgia, had taken Savannah several days before Christmas, and was now spreading devastation in the Carolinas. The Army of Tennessee, shrunken in men, arms, and spirit, had recently been defeated at the Battle of Franklin. Grant's forces had pinned down the other major Confederate force, the Army of Northern Virginia, in the Richmond-Petersburg area. In Virginia, and in every significant theater, Northern soldiers vastly outnumbered their Southern foes. Military prospects were undeniably bleak, and optimistic pronouncements in the Southern press sounded increasingly empty.[2]

The breakdown of government was equally debilitating. As one writer has observed, Richmond authorities had for some time been internally pursuing the road to ruin. Paper currency was almost worthless, and the monetary system was in disarray. A lack of confidence in the currency often made it impossible to procure vital supplies. By the fall of 1864 both the Quartermaster and the Subsistence Departments had run out of funds. Even if supplies could be bought, it was extremely difficult to transport and distribute them using the few worn-down railroads that the Confederacy still controlled.[3]

The unraveling of the government infrastructure was painfully evident in Montgomery. Strains and shortages made it harder than ever to carry on government business. W. W. Guy, the district commissary agent, had collected and purchased supplies since at least 1863. In January 1865, he issued a pessimistic appraisal. Guy estimated that a lack of funds had cost the Subsistence Department 200,000 pounds of bacon, 1,500 head of cattle, 10,000 bushels of wheat, and 12,000 hogs. He could not get any credit, had no money for the hospitals, and was unable to pay employees. The beleaguered agent had recently estimated the district debt at $1.5 million.

Colonel George Brent, assistant adjutant general to P. G. T. Beauregard, provided corroboration as 1865 opened. Writing Beauregard from Montgomery, he described the domino-like effect of insolvency. Transportation was moving slowly due to the "total want of quartermasters' funds," and impressment was impossible. The government owned some stock and cattle and more supplies could be obtained by a tax-in-kind commitment, but "one difficulty stares us right in the face—the want of money."[4]

Montgomery remained an important transportation and departmental junction, a place where war materials were stored and requisitioned. Government supplies arrived daily at the Montgomery and West Point and the Alabama and Florida railroad depots. Officials had belatedly connected the depots by rail, a move that expedited the flow of supplies, cut drayage costs, and—importantly from the standpoint of Montgomerians—settled much of the dust. Even so, no railroad linked Selma with Montgomery, and this major gap in the Southern network was extremely inconvenient. The fifty-mile distance was spanned by boats on the Alabama River and by wagons moving overland. Ordnance and foodstuffs passed over the wharf. On one typical

January day, stevedores unloaded twelve guns, six caissons, five horses, and seventy-one boxes of ammunition from the *Gertrude.*

The city remained an important transfer point for soldiers. Most belonged to the much-diminished Army of Tennessee in Mississippi. They were needed in North Carolina, and some regiments were brought up the Alabama River. In early January, 700 soldiers of the Forty-first, Forty-second, and Forty-third Georgia Infantry Regiments disembarked from the *Southern Republic.* Others reached Montgomery after being routed through Mobile and then transported on the Alabama and Florida Railroad line. One local resident remarked, "our city has been alive with the stir of passing troops."[5]

Post officials continued their efforts. Commandant Walter Jones, well known to Montgomerians, provided Richmond with monthly reports. At the recently opened government shoe shop on Tallapoosa Street, quartermaster employees turned out over a hundred pairs of shoes daily. Quartermaster bureau captain William Gillaspie alerted local women that uniforms were needed. Conscription Bureau officials searched for deserters and those illegally avoiding service—a group whose membership had increased across the South. Taking note of stragglers and deserters removed from the streets, the *Mail* noted that the bureau seemed to be working with "oiled wheels."[6]

Major William Price, a superintendent with the Niter and Mining Bureau, directed operations from his Market Street office. He asked for lead, promised compensation, and voiced the hope that "Montgomery will not be behind Mobile in this matter."[7] Several miles outside of the city, on the Lower Wetumpka Road, Charles Clapp continued to supervise niter cultivation. Niter, or saltpeter, took about three years to mature. Blacks almost exclusively composed the labor force. Little niter had actually been produced, but an observer predicted large yields, and reflecting on the operation's small origins, wondered about "the size to which the small beginning has been carried."[8]

At the arsenal, the vigilant Captain Charles Wagner fought his own losing battle. A recent estimate placed production each month at 6 sets of horse harnesses, 10,000 infantry accouterments, 3,000 haversacks, and 8,000 cedar canteens. Materials and labor, as in the past, remained woefully lacking. Some formerly exempted arsenal employees had been forced into the undermanned Southern armies. Wagner depended heavily on the black population, and in the final days he advertised for slave workers, promising rations, clothes, and board. J. R. Waddy, an ordnance officer who had inspected arsenals at Augusta, Macon, Columbus, and Mobile, arrived in January. A disappointed Waddy decided that only "a limited amount of work" had been completed when the Montgomery operation was "compared with the other arsenals visited by me."[9]

By early 1865, Montgomery had more soldiers in local hospitals than did any other site in Georgia, Alabama, or Mississippi. Surgeon Watson Gentry, overseeing medical care, frequently visited all six hospitals, where over thirty surgeons and several hundred staff members—including matrons, cooks, druggists, and laundresses—cared for a total of about 2,000 patients. Surgeon Gentry enjoyed the luxury of having numerous medical officers and even mentioned to medical director Samuel Stout that some of them could be transferred. Still, he worried that an attack on Mobile might send evacuated hospital patients to crowded Montgomery. As matters stood, there were more patients than beds, and some were forced into tents pitched near Edmund Harrison's home at the corner of Washington and Bibb Streets—the former residence of Jefferson and Varina Davis.

The scene at the four major hospitals—General, Ladies, Madison, and Concert Hall—had changed little or not at all. On the outskirts, the less seriously sick and wounded men convalesced at either Stonewall or Watts, the tent hospitals. In March, Surgeon William Cole at Stonewall Hospital offered his resignation. His wife was sick, duties in Montgomery had separated them for three and a half years, and he described his neglect of her as "deeply criminal," although he had "acted on *principle wholly from the beginning* of the revolution." [10] Gentry expressed regret at losing Cole, but in another case, he was relieved to transfer a certain hospital steward who "has made himself so objectionable that no one . . . wants anything to do with him."[11]

On the day after Christmas in 1864 the annual Christmas benefit banquet at Ladies Hospital was held for the last time. Philanthropic efforts on behalf of soldiers and the poor continued. Citizens also supplied the straw or hay needed to refill beds at Stonewall Hospital. Contributions were forwarded in January when the linen matron at Concert Hall Hospital advertised the need for bandages. Montgomerians crowded the theater on two February nights to benefit the sick and wounded soldiers of the Army of Tennessee. Women sang songs, and over $12,000 was raised.

The collection taken up at St. John's Episcopal Church on the first Sunday in March was donated to residents of Columbia, South Carolina. Two weeks earlier Sherman's troops had entered the city and burned much of Columbia. Montgomerians closed businesses and observed a "prayer and fasting" day on Friday, March 10. Two services were held that day at a recently established Methodist church on Herron Street. The *Mail* urged soldiers to fill the "little church to overflowing." Ellen Blue, a resident and an avid sympathizer, ate sparingly and drank only one cup of coffee before evening. Only poor health kept her from abstaining completely on the last Confederate fast day.[12] Late in March, women prepared and served food to paroled prisoners at Ladies Hospital. The poignant scene revived "a recollection of a more healthful season of the spirit of Southern independence."[13]

The state legislature gave Meyer Lehman of Lehman, Durr and Company a unique service to perform. In December 1864, legislators authorized $5 million for the relief of Alabama soldiers in federal prisons. Commerce with the United States government had been forbidden, but more and more items were being traded through the lines. The legislators planned for the state to generate revenue by purchasing cotton and shipping it to cotton buyers. Someone familiar with Northern cotton connections was needed to make arrangements. Governor Watts brought Lehman's qualifications to the attention of Jefferson Davis. The executive described the entrepreneur as "a man of established character" and, although a foreigner, "one of the best Southern patriots." Watts asked the Reverend Isaac Tichenor to assist on the mercy mission. Davis approved the plans, and Lehman and Tichenor traveled to Richmond, where they received passports.[14]

Grant spent much of January at his headquarters at City Point, Virginia. Writing him there, the Montgomerians urged him as a soldier to sympathize with "those brave men who by the fortunes of war are held as prisoners."[15] Lehman and Tichenor assured the general that their concerns were humanitarian and not military or political. Grant did not cooperate. He never replied except to have Richmond authorities informed that only commissioners of exchange could make such arrangements. On March 7, after the mission had failed, Davis wrote Watts from Richmond, "every facility was afforded the agent that was possible under the circumstances."[16]

The Confederacy's death watch in Montgomery continued under difficult circumstances. At Hamner Hall, where Principal Avery Shepherd had reluctantly raised tuition to meet expenses, girls proceeded with the study of English, French, music, embroidery, and drawing. In a culture that prized the social graces, the amenities could not be overlooked even in the most difficult of times. Professor J. St. Maur Bingham accepted pupils at his Dancing Academy, where he enthusiastically demonstrated the "new and fashionable" dances. In these financially stringent times, Bingham declared, tuition was "positively payable in advance."[17] Hamner Hall music professor T. N.

Caulfield offered singing lessons and was described as "fully competent to form the voice."[18]

In 1860, when the Montgomery Theater had opened, residents had viewed it as a crowning touch to their city. The theater at the corner of Perry and Monroe Streets by 1865 offered a metaphor for the general deterioration in Alabama's capital. A dwindling number of citizens watched inferior plays in increasingly uncomfortable surroundings. Even Manager William Crisp—redoubtable, talented, and long suffering—could not reverse the trend. Some plays, such as *Lucretia Borgia, the Poisoner,* were well received. Yet patrons tired of the repertoire, the poor accommodations, and, often, the inferior perform-ance. On December 28, 1864, a small audience watched the drama *Richelieu; or, The Conspiracy.* Thomas Hamilton, one of the more popular actors, por-trayed the chief minister of King Louis XIII in what was to be the last play of the season. Montgomerians could not know that they were witnessing the last production of the war years. One critic, referring to the "comfortless building, a piano rather out of tune—a squeaking violin, and an old clarinet," doubted they would have cared.[19]

In January the flooding Alabama River left its banks. Boats were needed to pass over some inundated streets and lots. The high water made rabbits and game easy prey for hunters. Wood floating down the river provided timely fuel for the poor. By late January temperatures had plunged, and one resident observed, "It is cold enough to pass for winter on the mountains of Vir-ginia."[20] Chaos reigned during the twilight of the Confederacy. "The great all-absorbing question that now agitates the public mind," according to one civic-minded individual, was "whether the beautiful city of Montgomery ought to be called a cow-yard."[21]

Trade and commerce, long stagnant, remained in the doldrums at the start of 1865. M. A. Jones, a widow, offered oysters at Forrest Restaurant, and cus-tomers enjoyed "all the luxuries of the season" at the Rialto Restaurant.[22] The Mobile Coffee House claimed to serve meals "at all hours."[23] The con-sumption of beer, wine, and harder spirits continued unabated. Joseph Bihler dispensed lager beer at the Lafayette House throughout the Confederacy's final months.

Benjamin Barton peddled the most recent (and last) edition of the *Con-federate States Almanac* from his bookstore, and Joel White catered to readers' requests at Pfister and White's. Samuel Wreford, at the One Armed Man's Dry Goods store, advertised coffee for "those who consider price no object."[24] Many stores had closed, but a few actually opened in the last months of the war. William Perry began selling confectioneries from a Commerce Street address in January and boasted that "service on the field ever since the war commenced" had earned him customer loyalty. Citizens took an interest in Perry's inventory, which included French, English, and Confederate stationery, pins, laces, toilet soaps, and "in fact a thousand and one things that everybody in the city is sure to want."[25]

It was also true that the standard pattern of exchanging money for products or services remained extremely unsettled. Druggist H. B. Metcalf discontinued his credit policy and demanded cash payments for prescriptions. Doctors combated inflation by setting higher fees. Meeting on January 17, fifteen of the best known doctors, including William Baldwin, Edward Semple, Abraham Gindrat, Job Weatherly, Samuel Seelye, and Samuel Norton, signed a guildlike manifesto establishing standard rates for visits and care. President William Gilmer of the Red Mountain Iron and Coal Company (formerly the Alabama Arms Manufacturing Company) presided over a meeting of stockholders two weeks later. In the meantime, production of the Enfield rifle had belatedly begun at the Gilmers' gun factory. A visitor to the manufactory endorsed the product in unequivocal terms: "We do not think a better gun has been made or imported into the Confederacy."[26]

Three years had passed since Albert Strasser and John Callahan had begun providing prosthetic limbs. An Arkansas soldier who had been a customer wrote of "the ease and perfect agreeableness of the one [limb] I am now using."[27] Captain John Travis, of "Travis Gun" fame, opened a pistol and rifle gallery under the Exchange and promised lessons to those wishing "to acquire a thorough knowledge of the art."[28]

From Columbia, South Carolina, Emma LeConte wrote, "I wonder if the new year is to bring us new miseries and sufferings. I am afraid so."[29] Many Montgomerians felt as she did. Citizens looked longer and harder before buying and paid more for commodities. Some merchants refused to take certain treasury notes. Given the slightest opportunity, speculators gouged. Shortages were endemic. The public depended increasingly on auctioneers, who located items often not available in stores. W. Broadbridge, "indefatigable caterer for universal comfort," offered watches, jewelry, tobacco, and other goods.[30] Auctioneers also supplied buggies, horses, and mules.

Broadbridge did not sell slaves; some auctioneers continued to do so. A few individuals placed bids at the Artesian Basin in January for field hands, shoemakers, plasterers, and wagoners. From his Market Street slave depot, Thomas Frazer made available a mulatto girl who could serve as a lady's waiting maid or nurse. Mason Harwell offered for sale a shoemaker, a blacksmith, a wagoner, and a cook, all slaves. Other individuals attempted to sell property. Numbers of refugees had recently arrived from Mobile. An established citizen advertised a home outside the city as representing "a good opportunity for refugees." Most found few "opportunities" in a city of economic collapse, destitution, and little hope.[31]

The slave population, however, did have hope. A twenty-one-year-old black man had recently been advertised as a "No. l. Negro man" adept as a bar keeper or "store boy." For him, and for over 4,000 other blacks, bondage was nearing an end. Slaves had generally concealed their desire for freedom. As the war ended, more blacks than ever "hired their own time" out. Reacting to the trend, the city council early in 1865 approved an ordinance that declared the wages earned by slaves a "great evil." Slaves had been exercising more and more privileges throughout the South, and Montgomery was no exception.[32] The police were authorized to arrest those who "habitually go at large in the city."[33]

On the streets, Montgomerians spoke of "rights," "tyranny," and the forfeiture of their "liberties." By 1865 they could just as easily have meant the Confederate States of America as the administration of Abraham Lincoln. There was a backlog of complaints. Conscription Bureau officials were heavy-handed. Confederate agents continued to impress goods. Prized carriage horses and slaves were seized in the name of the Confederacy. Several months earlier Sallie Sanford had objected when a Confederate official removed a servant from her household. Her husband, a soldier writing from Petersburg, Virginia, reacted angrily and vowed to challenge the "absurd" and "wrongful" act of "incompetent officials."[34] Montgomerians also felt aggrieved because impressment officials had in the past paid them prices consistently lower than market value for commodities and produce. Sometimes government representatives gave them no money at all but merely certificates authorizing future payment. In short, residents had many reasons, as one military official noted, to "evade the impressing officer every possible way."[35]

The war was never out of mind. Acquaintances of Virgil Murphey, fearing that he was dead, were relieved to learn that he was confined at Johnson's Island Prison on Lake Erie. Murphey had been missing since the Battle of Franklin in November 1864. Willie Baldwin, the nineteen-year-old son of William and Mary Baldwin, had been killed in the same battle. Montgomerians took an interest in Foreman's Battery, which was displayed at the capitol. With fifteen barrels and mounted on a wheeled frame, the formidable weapon could fire sixty balls a minute. One observer declared that Foreman's Battery might "enable us to meet an invading force of ten times our number." Fighting words and bravado remained, but nothing could mitigate the reality of defeat. In February, the fall of Charleston elicited both despair and resignation.[36]

The city council had continued to meet frequently during the war. Walter Coleman, as mayor, convened the aldermen as 1865 began. Various ideas for improvements were discussed. Several private citizens petitioned city government to declare the Forrest Barroom a "nuisance" and to close it.[37] Throughout the war, councilmen fielded complaints, and 1865 was no different. One controversy brought to their attention related to the exorbitantly high prices charged by hackmen. The *Advertiser,* outraged, protested that "none of these sooty Jehus pretend to charge less than $25 to go to a funeral." By repealing city code provisions allowing bondsmen to hire themselves out, the council passed one of the final ordinances directed exclusively at slaves in the South.

Some dilemmas seemed insoluble. The numbers of the impoverished rose steadily, and suffering reached unprecedented levels. Samuel Norton, protector of the poor, had recently informed the Presbyterian congregation that the underfed and underclothed were living in cellars. Refugees were among the poorest. Those who had left their homes and cities had begun arriving as early as 1862. Given high prices in Montgomery, the *Mail* asked why they did not relocate elsewhere. By 1865 perhaps as many as one person in three was a transient. Although it cannot now be determined with certainty, the mortality rate almost certainly increased. Early in the year undertaker John Newbold collected $200 from the city for interring the indigent.[38]

The *Mail*'s editor called on the city council to give the police a raise. After all, officers ran "a daily risk of having their heads broken by a set of drunken deserters, stragglers and thieves."[39] Beat officers, overseen by City Marshal Isaac Maxwell and Deputy Marshal Thomas Reed, were seldom idle day or night. As usual, the docket of the mayor's court was crowded. James Curry's notoriety reflected both his Northern background and his criminal proclivities. In January the "consummate villain," who was accused of stealing a pocketbook and a gold watch, appeared before Mayor Walter Coleman.[40]

Slaves committed a variety of small crimes and were severely punished. A slight measure of real justice was meted out when a citizen was fined fifty dollars for administering more than 400 lashes to a female slave accused of stealing some silver spoons. Women consistently crossed the bounds of the law. Possibly more women resorted to prostitution as a result of hard times, but in any case efforts to halt the practice failed. "Madame" Lou Champion was the acknowledged proprietress of a "well known resort for those misguided young men who lust after the so-called pleasures of the world."[41]

Eight days into 1865, the Southern capital of Richmond was described as being "full of people, and suffering, and crime."[42] Comparable chaos reigned in Montgomery. Soldiers caused trouble. One resident complained of "too many drunken hospital rats floating about the city."[43] According to another, soldiers' days were "spent in idleness and dissipation" and "their nights . . . devoted to debauchery and crime."

Not surprisingly officials sensed that there would be trouble when the Army of Tennessee passed through. A circular declared that soldiers camping near the city could enter only with a pass.[44] Arriving by steamboat in late January, members of the Fifteenth Texas Infantry Regiment were among those who settled down on the city's edge. Hardship and defeat had diminished their respect for authority, and many ignored orders to remain in camp. Numbers of Texans and Arkansans began their night with drinking and dancing at the Lighthouse, a river beer saloon. The situation degenerated when the soldiers found some whiskey in a Dutchman's nearby grocery, "soon commenced clerking for him," and carried on late into the night.[45]

Several days later, in early February, a merchant thanked the City Guard for dispersing a band of "riotous soldiers" in front of his store and thereby "saving my property." The City Guard, an unofficial volunteer body, assisted the police.[46] Order had never been so precariously balanced. On Tuesday, February 14, drunk and rowdy soldiers tried to force their way into a benefit concert at the theater. That same evening unidentified parties disrupted services at a black church and forced adjournment. At least four Confederates spent the night of March 6 in the Monroe Street jail. Police arrested them for drunkenness, a "fact none of them seemed inclined to dispute," and they paid a five-dollar fine the next day.[47]

Soldiers were sometimes on the receiving end of violence. The watchman at the Exchange Hotel shot and seriously wounded Lieutenant T. L. Loyd on the evening of February 20. Several nights later, a drunken soldier from the Seventh Tennessee Infantry fell from a fourth story window at the Exchange, losing a few teeth and breaking his jawbone in the process. Private William Warren, a Georgian, was convicted of bigamy on February 27. Judge Benajah Bibb considered Warren's plea for leniency in criminal court but sentenced him to three years in the penitentiary. Warren, in tears, thanked the judge for showing him mercy.[48]

Such compassion was not extended to L. C. Poole. Poole, a private in the Fifty-third Alabama Infantry, had been incarcerated in the city jail pending trial for the murder of George Laprade of Montgomery. Strong feelings were expressed locally, and William Chilton, Jr., the defendant's lawyer, asked for a change in venue soon after the opening of circuit court. The entreaty was refused. The jury deliberated overnight on February 21 before finding Poole guilty of first degree murder. At the sentencing several days later, Poole maintained he knew no more about Laprade's death than "any man in the room." Yet he well understood the rigors of the city jail dungeon. After a difficult stay there, he appealed for better treatment. Judge Bibb sentenced Poole to death by hanging on March 31 but ordered him to be handled less severely during incarceration prior to execution.[49]

Military reverses and hardships on the home front had undermined Southern morale. The populace desperately desired peace. Many called for an end to the conflict. Philosophical notions of sovereignty and nationhood seemed less important than hunger, impoverishment, and death. Peace societies had formed in Alabama and all Southern states. It is impossible to determine whether Montgomery had one. By 1865, certainly, opposition to continued hostilities had increased significantly.

A number of citizens met in early January to discuss terminating the war on terms offered by the Lincoln administration. A correspondent of the *Mobile Advertiser and Register* described them as a "little clique of submissionists."[50] That was probably an understatement. In late January the Davis administration appointed commissioners to discuss a peace arrangement with the United States. Three Southern emissaries met with President Lincoln and Secretary of State William Seward aboard a transport ship at Hampton Roads on February 3. Nothing was resolved, however, and the war continued. Noting the impasse at Hampton Roads, the *Mail* predicted that the upcoming spring would "usher in a more vigorous prosecution of the invasion policy than ever."[51]

Women in particular were weary of the war. In Richmond, women had rioted in 1863 because of lack of food. Suffering at home also provoked violence in Atlanta, Columbus, Mobile, and Augusta, Georgia. Although conditions were bad in Montgomery, violent protests did not take place. Some women continued to comfort soldiers and remained loyal to the Southern cause. Many more women were bitter, disconsolate, and ready to abandon the

Confederacy. The soldier husband of Mary Boyd, for example, had been a railroad worker before the war. From the outset, she and their three girls—Lenora, Elonza, and Mary—received public assistance. Mary Boyd and hundreds like her longed for the conflict's end. Years later one local woman who had lived through the war told an interviewer, "That time is a blank horror in my life."[52]

On the night of Saturday, February 25, a large crowd gathered at the theater for a crisis meeting. Benajah Bibb, the criminal court magistrate, told the crowd that the choice was between independence or degradation and that he favored continuing the fight. Governor Watts spoke for two hours and exaggerated Southern strength. He maintained that although the enemy had larger numbers of troops, Southern soldiers were superior in the field. This argument, which many had accepted at one time, was no longer convincing. A sense of desperation prevailed. Captain Ben Lane Posey, rising from the crowd, sounded the most controversial note. He introduced a resolution that recommended arming slaves and promising emancipation to the faithful. Another citizen disagreed and, amid much cheering, contended that if white men could not earn independence, then it was not deserved. Several Confederate officers spoke. James Clanton, by 1865 a brigadier general, called for "severe invective against everything which savored of yielding to Yankee demands." The crowd greeted Lieutenant Colonel Mike Woods, back only a few weeks from Johnson's Island prison in Ohio, with loud applause. Lieutenant Colonel John Gaines, an officer from the Fifty-third Alabama Cavalry who had lost a leg at Waynesboro, North Carolina, created the greatest stir. He stood on crutches before the crowd and urged continued resistance.[53]

A few days later citizens at the theater listened as the Reverend Isaac Tichenor summarized the efforts that he and Meyer Lehman had made to provide for the prisoners. It was fitting that a clergyman delivered one of the final Confederate eulogies. Tichenor expressed his high regard for Jefferson Davis and the residents of Richmond. He considered fighting far preferable to accepting "submission to Abraham Lincoln, and his black cohorts."[54] The meeting then adopted resolutions establishing a society to promote the cause. The following day, citizens meeting at the First Baptist Church created the Society of Loyal Confederates. Charter members pledged "to work out the independence and salvation of our country." Salvation for the South seemed possible despite the demise of hopes for independence.[55]

10

A City Surrendered

In 1865 Montgomery was one of five capitals controlled by Confederate officials. Change had come quickly. After being defeated at Franklin and Nashville late in 1864, the Army of Tennessee moved toward North Carolina to meet Sherman. The shift left north and central Alabama vulnerable. Union forces had controlled Mobile Bay since September 1864, and by early 1865 General Edward Canby was completing plans to assault Mobile itself. Grant considered having Canby proceed from Mobile and attack Selma and Montgomery. As 1864 ended, Henry Halleck, the chief of staff, told Grant that there were valuable concentrations of material at both points and emphasized the importance of railroads. Several weeks later, in mid-January, he assured the Union field commander that both Selma and Montgomery could be taken that winter. Grant responded from his headquarters in City Point, Virginia, within hours of receiving Halleck's communication. He concurred with the estimate made by the chief of staff. If Mobile fell, Grant believed, Selma and Montgomery could easily be reached. He was anxious for the campaign to begin and proposed "destroying everything useful for carrying on war."[1]

Canby eventually forced Mobile to capitulate, but he never advanced on Montgomery. Even so, Union strategists made a strong case for conducting a campaign into central Alabama. Grant wrote General George Thomas of the Army of the Cumberland that an advance could tie up Confederate forces and could ensure Canby's success at Mobile. Lines of communication and military resources could be eliminated in this untouched region. Coal and iron were produced in Shelby County. Further south, at Selma, ordnance workers turned out heavy cannon and ammunition at a large arsenal works. Plate armor and machinery were produced at a naval foundry there, and two railroads connected the important juncture to eastern points. Grant had speculated for some time about Montgomery, and he clearly understood the city's significance as a railroad link. A move to destroy manufacturing centers, railroads, and any military opposition in one sweep, he realized, would cripple the already weakening Confederacy. It was easy to justify extending the offensive to Selma and beyond, and success seemed likely, given the absence of any large Confederate forces. The war had brought little physical damage to the Black Belt, which stretched from Montgomery through central Alabama into Mississippi. Open and inviting, the region remained, as the war reached its conclusion, one of the last critical areas to have escaped invasion.

Union confidence was matched by Confederate despair. The situation in the Carolinas called Alabama's security into question. Regiments that might otherwise have been available were transferred to oppose Sherman's advancing forces. Alabama kept at home little more than the scattered cavalry command of General Nathan Bedford Forrest. Montgomery had recently been designated the headquarters of the Military Division of the West.

On February 17, writing from Meridian, Mississippi, General Richard Taylor made a discouraging report to Colonel George Brent in Montgomery. Taylor now commanded the Army of Tennessee. Conceding that neither Montgomery nor Selma could "resist anything more than a mere cavalry raid," Taylor wondered whether valuable machinery and weapons should be sent east. The capital's precarious status led to removal of the headquarters to Macon, Georgia, in mid-February.[2]

Brigadier General Daniel Adams, commanding the District of Alabama, assumed a prominent role in Montgomery's defense. In early March, Adams warned Governor Watts that, according to informed sources, "there is not a shadow of a doubt" that the enemy "contemplate a raid on Montgomery."[3] Watts had long feared for the city's security. Several military approaches were possible. If Mobile fell, Selma and Montgomery seemed logical and vulnerable objectives for troops moving up from the south. Federal forces in the Tennessee Valley and Mississippi also presented a threat. On March 3, Watts

General Daniel Adams, who gave
orders to abandon Montgomery in
April 1865, photograph c. 1860.
*Courtesy of Fouts Commercial
Photography, Montgomery, Alabama.*

issued a proclamation that began, "Alabama is now threatened on the North, on the South and on the West."[4]

Whether, how, and when the enemy would advance were questions openly asked. The Reverend Isaac Tichenor spoke to citizens in early March after he and Meyer Lehman returned from their futile attempts to arrange for the sale of Confederate cotton. Occupation by the enemy had been a topic of discussion before, but it had never seemed so likely. Anticipating the possibility, Tichenor declared that anyone who took a loyalty oath would be doing nothing less than dishonoring God. Surgeon Watson Gentry mentioned anxiety in a letter early in March to Samuel Stout. Gentry did not expect the enemy, but "much talk & fear is manifested here by the citizens & officials with reference to the coming of the Yankees."[5]

There was cause for alarm. In mid-February, plans for a cavalry strike into central Alabama had been approved. Major General James Harrison Wilson was to command the operation. General Wilson, at twenty-seven, had served on Grant's staff at Vicksburg and Chattanooga and had participated as a field commander in the Wilderness campaign. He was with General George Thomas more recently at the battle of Franklin. Early in 1865 his command established winter quarters on the Tennessee River near the borders of Alabama, Tennessee, and Mississippi. Wilson, a man whose military instincts caused him to be bold but not reckless, proposed moving south and destroying factories, government stores, and railroads. Cavalry raids were nothing new. Both sides had conducted them. Even so, the Union high command had committed itself to doing something different. Wilson's plans represented not quick forays, like those previously undertaken, but an invasion.

The expedition began in March when some 13,500 cavalrymen, artillery batteries, and supply wagons left Chickasaw Landing, Alabama, on the Tennessee River. On March 22 each mounted soldier carried a seven-shot repeating Spencer carbine. Selma, the main objective, lay 180 miles to the south. Three divisions, led by Generals Edward McCook, Eli Long, and Emory Up-

Major General James Harrison Wilson, who accepted the surrender of Montgomery, photograph c. 1860. *Courtesy of the Library of
Congress, Washington, D.C.*

ton, traveled by three different routes and moved unopposed through the
Tennessee Valley. The troops began making good Wilson's promise. At Ox-
moor (Shelby County), they destroyed the Red Mountain Iron Works owned
by William and Frank Gilmer and, at Brierfield in Bibb County, the Bibb
Naval Furnace. By March 31, the divisions had reached Montevallo. There
they overcame slight opposition, and the next day at Plantersville, twenty
miles from Selma, Confederate opposition crumbled. On the afternoon of
Sunday, April 2, the troops assumed battle positions outside Selma.

Meanwhile Confederate forces made preparations under General Nathan Bedford Forrest, a daring and successful cavalry commander. Forrest assembled somewhere between 4,000 and 7,000 troops at Selma. The town, situated on the north bank of the Alabama River, was ringed by extensive fortifications, but soon after Wilson's forces attacked at about 5:00 P.M. on Sunday, it became apparent that there were not enough troops to man them. Despite significant opposition, Wilson's troops overwhelmed resistance, and the battle was over by sundown. Some citizens had already evacuated. Others fled in the chaos of Sunday night. A few drowned swimming the Alabama River. A fire broke out that night and destroyed five city blocks. Over the next few days, the extensive arsenal, government warehouses, niter works, and railroad property were burned. It mattered little that Forrest had escaped.[6]

Wilson's orders gave him some discretion after the capture of Selma. He could decide to help General Edward Canby at Mobile, but the port's collapse was already all but complete. The remnants of Forrest's cavalry had headed northwest, but little could be achieved by giving chase. On the other hand, a move to the east—toward Montgomery and Columbus—held the promise of much bigger rewards. Wilson decided on this course of action. Montgomery lay on the south side of the river, and on April 9, one week after the battle, the corps began crossing. The first capital of the Confederacy lay three days and fifty miles to the east.

Montgomerians soon learned of Selma's fate and correctly guessed the enemy's subsequent moves. Projections based on the events at Selma were disconcerting at best. On Sunday, April 2, Ellen Blue recorded the "anxiety felt about the proximity of the raiders." Montgomery's residents had so far been spared the trauma experienced by those in overrun or occupied cities. Yet, as Blue realized, the city was "left almost entirely at the mercy of the enemy."[7]

Although Selma had been taken easily, officials planned to defend Montgomery. General Daniel Adams, from Louisiana, and Brigadier General Abraham Buford, from Kentucky, would direct the defense. Adams's experience and bravery were well established. He had lost the sight of one eye at Shiloh and had been wounded at Perryville and again at Chickamauga. More recently, Adams had commanded the troops that retreated before Wilson's forces converging on Selma. General Abraham Buford was in charge of Confederate cavalry forces in Alabama. Buford, who had graduated from West Point, was seasoned on western battlefields. As April opened, the two officers, with about 1,800 soldiers in their command, waited at Montgomery. At least fortifications were in place, evidence of progress since Lovell Rousseau's raid the previous July. Redoubts and redans looped around the borders in a semicircle, and rifle pits and stockades punctuated the line. Several artillery pieces were also strategically situated. The trench lines, virtually complete, protected the eastern, western, and southern borders. The vision of John Vinet of the Engineering Bureau was obvious. The Confederate troops, somewhat thinly spread, who took their positions behind these fortifications were representative of Confederates elsewhere. They were tired, all but beaten, and war weary but resigned to the prospect of further battle.

The situation was extremely discouraging. In Montgomery as elsewhere, the Confederacy's lack of soldiers was appallingly evident. Little could be expected from the civilian population. Military exemptions had been repealed in the last few years, and conscription authorities had flung a wide net. Unlike earlier stages of the war, when some conscription-age men were conspicuously present, relatively few local males were not in the field. The Alabama Rebels, a skeletal and disillusioned company, had performed provost guard duty. The Montgomery Guards were long since defunct. One observer described the totally untested Firemen's Guard as "nothing more than an organization of citizens." The Watts Cadets, a group of recently organized teenage boys, had no experience beyond the oversight of slaves working on the fortifications.[8]

If the city's fall was inevitable, as most observers believed, the damage might be minimized. About 90,000 bales of cotton were stored in the warehouses and amounted to a firetrap. At the orders of post commandant Walter Jones, removal efforts began. On April 1, Governor Watts issued special orders closing all establishments that sold beer or liquor. The liberties taken by inebriated Confederate troops locally were well documented. What the victorious enemy might do was potentially much worse.

The councilmen met on April 3 and 4 to determine how best to save Montgomery. Only a week earlier they had been occupied with such routine matters as reminding the wharfinger of his duties and reimbursing a citizen for work completed on the jail. The agenda had changed dramatically. The aldermen added fifty blacks to the firefighting force and considered a petition asking for the destruction of all liquor before the enemy arrived.

The closing of the saloons, at the orders of Governor Watts on April 1, seemed a step in the right direction. It seemed equally important to destroy all the spirits in private possession. Within days a committee composed of civilian and military personnel—including Ministers Isaac Tichenor, Holland

McTyeire, and John Mitchell—had been authorized to collect and dispose of all liquor supplies. Enemy troops might rout the opposition and ransack the town, or the city might surrender without contest. Either way, if Union troops did not have access to liquor, Montgomery would benefit.[9]

That there would be a defense became more and more open to question. Governor Watts and General Adams issued proclamations on April 4. Adams began by promising "to make [a] full defense of the city." He drew attention to the strong fortifications and asked for volunteers. Watts's message "to the people of Alabama" was a call to arms. He mentioned encroachments from the south and west, recalled the setback at Selma, and warned that the enemy "may attempt to occupy Montgomery." The governor referred to Adams's determination to hold the city and declared that Montgomery would not be surrendered as "long as there is a reasonable chance of defending it." He pleaded for volunteers to keep up the fight.[10] Adams and Watts both understood that there were not enough soldiers. So did General Buford, who felt able several days later, on April 7, to tell Secretary of War John Breckinridge only that he would "make the best fight possible."[11]

Some citizens, acting from an exaggerated sense of honor or from an underestimate of the enemy's power, wanted military officials to challenge Union forces. Others grasped the odds and foresaw the consequences of an initiative. Montgomerians, conditioned by four years of talk about "Vandals" and "Huns," expected the worst. Defense risked, invited, and probably insured the capital's destruction. Although most people had been patriotic and persevering, Montgomery's populace was not willing to take any risk. News of Richmond's recent evacuation had reached the city, and Montgomerians understood that the war was over.

Charles Linn, who ran a grocery, feared looting and losses. Charles May could only assume that cavalrymen would appropriate the saddles and harnesses he sold in his Market Street store. Thomas Powell, the owner of a slave depot, obviously had other reasons to be concerned. General Adams had promised in his April 4 circular that "no effort will be spared on the part of the officers, soldiers, or citizens to make full defense."[12] Montgomerians were skeptical of such a course of action. They found little consolation in Governor Watts's assurance that Wilson's force "does not exceed nine thousand."[13]

Within days of its conclusion, the war had finally reached Montgomery. Residents were more fearful than defiant in the final hours of the Confederacy's life. Shops closed, school was dismissed, and people fled. They hid china, silver, money, and anything of value. Hogs, cows, and horses were secured outside the city. One ingenious individual converted his home into a barn and housed a mare about to foal in a bedroom. Sarah and Charlotte Follansbee, teachers at Home School, secreted a considerable sum of gold in their home. Samuel Wreford was either mercenary, devoted to the public welfare, or both. Advertising on April 8, Wreford pronounced himself "calm and collected." The proprietor of the One Armed Man's Dry Goods store promised that he would remain open at his Market Street location. Some people boarded Montgomery and West Point cars and traveled toward Columbus. These emigrants included the editors of the *Memphis Daily Appeal*, who packed up the presses and moved for the fifth time.[14]

In the meantime, moving east from Selma through the Black Belt, the Northern cavalry drew nearer. Wilson's forces, joined by many slaves who had taken up with the army, spent the night of April 10 at Benton, passed through the village of Lowndesboro the next day, and settled down on the evening of Tuesday, April 11, near Catoma Creek. They were five miles west of Montgomery. Little opposition had been mustered by Confederates since Wilson left Selma. His men moved almost casually through what their commander described as the "richest planting district in the South." In contrast, Wilson expected a "sharp fight" at Alabama's capital.[15]

On April 7, General Adams telegraphed Secretary of War Breckinridge. Although the details of his message are not known, it is clear that he asked for more troops. From Danville, Virginia, where President Davis had set up a temporary government, the executive promised help "as far as practicable." In fact, however, the defense of Montgomery was not militarily viable. Sometime between April 8 and 12, Adams received orders from General Richard Taylor, commanding the Army of Tennessee, to retreat toward Columbus if Wilson threatened to attack in force. Adams began preparations to do so.[16]

In the next few days city authorities paradoxically carried on more fruitful negotiations with Federal officials than with Confederates. Acting on the assumption that Southern forces would withdraw, aldermen appointed a committee to negotiate with the advancing Union foe. Mayor Walter Coleman headed the committee, which met with General Adams on Monday, April 10, to discuss how best to deal with the invaders. The talks were anything but amicable. Adams was emphatic and inflexible. One point of contention concerned the cotton. The committee argued that by burning the warehoused cotton, Adams would be placing the city in grave danger. Adams flatly stated that the cotton would be destroyed regardless of risks. Differences of opinion extended to plans to negotiate with the enemy. Leaving city officials in limbo, Adams refused to confirm or deny that he planned to defend Montgomery. Even in the event of evacuation, he promised to arrest anyone attempting to take a flag of truce to Federal forces.

Later on Monday, Adams's intentions became clear. Troops left the trenchworks and the city. That the warehouses and cotton would be burned became public knowledge. James Stow, a local Unionist and chief engineer of the Fire Department, was one of those who felt outraged. He resented Confederate authority on principle, and he also believed that setting a fire jeopardized the city's safety. All he could do was place local firemen on standby. Most were slaves who belonged to Alabama Fire Engine Company Number Two.

On the afternoon of Tuesday, April 11, Confederate soldiers applied torches. The warehouses in the Commerce Street area burned quickly. The cotton blazed into an inferno that threatened to spread out of control. Hundreds watched as the warehouses first crumbled and then collapsed. Sarah Follansbee, watching from a distance, called the spectacle a "huge conflagration." [17]

Firemen labored desperately, and the efforts of the black firefighters were crucial. Fortunately, winds were light and came from the east. An observer later attributed Montgomery's survival to a "miracle" that was "almost providential." The *Mail* called the black firemen "brave fellows, reckless of life and limb," who "met the furious flames at every advance and kept the conflagration in check." By nightfall, the fires were out, and the warehouses, which had been brimming with cotton hours only before, lay in smoldering ruins. As dark settled on Tuesday, the situation was grim. A survey revealed that the warehouses of Lehman and Durr, Frank Gilmer, Barrett, Micou and Company, and other firms were in ruins. Cotton bales lay at random across streets where they had been placed as barricades. Retreating soldiers left spiked artillery behind in the trenches. [18] The fall of Montgomery was certain before Adams and Buford withdrew. The Confederate command's departure was now little more than a formality. Samuel Wreford had promised to keep his One Armed Man's Dry Goods open until "the danger becomes more imminent." The moment had arrived. [19]

Fortune and firefighting skill saved Montgomery on Tuesday, April 11. Early the next morning diplomacy was used to the same effect. In these final hours Mayor Coleman and the committee contacted the Union command and a meeting was arranged. William Bibb and Lewis Owen belonged to the ten-man committee. As Unionists, they might conceivably provide leverage when dealing with the Federal forces. General Edward McCook commanded the advance troops. Around three in the morning of Wednesday, April 12, the committee met with Union representatives. Although Montgomery's delegation was in no position to bargain—over thirteen thousand soldiers were at the city gates—the two sides reached an agreement. No resistance would be offered, and Federal troops would respect private and public property. In the meantime, the citizens waited. As one observer attested, Tuesday night passed in "dreadful suspense." A published note, signed by Mayor Coleman, ended the uncertainty early Wednesday by informing the public of the conditions of surrender.[20]

Four years earlier the inauguration of Jefferson Davis had afforded the city the most extraordinary day in its history. In a different sense, Wednesday, April 12, was equally momentous. The honor of entering Montgomery fell to the Fourth Kentucky Cavalry under Colonel Wickliffe Cooper. At 4:40 A.M., Union troops placed the Fourth Kentucky Regiment's standard in front of the capitol. Cooper's command represented merely the advance units. Several hours later, at about 8:00 A.M., Mayor Coleman and the city council formally surrendered Montgomery. Established protocol was observed. General McCook delivered his speech very close to the spot where Jefferson Davis had given his inaugural address. The war was all but over, he informed a large crowd, and in Montgomery, where some believed that it had really started, no revenge would be exacted. A large crowd heard McCook promise fair treatment and protection. The American flag was raised above the capitol.

Entering from the west on Hayneville Road, troops marched through the city for much of the morning. The ranks of blue-clad cavalrymen seemed endless. As Captain Charles Hinricks of the Tenth Missouri Cavalry recalled, "We put on all the style possible and marched according to regulations."[21] Sarah Follansbee was awakened that Wednesday morning by Milly, a servant, who excitedly announced that the "Yankees" had arrived. The two women watched as hundreds passed. Wagons, martial bands, and columns of soldiers with flying banners moved by—the Fourth Indiana, First Wisconsin, Ninety-eighth Illinois, Fifth Iowa, Third Ohio, Fourth Michigan, and Seventh Pennsylvania Regiments. Some units accepted bouquets from Montgomerians grateful that their city had been spared. The sentiments of rejoicing blacks were not in doubt.[22]

Montgomery became a Union post. It was ironic, galling, or fitting, depending on the observer's point of view, that the Exchange Hotel, where Jefferson Davis and other luminaries had made their headquarters, now housed

General McCook. General Wilson arrived later in the day and set up his command at James Powell's home on the corner of Moulton and Church Streets. Colonel Wickliffe Cooper of the Fourth Kentucky became post commander, and his regiment, with detachments from the First Wisconsin and the Third Iowa Regiments, formed the provost guard. To the relief of many, most of the Federal soldiers marched through town and camped three miles east of the city on Three Mile Branch. Few soldiers remained in Montgomery. Those who did were generally well behaved. Wilson had promised that anyone who violated the code of "Christian soldiery" would be punished strictly.[23]

The city that had escaped the worst of the war continued to exercise its special charm. Its occupation was brief and largely uneventful. Major Stephen Shipman, the officer of the day, assumed responsibilities as head of the provost guard. He directed operations from the governor's office in the capitol. Governor Watts had fled to Eufaula. Montgomerians, fearing for their property, pleaded with Union officials for protection. As one Union officer reported later, "the good order preserved during our stay was a subject of remark and congratulation by the citizens."[24] According to Francis Salter, a surgeon with the corps, "the inhabitants received the troops, if without manifestations of joy, at least without evidence of dislike."[25]

A few, including Dr. Samuel Seelye, actually welcomed the enemy. Having clandestinely opposed the war, Seelye extended various courtesies to the Federals. Major Shipman of the First Wisconsin Regiment visited the Seelye home and pronounced the family "pleasant and hospitable people." Shipman also met Thomas Glascock, a former supporter of Douglas, and commented that he "talks like a true Union man." The officer accepted a dinner invitation from Dr. Gustav Albright and enjoyed the "marked attention" of Sarah Abercrombie, a native of Massachusetts.[26]

James Powell and his family, although they harbored no Union sentiments, treated General Wilson with respect and displayed good manners. As the commanding officer recalled, Powell "knew how to be polite to unwelcome guests." The Montgomerian had little or no wine to offer Wilson. Like other residents, Powell had destroyed his private collection before the troops arrived. Occupation had finally done what the war never had: activity at the whiskey and beer saloons halted.

Some soldiers had wanted to destroy Montgomery because of its relationship to the Confederacy, but the city's attractions soon became apparent to the most vengeful. Wilson described the city as "very beautiful."[27] Captain

Charles Hinricks wandered about, visited a barbershop, and enjoyed a "genuine Confederate shave." The Exchange was still a landmark. When Hinricks learned that Jefferson Davis had stayed there, he made it a point to take a meal in the dining room. The captain decided that Montgomery was "by far the most beautiful [city] I have yet seen."[28]

The place also impressed Captain Louis Hosea, who wrote of the wide streets, impressive trees, and buildings that "show wealth." Altogether, Alabama's capital seemed to him a "lotus land, an Arcadia." Although Union troops had encountered hundreds of plantation slaves as they advanced from Selma, Hosea had not expected to see the multitudes of blacks in Montgomery. So many slaves volunteered for a "pioneer corps" that another Union soldier made them compete for admission on the basis of foot races. Hosea described the victors as composing "the crack athletic corps in the army."[29]

Federal troops stayed in Montgomery just over two days. From a military standpoint, there was no point in holding the city. Hard war could not tolerate idle occupation, and as Grant wished, Wilson quickly pushed on. As he had at Selma, Wilson did not leave until he had destroyed everything that might be of military use to the Confederacy, regardless of ownership. Some Montgomerians had more to lose than others. The worst fears of railroad president Charles Pollard were confirmed. No local resident had provided more services to the government than Pollard, and no one suffered as much monetarily from the occupation. Union forces destroyed both the Montgomery and West Point and Alabama and Florida depots, the machine and blacksmith shops, an oilhouse, the roundhouse, about twenty cars, and a car factory. Troops burned the government arsenal with the foundry and machinery and destroyed some small arms and government supplies. John Janney's foundry, where Confederate ammunition had been produced, met the same fate. Outside the city, on the Lower Wetumpka Road, Charles Clapp had supervised the niter works. The work of three years was obliterated in several hours.[30]

Ironically, Unionist David Carter counted more losses than most Montgomerians. Within hours of their arrival, Federal soldiers had visited his Monroe Street stables and nearby home. Carter had hidden what he could. Three horses, two bays and a black, were discovered and were taken from a lot adjacent to his home. His son, Walter, was forced from another horse. As a stable owner, Carter kept large stores of corn, hay, and fodder. Troops removed several thousand bushels of corn and a large quantity of hay and fodder. When Carter protested that he was a Unionist, he was gruffly ordered to move aside if he did not want to be struck over the head with a shovel. He followed orders. Soldiers also took three of his carriages to haul the Union's sick and wounded.

Carter's wife, Martha, and their daughter, Sally, suffered further humiliation. Sally was forced to give up a ring she was wearing. The Carters lost much more than others, but as their son Walter later testified, "it seemed as if they [Union troops] knew where everything was all over town." Stock was taken randomly and indiscriminately. Young Walter recalled that some of the corn was trampled and wasted. He said, "They didn't care what they done."[31]

Wilson had telegraphed General George Thomas from Montgomery that he planned to follow Adams and Buford toward Columbus. He assured Thomas that he would "accomplish what is expected of me by you and Grant." On Thursday, April 13, the day after his arrival, Wilson informed city authorities of his intentions to evacuate. By Friday, the next day, Union forces had pulled out. Over 140 sick and wounded soldiers were left behind at General Hospital in the care of Assistant Surgeon David Dome of the Seventeenth Indiana Mounted Infantry.[32]

As the soldiers departed, Montgomerians felt extraordinary relief. The élan and spirit of an earlier day, long since diminished, had now been irrevocably broken. From a sampling of local opinion, Captain Charles Hinricks "felt satisfied that [in] an early day the Confederate bubble would burst." A surgeon at Auburn, fifty miles to the east, soon concluded that the military should have made a stand at Montgomery.[33]

Some citizens agreed, but most—including the councilmen—condoned the decision to surrender. Although the aldermen had firmly supported the Confederacy, patriotism had its limits. In 1862, the *Mail* had praised the newly elected city council as a patriotic group whose members would never "voluntarily take a flag of truce of the enemy." By the spring of 1865, the council's only hope was that Federal forces would honor such a flag. They reflected a consensus of local opinion: to defend Montgomery would have been ill advised at best.[34]

General Daniel Adams had been exposed to the power, sweep, and fury of Wilson's troops at Selma. At the time when Selma was taken, the Confederates had more soldiers and enjoyed better fortifications. Southern troops had fought bravely but had been able to put up little more than a decent fight. There were fewer men at Montgomery, and the defenses were inferior to those at Selma. Union observers had reached the same conclusions. Captain Hinricks had compared local fortifications unfavorably to those at Selma. The

officer concluded that the Confederates "would not have delayed us an hour";
the cavalry could have charged in between redoubts and "captured or
drowned the whole outfit." Several days later, Hinricks's analysis was illumi-
nated by events at Columbus, where resistance was offered and Confederate
forces were routed.[35]

Montgomery had fallen. In the throes of defeat, citizens could find
some comfort in the fact that they and their city remained safe. The situation
could easily have been much worse. An observation of Union Major Eugene
Beaumont also represented reality. He wrote, "The Stars and Stripes are floating over the capitol of Alabama."[36]

Epilogue

In 1861 most white Montgomerians embraced secession and went to war, regretfully believing it a morally correct, constitutional, and necessary course of action. Bold words and allusions to gallantry were reiterated by people from all walks of life in settings as disparate as pulpits and saloons. When Robert E. Lee surrendered at Appomattox Courthouse on April 9, 1865, however, a conflict that had optimistically begun with a determination to defend sovereignty and to preserve a culture ended in despair and defeat.

The intervening years, 1861–1865, represented an unprecedented period. On a collective basis, the experiences of white and black Montgomerians were more similar than different from, for example, their counterparts in Macon, Georgia. There were connecting themes and cross-references in all Confederate cities where the population confronted the crucible of war. The daily routine in Alabama's capital was not unlike that experienced by residents of Raleigh, North Carolina. Montgomery was a microcosm, although what happened there was not replicated across the Confederacy.

The city maintained a veneer of normality throughout most of the war. A visitor might note the unremarkable nature of life in Montgomery. The favorable reaction of citizens to a blind phrenologist in 1862 was no different than what it would have been in 1852. The petty, outrageous, and controversial had its place. The circumstances of the marriage of Henry Hilliard to Eliza Ann Glascock Mays, the former nurse of Hilliard's recently deceased wife, caused a sensation. Rumors that their marriage was due to her pregnancy caused the previously much respected Hilliard to move to Augusta, Georgia. A populace that reached a consensus concerning the war's blame stridently disagreed over the moral appropriateness of the play *Camille, or the Fate of a Coquette*. Even as the momentous loomed, the mundane remained. In early September 1864 Sherman's troops entered Atlanta, and much of the city burned. In Alabama's capital, 150 miles to the west, a large crowd turned out for the horse races. On one level Montgomerians understood the epic historical nature of the period in which they lived. On a more elemental level, far removed from the battle lines and seemingly secure, ten thousand residents carried on with a minimum of interruptions.[1]

Yet the war framed life and exacted a devastating toll. There were cruel contrasts. With great fanfare in 1860 the theater opened and Montgomerians responded enthusiastically. Within a year, the Free Market, where the destitute turned for food, was on its way to becoming a place of equal institutional status. Concert Hall had been the scene of balls and other social events before Montgomerians had ever heard of Ulysses Grant, the Wilderness or Reseca. Its conversion to Concert Hall Hospital created a setting for despair, pain, and the stench of death. In the cemetery the elegant monuments of Montgomerians contrasted starkly with the weather-beaten pine markers of soldiers who had died in a local hospital far from home.

The lacerating forces of war were unsparing. Hundreds turned out for the funeral when the body of Lieutenant Tennent Lomax was returned home. He had been killed in June 1862 at the battle of Fair Oaks in Virginia. The uncertainty confronted by the family of Joseph Pollard was all too common. The son of Charles and Emily Pollard was killed at Murfreesboro as 1863 began. Falsely encouraged by recent reports of his safety, his mother suffered a neuralgic seizure when the definitive death notice arrived. Charles Pollard confided the next day, "everything that a father could ask for in a child, he was." Wounded at the battle of Winchester in Virginia, John Ledyard died at a Charlottesville hospital, and the soldier's remains were brought home in October. Bereaved relatives and friends buried John Ledyard at the family vault.[2]

Circumstances quickly stripped the lacquer from any romantic notions of war and revealed its unvarnished reality. Women could testify poignantly to unprecedented hardships. Theirs was a private war, sometimes futilely waged, to maintain a decent living standard for a family whose provider was often in uniform. Kindness, piety, and innocence were exalted virtues of the female sex. Other traits—perseverance, industry, and strength—were tested during the war. Arriving in summer 1864 at the Montgomery and West Point Railroad depot, corporal Sam Watkins saw "hucksters" selling oranges, watermelons, peaches, and more. An elderly woman peddled bread, fish, and boiled eggs. A one-legged veteran sold him a drink of whisky from a tin can. Such vignettes should take their place with the iconographic home-front images of basket-bearing women walking hospital halls.[3]

Alabama's capital, raised from a provincial setting and viewed in the context of the Confederacy, was a scene of human complexity. Under duress, some individuals emerged as magnanimous and philanthropic. Samuel Norton, benefactor of the poor, heroically battled the corrosive consequences of the war. In fact, there were infinite acts exemplifying compassion and sacrifice. Inevitably others stood revealed as guileful and avaricious. An obvious commitment to the Southern cause did not prevent extending humanity to the enemy. In the spring of 1862, Union prisoners, some extremely sick or severely wounded, were cared for at Soldiers Home Hospital. Confederate patriot Sophia Bibb explained, "they were suffering men and shall be made as comfortable as our Confederate soldiers." Differentiating the commendable from the contemptible was not always easy. Sophia Bibb (the local chapter of the Daughters of the Confederacy would be named in her honor) was a heroine. Her son, William Bibb, was the most outspoken Unionist in the city. Did his views make him any the less honorable? John Phelan had taken great satisfaction in the resounding victory at Bull Run in the summer of 1861. His thoughts were less clear following the death of one son at Seven Pines and another at Petersburg.[4]

The war was bitter, unforgiving, and for Montgomerians, seemingly interminable. A local woman wrote a long public letter to the *Advertiser* in 1864. She contrasted earlier days of sacrifice and national celebration with prevailing apathy. She declared the Ladies Aid Association dead in all but name and pointed disdainfully to "what our fervent zeal and homespun ardor have come to." By then Montgomerians were enduring the unacceptable home-front conditions compounded by military defeat. If great expectations rising in the Confederate capital reflected the Southern mein as the conflict opened, so did the descending arc of fatalism. The trajectory was complete by April 1865. The experience of other Southerners was no different, although in some places, there was more suffering. A comprehensive social history of the wartime South is overdue. That study inevitably would delineate the heroic and selfless. The pathos, deprivation, and eventual despair of the people would also be captured. The consequences of the rise, brief flourish, and lingering death of the Confederacy, in the place where that government was formed, are important and revealing. The situation, writ small in Montgomery, reflects the strengths, weaknesses, and with vivid resonance, the life of the greater Confederate home front.[5]

Four years of war ended in the spring of 1865. A conflict begun optimistically to defend sovereignty and preserve a culture ended in despair and defeat. More than 6,000,000 men died. The destruction of Southern cities, transportation systems, and various forms of property, meant recovery was years in the future. Atlanta, Richmond, and other cities were in ruins.

Montgomery shared no such fate but its citizens did not have to be shelled, overrun, burned, or occupied to feel the repercussions of war. The reaction to Union troops parading down Market Street in 1865 was more one of relief than bitterness. The four-year ordeal had ended. General Wilson's troops had marched into Montgomery on April 12, and two days later, on Friday, April 14, the soldiers left the city as quietly as they had entered it. A certain calm returned to the city life. Children went back to school, and on Sunday churchgoing Montgomerians found much to be thankful for even in defeat. Sam Werford, at the One Armed Man's Dry Goods, and other merchants, soon reopened their businesses. Nothing indicated a normal state of affairs more than activity at the saloons where customers seemed "anxious to make up for lost time."

Police struggled to keep order. Over a forty-eight hour period, April 18–19, there were two murders. Robert Carr, a well-liked soldier living near Montgomery, was shot and killed. Only the "firmness of the police" prevented a lynch mob from seizing the assailant who worked as a machinist at the Montgomery and West Point Railroad. City Marshall Thomas Maxwell was central to efforts. The *Advertiser,* circulating after a week's hiatus, pled for calm.[6] Mayor Walter Coleman soon wrote an undertaker John Newbold of a local woman's death. Because her husband had "been a Confederate soldier," the mayor promised to ask the city council to assume the expenses. Meantime, Coleman requested Newbold to provide a coffin and hearse. On a much lighter note, notice of a troupe's performance at the theater was posted. In fact, Montgomerians were fortunate to have a theater and a city much in its prewar state.

A shopkeeper on Market Street, a commission merchant down by the river, or the mother of three in her parlored home, may have reflected on an ultimate irony. A war fought more than any other issue over maintaining the institution of slavery had ended. In Montgomery, exploited slaves had created much of the considerable wealth. In what was literally their final hours as bondsmen, black fire fighters saved the city and that wealth from destruction.

Faced by the presence and immediacy of defeat, the population felt a sense of change. Soldiers would soon return from the war and take their place in a society that was fundamentally altered. Montgomery had been a prosperous place before the war, and it became that after the conflict, but not immediately. There was no restorative elixir, and Alabama's capital and its citizens faced an indefinite period of economic adversity.

Life changed for free persons of color. Eliza Lumpkin was representative. The free black who took in washing for a living would not have to worry about registering her place of residence, observing a curfew, or furtively associating with slaves. Postwar differences would be most dramatic for the former slaves. In a city where every other person was black, the war's end brought the prospect of extensive social change. Four years earlier, Laura Hill, a young slave girl, had watched as Confederate troops marched from Montgomery to war. She could not have guessed how the verdict of that conflict would impact her life and that of all Montgomery blacks after her. One of Laura Hill's daughters would teach at the Loveless School for blacks, but that would be in a time not yet imagined. For the moment, Montgomery's residents—whites and blacks—speculated about the present. The trials of the war were over and those of Reconstruction lay ahead.[7]

Notes

Abbreviations

ADAH   Alabama Department of Archives and History, Montgomery, Ala.

CP   Confederate Papers Relating to Citizens or Business Firms, 1861–1865

LR   Letters Received

NA   National Archives, Washington, D.C.

OR   U.S. War Department, *The War of the Rebellion: A Compilation of the Official Records of the Union and Confederate Armies* (Washington, 1880–1901)

RG   Record Group

1. Montgomery on the Eve of War

1. *Montgomery Weekly Mail,* October 19, 1860; *Montgomery Mail,* April 17, 1861; Leonard Mears and James Turnbull, *The Montgomery Directory for 1859–60, Containing the Names of the Inhabitants, A Business Directory, Street Directory* (Montgomery: Advertiser Book and Printing Office, 1859), 91. For a description of Montgomery on the war's eve see Thomas C. DeLeon, *Four Years in Rebel Capitals* (Mobile, Ala.: Gossip Printing, 1890), 23–41; William Howard Russell, *My Diary North and South,* vol. 1 (London: Bradbury and Evans, 1863), 234–46; William C. Davis, *"A Government Of Our Own": The Making of the Confederacy* (New York: Free Press, 1994), 31–43.

2. *London Times,* May 30, 1861; for miscegenation see Gary Mills, "Miscegenation and the Free Negro in Antebellum 'Anglo' Alabama: A Reexamination of Southern Race Relations," *Journal of American History* 68 (June 1981), 16–32; G. H. Stueckrath, "Montgomery, the Capital of Alabama," *Debow's Review* 28 (January, 1860), 111–14; U.S. Bureau of the Census, *Eighth Census of the United States: 1860* (Washington, D.C.), 3–10; *Alabama State Census, Free Population: 1860,* 15, 89; *Alabama State Census, Slave Population: 1860,* 130–32, 135, 139, 151, 164; *Montgomery Advertiser,* December 10, 1862; for Goldthwaite see Thomas M. Owen, *History of Alabama and Dictionary of Alabama Biography,* 4 vols. (Chicago: S. J. Clarke, 1921), 3:674–75; for Jackson see 3:893; and for Seelye see 4:1524.

3. Mears and Turnbull, *Montgomery Directory,* 9, 5, 11, 16, 35, 83, 85, 88, 90, 97; *Montgomery Mail,* March 14, 21, 1861; for Knox see Owen, *Dictionary of Alabama Biography,* 3:992; for Glackmeyer see Glackmeyer, Surname File, ADAH.

4. *Montgomery Weekly Post,* December 5, 1860; *Montgomery Weekly Mail,* June 22, 1860; *Montgomery Mail,* March 11, 1860; *Montgomery Confederation,* February 5, 1860; Mears and

Turnbull, *Montgomery Directory,* 91, 94; for Yancey see Eric H. Walther, *The Fire-Eaters* (Baton Rouge: Louisiana State University Press, 1992), 48–78; for Elmore see Owen, *Dictionary of Alabama Biography,* 3:992; for Baldwin, 3:83; for Weatherly, 4:1735.

5. *Alabama State Census, Free Population: 1860,* 99, 29, 31, 163; Mears and Turnbull, *Montgomery Directory,* 83–97; for antebellum women see Anne Firor Scott, *The Southern Lady: From Pedestal to Politics, 1830–1930* (Chicago: University of Chicago Press, 1970); George C. Rable, *Civil Wars, Women, and the Crisis of Southern Nationalism* (Urbana: University of Illinois Press, 1989), 1–30.

6. Montgomery City Council Minutes (June 1856–September 1860), 431, ADAH; Mears and Turnbull, *Montgomery Directory,* 12–13, 39, 50, 82, 103–8; *Eighth Census of the United States, Manufactures: 1860,* 9, 13; for Janney see *Montgomery Advertiser,* November 20, 1909, and Janney Surname File, ADAH.

7. *Montgomery Mail,* April 12, 1861; *Montgomery Post,* February 6, 1861; *Montgomery Weekly Mail,* July 13, August 17, 1860; *Montgomery Weekly Advertiser,* August 15, 1860; Meyer and Emanuel Lehman Surname File, ADAH; Mears and Turnbull, *Montgomery Directory,* 92; n.a., *Centennial Lehman Brothers, 1850–1950* (New York: Spirol Press, 1950), 9–12.

8. *Montgomery Mail,* March 7, 1861; William Stanley Hoole, *Alias Simon Suggs: The Life and Times of Johnson Jones Hooper* (Tuscaloosa: University of Alabama Press, 1952); for Hilliard see Owen, *Dictionary of Alabama Biography,* 3:814; for Armand Pfister and Joel White see 4:1355, for Watts, 4:1732.

9. *Montgomery Confederation,* April 4, 1860.

10. *Montgomery Directory,* 67.

11. Stueckrath, "Montgomery, the Capital of Alabama," 113; for Anna Knox see Owen, *Dictionary of Alabama Biography,* 3:990.

12. *Montgomery Weekly Post,* December 5, 12, 1860; *Montgomery Weekly Advertiser,* April 14, December 26, 1860; *Montgomery Weekly Mail,* May 25, October 26, November 2, 1860; for Mitchell see Thomas A. Brown, *History of the American Stage* (New York: Dick and Fitzgerald, 1870), 249–50.

13. *Montgomery Weekly Mail,* September 21, 1860; *Montgomery Weekly Advertiser,* September 19, 1860; *Montgomery Weekly Post,* January 9, 1861; Mears and Turnbull, *Montgomery Directory,* 106; for Cobbs see Mattie Pegus Wood, *The Life of St. John's Parish: A History of St. Johns Episcopal Church from 1834–1955* (Montgomery, Ala.: Paragon Press, 1955), 24–25, 42–45, and Owen, *Dictionary of Alabama Biography,* 3:359–60; for Petrie, 4:1350–1351; for Tichenor, 4:1672, and Lee N. Allen, *The First 150 Years: Montgomery's First Baptist Church, 1829–1979* (Montgomery, Ala.: First Baptist Church, 1979), 50–51.

14. John W. A. Sanford, *The Code of the City of Montgomery* (Montgomery: Gaines and Smith, 1861), 33, 83–90; Montgomery City Council Minutes (September 1860–December 1866), 4–5; for slavery see Richard Wade, *Slavery in Cities: The South, 1820–1860* (London: Oxford University Press, 1964); Eugene D. Genovese, *Roll, Jordan, Roll: The World the Slaves Made* (New York: Pantheon Books, 1974).

15. Sanford, *The Code of the City of Montgomery,* 84; *Baltimore American and Commercial Advertiser,* February 21, 1861; *Montgomery Weekly Post,* April 3, 1860; *Alabama State Census, Slave Population: 1860,* 140, 147; Wade, *Slavery in Cities,* 56–57, 143–45.

16. *Alabama State Census, Free Population: 1860,* 27, 75, 78, 89, 112; Sanford, *The Code*

of the City of Montgomery, 83–90; see, for free blacks, Ira Berlin, *Slaves Without Masters: The Free Negro in the Antebellum South* (New York: Pantheon Books, 1974).

17. *Montgomery Weekly Advertiser,* August 22, 1860; Sanford, *The Code of the City of Montgomery,* 29–30, 76.

18. *Montgomery Weekly Advertiser,* September 26, 1860.

19. Ibid., September 5, 1860.

20. Sanford, *The Code of the City of Montgomery,* 48–49.

21. Montgomery City Council Minutes (1860–1866), 15; *Alabama State Census, Free Population: 1860,* 88.

22. *Montgomery Confederation,* June 22, 1860; *Montgomery Weekly Post,* January 2, 1861.

23. Sanford, *The Code of the City of Montgomery,* 86–87; *Alabama State Census, Slave Population: 1860,* 147.

24. Jacob Weil to Josiah Weil, May 16, 1861, Jake Weil Papers, ADAH; an excellent one-volume study of events leading up to the Civil War is James M. McPherson, *The Battle Cry of Freedom: The Civil War Era* (New York: Oxford University Press, 1988).

25. Basil Manly to children, February 26, 1861, in Basil Manly Papers, W. S. Hoole Special Collections, University of Alabama, Tuscaloosa, Ala.; Randall C. Jimerson, *The Private Civil War: Popular Thought During the Sectional Conflict* (Baton Rouge: Louisiana State University Press, 1988), 10; for Moore see Malcolm C. McMillan, *The Disintegration of a Confederate State: Three Governors and Alabama's Wartime Home Front, 1861–1865* (Macon, Ga.: Mercer University Press, 1986), 11; for Manly see Owen, *Dictionary of Alabama Biography,* 4:1152–53; for excerpts of his diary while in Montgomery see W. Stanley Hoole, ed., "The Diary of Dr. Basil Manly, 1858–1867," pt. 1, *Alabama Review* 4 (April 1951), 127–49, and "The Diary of Dr. Basil Manly, 1858–1867," pt. 2, *Alabama Review* 4 (July 1951), 221–36.

26. *Montgomery Confederation,* February 29, 1860.

27. *Montgomery Weekly Confederation,* February 22, 1860.

28. Walther, *The Fire-Eaters,* 48–76; for Hilliard see Evans Johnson, "A Political Life of Henry W. Hilliard" (M.A. thesis, University of Alabama, 1947); for secession see William L. Barney, *The Secessionist Impulse: Alabama and Mississippi in 1860* (Princeton: Princeton University, 1974); Durward Long, Jr., "Alabama in the Formation of the Confederacy (Ph.D. diss., University of Florida, 1959).

29. William R. Smith, *The History and Debates of the Convention of the People of Alabama,* reprint ed. (Spartanburg, S.C.: Reprint Company, 1975), 10; McMillan, *Disintegration of a Confederate State,* 12; Frederick M. Beatty, "William Lowndes Yancey and Alabama Secession" (M.A. thesis, Auburn University, 1990), 96–98.

30. John J. Seibels to Stephen Douglas, June 5, 1860, Stephen Douglas Papers, Special Collections Department, University of Chicago Library, Chicago, Ill.; for Seibels see Willis Brewer, *Alabama: Her History, Resources, War Record, and Public Men,* reprint ed. (Spartanburg, S.C.: Reprint Company, 1975), 459–460.

31. *Montgomery Weekly Advertiser,* April 4, June 20, 1860; for muster and occupation of True Blues members see *Montgomery Mail,* February 28, 1861; John W. Napier III, "Martial Ante-bellum Military Activity," *Alabama Historical Quarterly* 29 (Fall and Winter 1967), 112, and "Montgomery During the Civil War," *Alabama Review* 39 (April 1988), 109; for

Arrington see Owen, *Dictionary of Alabama Biography,* 3:60; for Clanton, 3:327; for Winter see Winter Surname File, ADAH.

32. McPherson, *Battle Cry of Freedom,* 117–22.

33. *Montgomery Weekly Advertiser,* June 27, May 23, 1860; Hoole, *Alias Simon Suggs,* 134–39; for Reid see Owen, *Dictionary of Alabama Biography,* 4:1424; Durward Long, "Political Parties and Propaganda in Alabama in the Presidential Election of 1860," *Alabama Historical Quarterly* 25 (Spring and Summer 1963), 122–30.

34. *Montgomery Weekly Mail,* August 10, November 2, 1860; *Montgomery Weekly Advertiser,* July 18, October 3, 1860; for Bethea see Owen, *Dictionary of Alabama Biography,* 3:140; for Gabriel DuVal, 3:524–25; for Holtzclaw, 3:836.

35. John Seibels to Stephen Douglas, September 14, 1860, Douglas Papers, University of Chicago; *Montgomery Mail,* November 3, 1860; Robert W. Johannsen, *Stephen A. Douglas* (New York: Oxford University Press, 1973), 798–801.

36. David R. Barbee and Milledge L. Bonham, Jr., "The Montgomery Address of Stephen A. Douglas," *Journal of Southern History* 5 (Fall 1939), 529–52; Johannsen, *Stephen Douglas,* 801; *Montgomery Weekly Advertiser,* November 14, 1860.

37. *Montgomery Weekly Mail,* November 16, 1860; for Phelan see Benjamin B. Williams, "Nineteenth Century Authors," *Alabama Historical Quarterly* 37 (Summer 1975), 140; Durward Long, "Unanimity and Disloyalty in Secessionist Alabama," *Civil War History* 11 (March 1965), 257–62.

38. *Montgomery Advertiser,* November 13, 1860; McMillan, *Disintegration of a Confederate State,* 75–76.

39. *Montgomery Weekly Advertiser,* November 21, 13, 1861; *Montgomery Mail,* November 16, 1861.

40. *Montgomery Weekly Confederation,* December 21, 1860; *Montgomery Weekly Post,* December 12, 1860; Henry W. Hilliard, *Politics and Pen: Pictures At Home and Abroad* (New York: G. P. Putnam's Sons, 1892), 309–10; Evans Johnson, "Henry W. Hilliard and the Civil War Years," *Alabama Review* 17 (April 1964), 105–6.

41. *Montgomery Weekly Advertiser,* November 14, 28, 1860.

42. *Montgomery Mail,* January 11, 1861; *Montgomery Weekly Advertiser,* December 19, 1860.

43. Smith, *History and Debates,* 20; McPherson, *Battle Cry of Freedom,* 127–28; see Ralph A. Wooster, *The Secession Conventions of the South* (Princeton, N.J.: Princeton University Press, 1962), 51–53.

44. E. Lewis to Mr. Kerr, January 11, 1861, E. Lewis Papers, ADAH; *Montgomery Mail,* January 12, 1861; *Montgomery Weekly Advertiser,* January 16, 1861.

45. *Montgomery Mail,* February 6, 1861; *Montgomery Weekly Mail,* January 11, 1861; *Montgomery Weekly Post,* January 30, 1861; *Montgomery Advertiser,* November 13, December 11, 1910; John E. Johns, *Florida During the Civil War* (Gainesville: University of Florida Press, 1963), 26–33; for military career of Lomax see Joseph Wheeler, *Alabama in Confederate Military History,* vol. 8 (Wilmington, N.C.: Broadfoot Publishing, 1987), 679–82.

46. *Montgomery Mail,* January 28, 1861; Ludwell H. Johnson, "Fort Sumter and Confederate Diplomacy," *Journal of Southern History* 26 (November 1960), 442.

47. *Montgomery Mail,* January 19, 1861.

48. Ibid., February 15, 17, 22, 1861.

49. Ibid., January 29, 28, 23, February 2, 1861.

50. *Montgomery Confederation,* January 31, 1861.

51. *Montgomery Mail,* January 12, 1861; for Wallacks see Brown, *History of the American Stage,* 375.

52. Caleb Huse, *The Supplies for the Confederate Army: How They Were Obtained in Europe and How Paid For* (Boston: T. R. Marvin, 1904), 89.

53. Manly to Basil Manly, Jr., February 5, 1861, Manly Papers, University of Alabama; Smith, *History and Debates,* 189.

54. Armand J. Gerson, "The Inception of the Montgomery Convention," *Annual Report of the American Historical Association* (1910), 181–87; *Journal of the Convention of the People of South Carolina Held in 1860–61* (Charleston: Evans and Cogswell, 1861), 99–100, in South Carolina Pamphlets Collection, South Caroliniana Library, Columbia, S.C.; Charles R. Lee, *The Confederate Constitutions* (Chapel Hill: University of North Carolina Press, 1963), 8–9, 16.

55. Gabriel Duval to Samuel Marks, January 13, 1861, Thomas Winfrey Oliver Papers, ADAH; Emory Thomas, *The Confederate Nation, 1861–1865* (New York: Harper and Row, 1979), 51.

56. Lucretia Davidson to daughter, January 11, 1861, Lucretia Bailey Davidson Papers, ADAH; Jefferson Franklin Jackson, "Was the Execution of Charles I Justifiable?" and "Was the French Revolution Beneficial to France?" in Jefferson Franklin Jackson Papers, ADAH.

2. The Capital of the Confederacy

1. Basil Manly to son, February 5, 1861, in Manly Papers, University of Alabama; the definitive study of Montgomery while the city was the seat of government is Davis, *The Making of the Confederacy;* see also Rembert W. Patrick, *Jefferson Davis and His Cabinet* (Baton Rouge: Louisiana State University Press, 1944); Charles R. Lee, *Confederate Constitutions,* 50–53; two contemporary accounts of Montgomery during the Provisional Capital period are John B. Jones, *A Rebel War Clerk's Diary* (Philadelphia: J. B. Lippincott, 1866), 35–45, and Mary Chesnut, *Mary Chesnut's Civil War,* ed. C. Vann Woodward (New Haven: Yale University Press, 1981), 8–62, 319–24.

2. *New Orleans Delta,* March 5, 1861; Charles R. Lee, *Confederate Constitutions,* 52.

3. *New York Herald,* February 23, 1861.

4. *Charleston Daily Courier,* February 13, 1861; Weekly *Vicksburg Whig,* February 13, 1861; Thomas Cobb to Marion, March 4, 1861, in Augustus Longstreet Hull, ed. "The Correspondence of Thomas Reade Rootes Cobb, 1860–1862," *Publications of the Southern History Association* (May 1907), 252; Davis, *The Making of the Confederacy,* 72–77, 80–82; Charles R. Lee, *Confederate Constitutions,* 52–53.

5. *Montgomery Weekly Advertiser,* February 20, 1861; *Montgomery Advertiser,* February 19, 1861; *Montgomery Weekly Post,* February 13, 1861; *New York Herald,* February 18, 1861; *Columbus Enquirer,* February 19, 1861; Alexander Stephens to brother, February 11, 1861,

Alexander Stephens Papers, Special Collections Department, Robert Woodruff Library, Emory University, Atlanta, Ga.; Davis, *The Making of the Confederacy,* 149–52; the most recent biography of Davis, as of this printing, is William C. Davis, *Jefferson Davis: The Man and His Hour* (New York: Harper Collins, 1991); for Stephens see Thomas E. Schott, *Alexander H. Stephens of Georgia: A Biography* (Baton Rouge: Louisiana State University Press, 1988).

6. *Montgomery Advertiser,* February 19, 1861; *Charleston Mercury,* February 22, 1861; *New Orleans Daily Picayune,* February 22, 1861; *Montgomery Mail,* February 19, 1861; Henry D. Capers, *The Life and Times of C. G. Memminger* (Richmond: Everett Waddey, 1893), 307.

7. *Montgomery Advertiser,* February 19, 1861; *Montgomery Weekly Mail,* February 22, 1861; for copy of inaugural address see Jefferson Davis, *The Papers of Jefferson Davis: Vol. 7, 1861,* edited by Lynda L. Crist and Mary Seaton Dix (Baton Rouge: Louisiana State University Press, 1992), 45–50; Charles R. Lee, *Confederate Constitutions,* 80–81.

8. Ellen Jackson to Mary Noyes, February 19, 1861, Jefferson Franklin Jackson Papers, ADAH; *Richmond Dispatch,* February 23, 1861; *New Orleans Daily Picayune,* February 22, 1861; Archibald McIntyre Surname File, ADAH; Davis, *The Making of the Confederacy,* 37, 162–67.

9. Jefferson Davis to Varina Davis, February 20, 1861, Davis, *Papers: Vol. 7, 1861,* 53.

10. Raphael Semmes, *Service Afloat; or, the Remarkable Career of the Confederate Cruisers Sumter and Alabama During the War Between the States* (New York: P. J. Kennedy and Sons, 1903), 83; *New Orleans Delta,* March 10, 1861; DeLeon, *Four Years in Rebel Capitals,* 25; Dunbar Rowland, ed., *Jefferson Davis Constitutionalist: His Letters, Papers, and Speeches,* vol. 9 (Jackson: Mississippi State Department of Archives and History, 1923), 423; Davis, *The Making of the Confederacy,* 176, 197.

11. Jefferson Davis to Varina Davis, February 20, 1861, Davis, *Papers: Vol. 7, 1861,* 153–54; *Atlanta City Guardian,* March 1, 1860; DeLeon, *Four Years in Rebel Capitals,* 24.

12. *Charleston Mercury,* February 8, 1861; John B. Jones, *Rebel War Clerk's Diary,* 36; James F. Sulzby, Jr., *Historic Alabama Hotels and Resorts* (Tuscaloosa: University of Alabama Press, 1960), 124–25.

13. DeLeon, *Four Years in Rebel Capitals,* 26.

14. Ibid., 37; "Report on the Committee for Public Buildings," Alabama Historic Commission Office, Montgomery, Ala.; *Montgomery Mail,* February 11, 1861; Chesnut, *Mary Chesnut's Civil War,* 56.

15. *London Times,* May 30, 1861.

16. *Richmond Examiner,* May 13, 1861; Henry D. Capers, *Life and Times of C. G. Memminger,* 310.

17. Henry D. Capers, *Life and Times of C. G. Memminger,* 310–11.

18. John B. Gordon, *Reminiscences of the Civil War* (New York: Charles Scribners' Sons, 1904), 17; Nathaniel C. Hughes, Jr., *General William J. Hardee, Old Reliable* (Baton Rouge: Louisiana State University Press, 1965), 70–71; T. Harry Williams, *P. G. T. Beauregard: Napoleon in Gray* (Baton Rouge: Louisiana State University Press, 1954), 49–50; Joseph Howard Parks, *General Edmund Kirby Smith, C.S.A.* (Baton Rouge: Louisiana State University Press, 1954), 122; Craig L. Symonds, *Joseph E. Johnston: A Civil War Biography* (New

York: W. W. Norton, 1992), 97–98; *Montgomery Mail*, March 20, 1861; *Montgomery Advertiser*, April 8, 1861.

19. Hillary Herbert, "Grandfather Talks About His Life Under Two Flags," typescript, Hillary Herbert Papers, Southern Historical Collection, Chapel Hill, N.C.; *New Orleans Daily Picayune*, April 9, 1861, *Montgomery Mail*, February 21, 23, 1861; *London Times*, May 30, 1861; DeLeon, *Four Years in Rebel Capitals*, 38.

20. James M. Morgan, *Recollections of a Rebel Reefer* (Boston: Houghton Mifflin, 1917), 37–38; Drew Gilpin Faust, *The Creation of Confederate Nationalism: Ideology and Identity in the Civil War South* (Baton Rouge: Louisiana State University Press, 1988), 11–14.

21. *Montgomery Weekly Post*, February 20, 1861; *Montgomery Mail*, February 6, March 9, 1861.

22. Thomas Cobb to Marion, February 8, 1861, in Hull, "Correspondence of Thomas Reade Rootes Cobb" (May 1907), 167; Davis, *The Making of the Confederacy*, 269–70.

23. Thomas Cobb to Marion, February 8, 1861, in Hull, "Correspondence of Thomas Reade Rootes Cobb" (May 1907), 169.

24. Chesnut, *Mary Chesnut's Civil War*, 11.

25. Thomas Cobb to Marion, February 28, 1861, in Hull, "Correspondence of Thomas Reade Rootes Cobb" (June 1907), 244–45.

26. Alexander Stephens to brother, March 1, 1861, Stephens Papers, Emory University.

27. Chesnut, *Mary Chesnut's Civil War*, 17; *Montgomery Weekly Post*, March 5, 1861; *Montgomery Mail*, March 6, 1861; for Varina Davis see William C. Davis, *Jefferson Davis*, 95–98, 313, 335; Bell Irvin Wiley, *Confederate Women* (Westport, Conn.: Greenwood Press, 1995), 83–129.

28. Charles R. Lee, *Confederate Constitutions*, 82–127; McPherson, *Battle Cry of Freedom*, 138–40.

29. *Montgomery Weekly Post*, April 3, March 5, 1861; *Montgomery Advertiser*, March 5, 13, 1861; *Charleston Mercury*, April 6, 1861.

30. *Montgomery Advertiser*, April 6, 1861.

31. *New Orleans Picayune*, April 7, 1861; *Montgomery Mail*, April 10, 1861; *Montgomery Advertiser*, April 15, 1861.

32. *Montgomery Mail*, March 28, 1861.

33. Ellen Jackson to Mary Noyes, February 19, 1861, Jefferson Franklin Jackson Papers, ADAH.

34. Leroy Pope Walker to P. G. T. Beauregard, April 11, 1861, *OR*, ser. 1, vol. 1, 301; Williams, *P. G. T. Beauregard*, 56–60; William C. Harris, *Leroy Pope Walker: Confederate Secretary of War* (Tuscaloosa, Ala.: Confederate Publishing, 1962), 34–38.

35. Basil Manly to son, April 11, 18, 1861, Manly Papers, University of Alabama; *Montgomery Advertiser*, April 13, 15, 1861; *Montgomery Mail*, April 13, 1861.

36. *Journal of the Congress of the Confederate States of America (1861)* (Washington: Government Printing Office, 1904), 160–69; hereafter cited as *Journal of the Confederate Congress; Charleston Mercury*, May 2, 1861.

37. *Montgomery Weekly Confederation*, May 10, 1861; for women and views on Southern rights and slavery see Rable, *Civil Wars*, 32–44.

38. *Journal of the Confederate Congress (1861)*, 168.

39. *Charleston Courier,* February 5, 1861; Charleston *Mercury,* April 29, 1861; Thomas Cobb to Marion, February 10, 1861, in Hull, "Correspondence of Thomas Reade Rootes Cobb" (May 1907), 170; Patrick, *Jefferson Davis and His Cabinet,* 320.

40. *Montgomery Confederation* quoted in *Montgomery Weekly Post,* February 13, 1861; for Cobb in Montgomery see William B. McCash, *Thomas R. R. Cobb, 1823–1862: The Making of a Southern Nationalist* (Macon, Ga.: Macon University Press, 1983), 209–48; Davis, *The Making of the Confederacy,* 146–47, 279.

41. Russell, *My Diary North and South,* 255; "Report on the Committee for Public Buildings," Alabama Historic Commission, Montgomery, Ala.; for Harrison see Owen, *Dictionary of Alabama Biography,* 3:760.

42. *London Times,* May 30, 1861; Russell, *My Diary North and South,* 237–58; for Russell see Martin Crawford, ed., *William Howard Russell's Civil War Private Diary and Letters* (Athens: University of Georgia Press, 1992), xvii–xlvii; Davis, *The Making of the Confederacy,* 378–81.

43. *New Orleans Delta,* March 10, 1861; *Montgomery Advertiser,* March 8, 1861; DeLeon, *Four Years in Rebel Capitals,* 28; Davis, *The Making of the Confederacy,* 263–65.

44. *Charleston Mercury,* May 3, 1861; *Montgomery Advertiser,* March 21, 1861; Faust, *The Creation of Confederate Nationalism,* 14.

45. Chesnut, *Mary Chesnut's Civil War,* 63; Alexander Stephens to brother, March 5, 1861, Stephens Papers, Emory University; *Charleston Mercury,* March 22, 25, 1861.

46. George W. Reese, ed., *Proceedings of the Virginia State Convention, 1861,* vol. 4 (February 13–May 1, 1861) (Richmond: Virginia State Library, 1965), 388–89, 372; for Richmond in 1861 see Emory Thomas, *The Confederate State of Richmond: A Biography of the Capital* (Austin: University of Texas Press, 1971), 15–31; Thomas, *Confederate Nation,* 99.

47. Augustus Longstreet Hull, ed., "Thomas R. R. Cobb Extracts from Letters to His Wife, February 3, 1861–December 10, 1862," *Southern Historical Society Papers* 28 (1900), 288; *Charleston Mercury,* May 7, 1861; for Hunter see Henry H. Simms, *Life of Robert M. T. Hunter: A Study in Sectionalism and Secession* (Richmond: The William Byrd Press, 1935); John F. Fisher, "Statesman of the Lost Cause: The Career of R. M. T. Hunter, 1869–87" (M.A., thesis, University of Virginia, 1966); Ezra J. Warner and W. Buck Yearns, *Biographical Register of the Confederate Congress* (Baton Rouge: Louisiana State University Press, 1975), 127–28.

48. Chesnut, *Mary Chesnut's Civil War,* 61.

50. William Boyce to R. M. T. Hunter, February 5, 1861, Robert M. T. Hunter Papers, Special Collections Department, Alderman Library, University of Virginia, Charlottesville, Va.; *Journal of the Confederate Congress (1861),* 1:173–74.

50. *Montgomery Weekly Post,* May 15, 1861; *Montgomery Weekly Advertiser,* May 15, 1861; John B. Jones, *Rebel War Clerk's Diary,* 41; Jerrell H. Shofner and William Warren Rogers, "Montgomery to Richmond: The Confederacy Selects a Capital," *Civil War History* 10 (June 1964), 159; Thomas, *Confederate Nation,* 102; for secession debate in Virginia and Upper South states see Daniel W. Crofts, *Reluctant Confederates: Upper South Unionists in the Secession Crisis* (Chapel Hill: University of North Carolina Press, 1989).

51. Alexander Stephens to brother, May 4, 1861, Stephens Papers, Emory University;

John B. Jones, *Rebel War Clerk's Diary,* 41.

52. *Richmond Dispatch,* May 6, 1861; Varina Davis to Clement Clay, May 10, 1861, Clement C. Clay Papers, Special Collections, William R. Perkins Library, Duke University, Durham, N.C.; Shofner and Rogers, "The Confederacy Selects a Capital," 160; Davis, *The Making of the Confederacy,* 373, 388.

53. Varina Davis to Clement Clay, May 10, 1861, Clay Papers, Duke University.

54. Thomas Cobb to Marion, May 5, 1861, in Hull, "Correspondence of Thomas Reade Rootes Cobb" (November 1907), 325.

55. John B. Jones, *Rebel War Clerk's Diary,* 20; Fischer, "Statesman of the Lost Cause," 74–76.

56. *Journal of the Confederate Congress (1861),* 1:206.

57. Varina Davis to Clement Clay, May 10, 1861, Clay Papers, Duke University; John B. Jones, *Rebel War Clerk's Diary,* 43; *Charleston Courier,* May 16, 1861.

58. Thomas Cobb to Marion, April 29, 1861, in Hull, "Correspondence of Thomas Reade Rootes Cobb" (July 1907), 259; Jones, *Rebel War Clerk's Diary,* 35; Chesnut, *Mary Chesnut's Civil War,* 62.

59. Thomas Cobb to Marion, May 11, 1861, Thomas Cobb Papers, University of Georgia; Hull, "Thomas R. R. Cobb: Extracts from Letters to His Wife," 286.

60. *Charleston Courier,* May 14, 1861; *Journal of the Confederate Congress (1861),* 1:208–13, 242–43.

61. *Charleston Courier,* May 18, 1861; *Montgomery Advertiser,* quoted in *Atlanta Daily Intelligencer,* May 16, 1861.

62. *New Orleans Picayune,* May 14, 1861; *Charleston Mercury,* May 14, 1861; *Montgomery Weekly Advertiser,* May 15, 1861; *Montgomery Post,* May 15, 1861; *Montgomery Weekly Confederation,* May 24, 1861; Chesnut, *Mary Chesnut's Civil War,* 18.

63. *Columbus Enquirer,* May 22, 1861; *Journal of the Confederate Congress (1861),* 1:249–57; Davis, *The Making of the Confederacy,* 390–91; Shofner and Rogers, "The Confederacy Selects a Capital," 162–63.

64. Alexander Stephens to brother, May 22, 1861, Stephens Papers, Emory University; *Journal of the Confederate Congress (1861),* 1:257, 264.

65. Henry D. Capers, *Life and Times of C. G. Memminger,* 331.

66. Thomas, *Confederate Nation,* 100–101; Thomas, *The Confederate State of Richmond,* 33–34; Jefferson Davis, *The Rise and Fall of the Confederate Government* (New York: Thomas Yoseloff, 1958), 339–40; Shofner and Rogers, "The Confederacy Selects a Capital," 163–65.

67. *London Times,* June 18, 1861.

68. DeLeon, *Four Years in Rebel Capitals,* 28.

69. Hull, "Thomas R. R. Cobb: Extracts from Letters to his Wife," *Southern Historical Society Papers,* 286; Henry D. Capers, *Life and Times of C. G. Memminger,* 331–32.

70. *Richmond Dispatch,* June 1, 1861; *Journal of the Congress (1861),* 1:264; *Charleston Mercury,* May 30, 1861; *Montgomery Weekly Post,* June 5, 1861; Davis, *The Making of the Confederacy,* 395–96; Varina Davis, *Jefferson Davis Ex-President of the Confederate States of America: A Memoir,* vol. 2 (New York: Belford, 1870), 74.

71. *Montgomery Weekly Post,* February 20, May 15, 1861; *Montgomery Mail,* February 20, 1861; *Montgomery Weekly Advertiser* May 15, 1861.

3. A Military Post

1. For Confederate bureaucracy see Richard D. Goff, *Confederate Supply* (Durham, N.C.: Duke University Press, 1964); Horace H. Cunningham, *Doctors in Gray: The Confederate Medical Service* (Baton Rouge: Louisiana State University Press, 1958); Frank E. Vandiver, *Ploughshares into Swords: Josiah Gorgas and Confederate Ordnance* (Austin: University of Texas Press, 1952); for an overview of departments and their functions see Henry P. Beers, *The Confederacy: A Guide to the Archives of the Government of the Confederate States of America* (Washington, D.C.: National Archives and Records Administration, 1986).

2. *Montgomery Mail,* March 26, February 7, 1863, January 21, 1864; *Montgomery Advertiser,* June 30, July 13, 1864; n.a., *Memorandum of Armies, Corps, and Geographical Commands in the Confederate States 1861–1865* (n.p., n.d), 3–4.

3. Abraham Myers to Calhoun, March 18, 1863, February 13, 1861, Roll 3, and W. B. B. Cross to A. P. Calhoun, May 27, 1864, Roll 4, in Letters and Telegrams Sent by the Confederate Quartermaster General, 1861–1865, Microcopy 437, RG 109, NA; "Report of Employees by Captain Wm. Gillaspie AQM at Mont, Ala.," in Inspection Reports and Related Records Received by the Inspection Branch in the Confederate Adjutant and Inspector's Office (hereafter cited as Inspection Reports), RG 109, M437, NA; *Montgomery Mail,* October 26, 1862; April 9, 1863; *Mobile Daily Advertiser and Register,* April 16, 1864; Goff, *Confederate Supply,* 16; Beers, *The Confederacy,* 153.

4. Charles Pollard to Abraham Myers, December 16, 1861 (December 1861); Pollard to C. J. R___, November 5, 1861, Letters Received by the Confederate Secretary of War, 1861–1865, Microcopy 437, RG 109, NA (hereafter cited at LR [Confederate Secretary of War]); *OR,* ser. 1, vol. 17, pt. 2, 88, 660; Robert C. Black, *The Railroads of the Confederacy* (Chapel Hill: University of North Carolina Press, 1952), 5–6, 9, 73–74, 155, 180–84.

5. *Mobile Advertiser and Register,* September 6, 1864.

6. B. F. Jones to Samuel Cooper, December 12, 1864, in Inspection Reports, reel 9, RG 109, NA; Goff, *Confederate Supply,* 10, 16, 175.

7. B. F. Jones to Samuel Cooper, December 1, 1864, in Inspection Reports, RG 109, NA; "Report of Mack Copeland, Depot Commissary, at Montgomery, Ala.," in Inspection Reports, reel 9, RG 109, NA; *OR,* ser. 1, vol. 17, pt. 2, 660; *Montgomery Mail,* November 16, 1862; *Mobile Advertiser and Register,* June 2, 1864.

8. John Gill Shorter to George Randolph, July 29, 1862, John Gill Shorter Papers, ADAH.

9. John W. Mallet to Josiah Gorgas, July 31, 1862, William Stanley Hoole Papers, W. S. Hoole Special Collections, University of Alabama, Tuscaloosa, Ala.; *Montgomery Mail,* May 27, 1864; W. Stanley Hoole, "John W. Mallet and the Confederate Ordnance Laboratories, 1862–1865," *Alabama Review* 26 (January 1973), 33–39; Vandiver, *Ploughshares into Swords,* 61, 240.

10. Charles Wagner to Josiah Gorgas, February 10, 1863 (December 1862–April 1863) LR (Confederate Secretary of War).

11. *Montgomery Advertiser,* May 24, 1864.

12. *Montgomery Mail,* October 14, 1862; *OR,* ser. 1, vol. 10, pt. 1, 473; "Descriptive Muster and Pay Roll of Stewards, Ward Masters, Nurses and Cooks on duty in the Madi-

son House Hospital at Montgomery, Alabama," in Muster Roll for Hospitals, RG 109, NA; Glenna R. Schroeder-Lein, *Confederate Hospitals on the Move: Samuel H. Stout and the Army of Tennessee* (Columbia: University of South Carolina Press, 1994), 70–71, 74–77, 96, 103–4; Cunningham, *Doctors in Gray,* 62, 74–76; for Alabama hospitals see W. J. Donald, "Alabama Confederate Hospitals," *Alabama Review* 15 (October 1962), 271–75.

13. Julian Chisolm, *A Manual of Military Surgery for the use of Surgeons in the Confederate Army* (Richmond, Va.: West and Johnston, 1861), 389; Cunningham, *Doctors in Gray,* 184–207, 218, 225–26.

14. *Montgomery Advertiser,* June 3, 1864.

15. Edward Moren to wife, December 1, 1861, Edward Moren Papers, ADAH; vouchers from Luke Dickerson, in Confederate Papers Relating to Citizens or Business Firms, M346, RG 109, NA (hereafter cited as CP, NA).

16. *Montgomery Weekly Advertiser,* September 11, 1861.

17. William Gentry to Samuel Stout, December 23, 1863, Samuel H. Stout Papers, William R. Perkins Library, Manuscript Division, Emory University, Atlanta, Ga.; Cunningham, *Doctors in Gray,* 55–57; for Gentry see *Confederate Veteran* 27 (August 1919), 310; for Stout see Schroeder-Lien, *Confederate Hospitals on the Move.*

18. William Gentry to Samuel Stout, December 23, 1863, Samuel H. Stout Papers, Emory University; Courtney Clark to Samuel Stout, October 9, 1864, Samuel H. Stout Papers, The Center for American History, University of Texas at Austin, Texas; Donald, "Alabama Confederate Hospitals," 273–75; Cunningham, *Doctors in Gray,* 82–87.

19. William Gentry to Samuel Stout, May 21, 1864, December 23, 1863; Samuel H. Stout Papers, Emory University; *Montgomery Advertiser,* May 5, 1864; Schroeder-Lein, *Confederate Hospitals on the Move,* 100–01; Donald, "Alabama Confederate Hospitals," 274.

20. William Gentry to Samuel Stout, December 8, 1863, Samuel H. Stout Papers, Tennessee State Library and Archives, Nashville, Tenn.

21. Robert E. Campbell to Samuel Stout, March 15, 1864, Samuel H. Stout Papers, Southern Historical Collection, University of North Carolina, Chapel Hill, N.C.

22. William Gentry to Samuel Stout, May 21, 1864; Samuel Bemiss to Samuel Stout, January 15, 1864; Samuel H. Stout Papers, Emory University; for Bemiss see Schroeder-Lien, *Confederate Hospitals on the Move,* 82.

23. William Gentry to Samuel Stout, December 23, 1863; Samuel H. Stout Papers, Emory University.

24. *Montgomery Mail,* May 18, 1864; Cunningham, *Doctors in Gray,* 66.

25. William Gentry to Samuel Stout, May 21, 1864, Samuel H. Stout Papers, Emory University; *Mobile Advertiser and Register,* May 31, 1864.

26. *Montgomery Mail,* September 6, 1864; William Gentry to Samuel Stout, May 21, 1864, Samuel H. Stout Papers, Emory University.

27. *Montgomery Advertiser,* June 5, 1864; William Gentry to Samuel Stout, May 21, 1864, Samuel H. Stout Papers, Emory University.

28. *Montgomery Advertiser,* June 19, 1864.

29. *Montgomery Mail,* July 12, 1864.

30. William Gentry to Samuel Stout, May 21, 1864, Samuel H. Stout Papers, Emory University.

31. Ibid., August 26, 1864.

32. *Montgomery Mail,* January 13, 1864; October 22, 1862; *Montgomery Advertiser,* April 16, June 15, 1864; William Gentry to Samuel Stout, May 21, 1864, Samuel H. Stout Papers, Emory University; B. F. Jones to Samuel Cooper, December 1, 8, in Inspection Reports, RG 109, NA; "Report of Mack Copeland," in Inspection Reports," RG 109, NA; for Copeland see Owen, *Dictionary of Alabama Biography,* 3:400.

33. Edward Moren to wife, October 28, 1861, Moren Papers, ADAH.

34. *Mobile Advertiser and Register,* June 2, 24, September 6, 1864; *Montgomery Mail,* April 3, 1864; "Report of Camp & Garrison Equipage & Miscellaneous Stores on hand August 1864 by Captain Wm. Gillaspie at Montgomery, Ala.," in Letters Received by the Confederate Quartermaster General, 1861–1865, Roll 10, RG 109, NA; William Gentry to Samuel Stout, May 21, 1864, Samuel H. Stout Papers, Emory University.

35. George Brent to General P. G. T. Beauregard, December 18, 1864, *OR,* ser. 1, vol. 45, pt. 11, 704.

36. Charles Pollard to William Chilton, April 18, 1863 (December 1862–June 1863) LR (Confederate Secretary of War).

37. Charles W. Ramsdell, "The Control of Manufacturing by the Confederate Government," *Mississippi Valley Historical Review* 8 (December 1921), 248; J. W. Echols to Walter Jones, April 1864, Letters Received by the Confederate Adjutant and Inspector General, 1861–1865, Microcopy 474, RG 109, NA; *Montgomery Advertiser,* June 3, 1864.

38. *Montgomery Mail,* April 8, 1865; n.a., *Memorandum of Armies, Corps, and Geographical Commands in the Confederate States 1861–1865,* 3.

39. "Report of Mack Copeland, Depot Commissary at Montgomery, Ala.," in Inspection Reports, RG 109, NA; *Montgomery Advertiser,* July 13, 1864.

4. Life and Labor in Wartime

1. Charles East, ed. *The Civil War Diary of Sarah Morgan* (Athens: University of Georgia Press, 1991), 64–65; Gerald M. Capers, *Occupied City: New Orleans Under the Federals, 1862–1865* (Lexington: University of Kentucky Press, 1965).

2. William Sherman to Admiral David Dixon Porter, July 19, 1863, *OR,* ser. 1, vol. 24, pt. 3, 531; Mark Grimsley, *The Hard Hand of War: Union Military Policy Toward Southern Civilians, 1861–1865* (New York: Cambridge University Press, 1995), 154–60; Stephen V. Ash, *When the Yankees Came: Conflict and Chaos in the Occupied South, 1861–1865* (Chapel Hill: University of North Carolina Press, 1995), 16–19, 77, 91; Stephen R. Wise, *Gate of Hell: Campaign for Charleston Harbor* (Columbia: University of South Carolina Press, 1994), 29–32, 169–71; Gerald M. Capers, *The Biography of a River Town; Memphis: Its Heroic Age* (Chapel Hill: University of North Carolina Press, 1939), 148–49, 155; Walter T. Durham, *Nashville: The Occupied City* (Nashville: Tennessee Historical Society, 1985), 7, 12, 16–20, 46.

3. Thomas McClellan to wife, November 19, 1861, Thomas McClellan Papers, ADAH.

4. W. C. Corsan, *Two Months in The Confederate States, Including A Visit to New Orleans Under the Domination of General Butler* (London: Richard Bentley, 1863), 119–20; *Mobile Advertiser and Register,* April 21, May 31, 1864.

5. *New Orleans Delta,* March 24, 1861.

6. *Mobile Advertiser and Register,* March 31, 1864.

7. *London Times,* May 30, 1861; *Montgomery Weekly Mail,* June 28, 1862; *Mobile Advertiser and Register,* April 28, 1864; for McTyeire see Owen, *Dictionary of Alabama Biography,* 4:1140–41; Luther Leonidas Hill, *Sermons, Addresses, and Papers of Rev. Luther Leonidas Hill* (New York: Fleming H. Revell Press, 1919), 19–25.

8. Minutes of Presbyterian Church of Montgomery, Ala. (1857–1869), 113, in First Presbyterian Church Records, Department of Archives and Special Collections, Auburn University at Montgomery Library, Montgomery, Ala.; *Montgomery Advertiser,* June 25, 1871; Wood, *Life of St. John's Parish,* 45–56; William Warren Rogers, Jr., " 'In Defense of Our Sacred Cause': Rabbi James K. Gutheim in Confederate Montgomery," *Journal of Confederate History* 7 (Fall 1991), 113–22; Bertram W. Korn, *American Jewry and the Civil War* (Philadelphia: The Jewish Publication Society of America, 1951), 47–51.

9. Virginia K. Jones, ed., "The Journal of Sarah G. Follansbee," *Alabama Historical Quarterly* 27 (Fall and Winter 1965), 213–14, 222.

10. *Montgomery Mail,* October 11, 1861, August 13, 1860; Wood, *Life of St. John's Parish,* 39.

11. *Montgomery Weekly Advertiser,* July 10, 1861.

12. *Montgomery Mail,* October 11, 1861; *Montgomery Post,* June 28, 1861.

13. *Montgomery Advertiser,* January 5, 18, 1862; *Montgomery Mail,* October 11, 1861; *Prospectus of the Montgomery Military Academy* (Montgomery, Ala.: Montgomery Advertiser Book, 1862), 2–7; *Regulations and Rules of the Montgomery Military Academy, 1861* (Montgomery: Floyd and Warrock, 1861), 5–12, ADAH.

14. William Baldwin to John Gill Shorter, November 15, 1862, John Gill Shorter Papers, ADAH; *Montgomery Weekly Mail,* August 8, 1862; for Baldwin see Owen, *Dictionary of Alabama Biography,* 3:83.

15. *Montgomery Advertiser,* November 11, 1862.

16. *Montgomery Mail,* October 4, 1864; *Montgomery Weekly Advertiser,* August 7, 1861; Samuel Seelye Surname File, ADAH.

17. *Montgomery Post,* September 19, 1861.

18. Edward Moren to wife, January 26, 1862, Moren Papers, ADAH.

19. "Diary of Frances Woolfolk Wallace," 35, in Southern Historical Collection, University of North Carolina; *Montgomery Advertiser,* January 19, 21, 1863; June 18, 1864; *Montgomery Mail,* June 15, 1864; for Blind Tom see Brown, *History of the American Stage,* 362.

20. *Mobile Advertiser and Register,* June 19, 1864.

21. *Montgomery Mail,* December 11–17, 1862; *Montgomery Advertiser,* December 10, 1862, January 13, 17, 1863; for theater see Richard Barksdale Harwell, *Brief Candle: The Confederate Theater* (Worchester, Mass.: American Antiquarian Society, 1971); for Vernon see Brown, *History of the American Stage,* 366.

22. *Montgomery Mail,* February 13, 1864.

23. Ibid., April 13, January 4, 7, 9, 15, 1864; for Hamilton see Brown, *History of the American Stage,* 58, 159; for Crisp see James H. Dormon, Jr., *Theater in the Ante Bellum South, 1815–1861* (Chapel Hill: University of North Carolina Press, 1967), 168–71.

24. *Montgomery Mail,* November 25, 1862; *Baltimore American and Commercial,* February 21, 1861; *Mobile Advertiser and Register,* July 7, 1864.

25. Edward Moren to wife, December 1, 1862, Moren Papers, ADAH; *Montgomery Advertiser,* May 8, 1863, October 17, 1863; *Montgomery Mail,* October 25, March 27, 1864; Minutes of Presbyterian Church (1856–1869), 165–66; for slaves during the war see Genovese, *Roll, Jordan, Roll,* 128–33; Stephen V. Ash, *Middle Tennessee Society Transformed, 1860–1870: War and Peace in the Upper South* (Baton Rouge: Louisiana State University Press, 1988), 130–31; Clarence L. Mohr, *On the Threshold of Freedom: Masters and Slaves in Civil War Georgia* (Athens: University of Georgia Press, 1986), 68–75; Jacqueline Jones, *Labor of Love, Labor of Sorrow: Black Women, Work, and the Family from Slavery to the Present* (New York: Basic Books, 1985), 46–51.

26. *Montgomery Mail,* October 14, 1862.

27. Ibid., June 2, 9, March 20, July 26, 1864; November 22, December 2, 1862; *Montgomery Advertiser,* April 17, May 23, 1864.

28. *Montgomery Advertiser,* December 18, 1862.

29. *Montgomery Mail,* December 3, November 8, March 24, 1864, March 15, June 10, 1863; for Durr see Durr Surname File, ADAH

30. *Montgomery Mail,* February 6, 1863; *Montgomery Advertiser,* December 21, 1862.

31. *Montgomery Mail,* June 2, 1864.

32. Kate Cumming, *Kate: The Journal of a Confederate Nurse,* ed. Richard Barksdale Harwell (Baton Rouge: Louisiana State University Press, 1959), 89.

33. *New York World* quoted in *Montgomery Advertiser,* June 26, 1863, November 5, 1862.

34. *Montgomery Mail,* April 30, July 25, 1863; *Montgomery Advertiser,* January 30, 1862.

35. *Mobile Advertiser and Register,* June 28, 1864.

36. Vouchers from Stephen Hutchings and Joseph Williams, Charles May, A. Burrows, Felix Glackmeyer, in CP, NA; *Alabama State Census, Free Population: 1860,* 169; Mary A. DeCredico, *Patriotism for Profit: Georgia's Urban Entrepreneurs and the Confederate War Effort* (Chapel Hill: University of North Carolina Press, 1990), 30–40, 152–53.

37. *Mobile Advertiser and Register,* August 20, 1864.

38. *Montgomery Advertiser,* May 25, August 1, September 22, 1864.

39. Vouchers from Luke Dickerson, in CP, NA.

40. Silvester Bennett to John Gill Shorter, May 6, 1863, in LR (Confederate Secretary of War); *Montgomery Weekly Mail,* November 15, 1862; copy of pardon application from Charles Clapp to Andrew Johnson, August 1865, in Clapp Surname File, ADAH; vouchers from "Janney and Co., Manufacturers of Steam Engines and Mill Work," in CP, NA; *Montgomery Advertiser,* August 17, 1864; William Albaugh and Edward N. Simmons, *Confederate Arms* (Harrisburg, Pa.: Stackpole Co., 1952), 135–36; for Frank Gilmer see Armes, *The Story of Coal and Iron in Alabama,* 103–40.

41. *Montgomery Advertiser,* October 15, June 2, 1864; for cotton cards see Faust, *Mothers of Invention,* 48–49.

42. Douglas B. Ball, *Financial Failure and Confederate Defeat* (Urbana: University of Illinois Press, 1991), 161–91; Todd, *Confederate Finance,* 85–120; Stephen R. Wise, *Lifeline of the Confederacy: Blockade Running During the Civil War* (Columbia: University of South

Carolina Press, 1988), 80–81, 167–68, 175–77; Paul Escott, *After Secession: Jefferson Davis and the Failure of Confederate Nationalism* (Baton Rouge: Louisiana State University Press, 1978), 67, 122–23; Charles W. Ramsdell, *Behind the Lines in the Southern Confederacy* (Baton Rouge: Louisiana State University Press, 1944), 76–77.

43. *Columbus Enquirer,* September 30, 1862; *Montgomery Post,* October 1, 1861.

44. Edward Moren to wife, November 26, 1862, Moren Papers, ADAH.

45. *Montgomery Advertiser,* May 30, 1864; *Montgomery Weekly Advertiser,* April 1, 1863; *Montgomery Mail,* January 4, May 31, 1864; John Seibels to John A. Campbell, October 24, 1863, LR (Confederate Secretary of War).

46. *Mobile Advertiser and Register,* March 31, 1864.

47. *Montgomery Mail,* March 23, 1864; for currency situation see *Mail,* May 18, April 18, October 14, 19, 1864; *Montgomery Advertiser,* June 15, 1864; *Mobile Advertiser and Register,* June 8, 1864.

48. Edward Moren to wife, August 24, November 21, 1863, Moren Papers, ADAH; *Montgomery Mail,* October 14, 1862, October 14, December 28, 1864; Rable, *Civil Wars,* 92–96; Joseph Jacobs, "Some of the Drug Conditions During the War Between the States, 1861–5," *Southern Historical Papers* 33 (1905), 169, 175.

49. *Montgomery Advertiser,* July 11, 1864; *Montgomery Mail,* January 6, 1863; *Columbus Enquirer,* January 5, 1864; Kreutner Surname File, ADAH; Clinton, *Tara Revisited: Women, War and the Plantation Legend* (New York: Abbeville Press, 1992), 149–52; McMillan, *Disintegration of a Confederate State,* 83.

50. *Harper's Weekly Magazine,* June 25, 1864.

51. *Montgomery Mail,* November 16, December 6, 1864.

52. *Montgomery Mail,* March 18, 1863; September 22, 1864; *Alabama State Census, Free Population: 1860,* 15; Faust, *Mothers of Invention,* 238–47.

53. *Montgomery Mail,* February 7, 1864, July 2, December 27, 1864.

54. *Mobile Advertiser and Register,* November 8, 1864; *Montgomery County, Alabama White Marriage License Index (1817–1919),* Book 7, 1663, copy in the Alabama Department of Archives and History, Montgomery, Ala.; Kruetner Surname File, ADAH.

5. The Administration of a Confederate City

1. *Montgomery Mail,* February 28, March 1, 1861; *Montgomery Weekly Post,* March 6, 1861, *Montgomery Weekly Advertiser,* July 25, 1860.

2. *Montgomery Advertiser,* March 24, 1861.

3. Ibid., November 15, 1864; *Montgomery Mail,* December 2, 1862, December 6, 1864; Montgomery City Council Minutes (1861–1866), 177; for Coleman see Owen, *Dictionary of Alabama Biography,* 3:379; for Noble, 4:1283.

4. *Montgomery Mail,* May 15, 1863.

5. Montgomery City Council Minutes (1861–1866), 75; Sanford, *The Code of the City of Montgomery,* 40–46, 68–70, 76–77, 93–95; for an overview of city government functions elsewhere see Louis H. Manarin, ed., *Richmond at War: The Minutes of the City Council* (Chapel Hill: University of North Carolina Press, 1966), 1–6.

6. Montgomery City Council Minutes (1861–1866), 80.

7. Ibid., 81, 90, 93; *Montgomery Weekly Post,* May 22, 1861.

8. Montgomery City Council Minutes (1861–1866), 121–23, 242–43, 297–99, 317; Sanford, *The Code of the City of Montgomery,* 45–56, 65, 80–81, 94–99.

9. Montgomery City Council Minutes (1861–1866), 66–67, 88, 162, 184–91, 196, 198; Mears and Turnbull, *Montgomery Directory,* 38, 41, 73; for Thomas Hill see Hill Surname File, ADAH.

10. *Montgomery Mail,* November 29, 1862; Montgomery City Council Minutes (1861–1865), 51, 156, 159, 174, 199–200, 209.

11. Montgomery City Council Minutes (1861–1866), 115, 101, 145–47, 194, 250–52, 264, 268–69, 280, 283; *Montgomery Weekly Advertiser,* August 7, 1861; *Montgomery Advertiser,* June 15, 1864.

12. "Ladies of Montgomery" to Jefferson Davis, April 1862, LR (Confederate Secretary of War); *Alabama State Census, Free Population: 1860,* 20, 22, 24, 60, 62; *Montgomery Mail,* October 22, 1862; Drew Gilpin Faust, *Mothers of Invention: Women Of The Slaveholding South in the American Civil War* (Chapel Hill: University of North Carolina Press, 1996), 131–34; Rable, *Civil Wars,* 50–51, 62, 78–79.

13. *Montgomery Weekly Advertiser,* October 21, 1863; *Montgomery Mail,* October 26, 1862, April 9, 1863.

14. "Ladies of Montgomery" to Jefferson Davis, April 1862, LR (Confederate Secretary of War); List of Families in Montgomery County who are Entitled to Relief, March 1862, October 1864, in Military Volunteer Association Records, ADAH; *Alabama State Census, Free Population: 1860,* 99.

15. Anna Knox to Thomas Hill Watts, February 1864, in Applications for Military Service Exemptions File, ADAH.

16. Montgomery City Council Minutes (1861–1866), 175, 82–83, 100.

17. Ibid., 230–31, 179–80, 235, 271–72, 297–98.

18. *Montgomery Weekly Mail,* September 5, 1862; Montgomery City Council Minutes (1861–1866), 55–57, 131, 257–58; Sanford, *The Code of the City of Montgomery,* 54–59, 252.

19. *Montgomery Mail,* April 22, 1864; Montgomery City Council Minutes (1861–1866), 136–37; *Montgomery Mail,* April 21, 28, 1864; *Mobile Advertiser and Register,* July 7, 1864; Sanford, *The Code of the City of Montgomery,* 76–80.

20. Montgomery City Council Minutes (1861–1866), 86, 36, 98.

21. Sanford, *The Code of the City of Montgomery,* 48–49; *Montgomery Mail,* January 3, 6, 1863, March 18, 20, April 30, 1864.

22. Montgomery City Council Minutes (1861–1866), 135–37, 144, 147.

23. *Montgomery Advertiser,* November 9, 1863.

24. Montgomery City Council Minutes (1861–1866), 65, 106–7, 172, 254; *Montgomery Mail,* February 2, 1864.

25. Kenneth Radley, *Rebel Watchdog: The Confederate States Army Provost Guard* (Baton Rouge: Louisiana State University Press, 1989), 3.

26. *Montgomery Advertiser,* May 23, April 26, 1863.

27. William E. Bevens, *Reminiscences of a Private,* ed. Daniel E. Sutherland (Fayetteville: University of Arkansas Press, 1992), 87.

28. *Montgomery Mail,* December 22, 1864, May 15, 1863; *Montgomery Advertiser,* May 10, 23, 1863; Montgomery City Council Minutes (1861–1866), 168, 226.

29. *Montgomery Weekly Advertiser,* July 15, 1863; for Shorter see McMillan, *Disintegration of a Confederate State,* 27–30.

30. Montgomery City Council Minutes (1861–1866), 221–22.

31. Thomas Hill Watts to J. M. Withers, October 28, 1864, in Watts Papers, ADAH; John Gill Shorter to James Seddon, July 7, 1863, John Gill Shorter Papers, ADAH; *Montgomery Advertiser,* October 15, 1864; McMillan, *Disintegration of a Confederate State,* 96–97.

32. *New Orleans Delta,* May 12, 1861.

33. *Montgomery Mail,* April 16, 1862.

34. Petition of "Members of Dexter Fire Engine Co. No. 1," LR (Confederate Secretary of War); Montgomery City Council Minutes (1861–1866), 112, 255, 259, 289, 318; *Montgomery Weekly Mail,* June 28, 1862; Lee Ann Whites, *The Civil War As a Crisis in Gender: Augusta, Georgia, 1860–1890* (Athens: University of Georgia Press, 1995), 78–82.

6. Waging War on the Home Front

1. *Montgomery Weekly Confederation,* May 10, 1861.

2. *Montgomery Weekly Post,* March 27, May 8, June 22, July 17, 1861; *Montgomery Weekly Advertiser,* March 15, May 1, 1861; John Tyler, Jr., to John P. Figh and George M. Figh, LR (Confederate Secretary of War); William Boyrer, "Montgomery Parade March," Composed and Respectfully Dedicated to the Metropolitan Guards (Mobile, J. H. Snow, 1861), Lester S. Levy Collection of Sheet Music, Special Collections, Milton S. Eisenhower Library, The Johns Hopkins University, Baltimore, Md.

3. *Montgomery Weekly Post,* May 22, 1861.

4. *Montgomery Weekly Advertiser,* June 12, 1864; Montgomery City Council Minutes (1861–1865), 98; *Montgomery Weekly Post,* June 5, 1861; James I. Robertson, Jr., *Civil War Virginia: Battleground For a Nation* (Charlottesville: University Press of Virginia, 1991), 26; Eleanor Lee Templeman, "In the Beginning . . . " *Arlington Historical Magazine* 1, no. 4 (October 1960), 4, 43–48.

5. *Montgomery Weekly Post,* June 5, May 8, 1861; *London Times,* May 30, 1861.

6. *Montgomery Weekly Post,* May 15, 1861; Jimerson, *The Private Civil War,* 128–29.

7. *Montgomery Mail,* April 18, 1861; *Montgomery Weekly Confederation,* May 10, 1861.

8. Jacob Weil to Josiah Weil, May 16, 1861, Weil Papers, ADAH.

9. *Montgomery Advertiser,* April 15, 1861; *Montgomery Post,* May 25, 1861; *Montgomery Weekly Post,* May 1, 8, 15, 1861; Rable, *Civil Wars,* 48.

10. John D. Phelan to William P. Browne, August 12, 1861, William P. Browne Papers, ADAH; for a typically nonobjective comparison of Southern and Northern soldiers see *Montgomery Weekly Advertiser,* May 8, 1861.

11. *Journal of the Confederate Congress* (1860), 1:168; Faust, *Confederate Nationalism Ideology and Identity,* 22–29; Richard E. Beringer, Herman Hattaway, Archer Jones, and William N. Still, Jr., *The Elements of Confederate Defeat: Nationalism, War Aims, and Religion* (Athens: University of Georgia Press, 1988), 32–42; James W. Silver, *Confederate Morale and Church Propaganda* (Tuscaloosa: Confederate Publishing, 1957), 31; William E. Wight, "The Churches and the Confederate Cause," *Civil War History* 6 (December 1960), 361–62, 373.

12. Edward Moren to wife, n.d., Moren Papers, ADAH; *Montgomery Post,* July 25, 1861.

13. J. S. Dill, *Isaac Taylor Tichenor: The Home Mission Statesman* (Nashville: Sunday School Board Southern Baptist Convention, 1908), 93–94; for Tichenor see Alan L. Walker, "Three Alabama Chaplains, 1861–1865," *Alabama Review* 16 (July 1963), 178–80.

14. Bertram W. Korn, *American Jewry and the Civil War* (Philadelphia: Jewish Publications Society of America, 1951), 48; for Gutheim see Rogers, " 'In Defense of Our Sacred Cause,' " 113–22.

15. M. J. Solomons Scrapbook Collection (1861–1863), Duke University Special Collections, Durham, N.C.

16. Caroline Hausman to John Gill Shorter, October 1861, in Hausman Surname File, ADAH; Kate Morrissette, "Social Life in the First Capital of the Confederacy," 21–24, unpublished manuscript on file at Landmarks Foundation, Montgomery, Ala.; *Montgomery Post,* June 4, 1861; *Montgomery Weekly Post,* May 8, June 5, 1861; Marielou Armstrong Cory, *The Ladies' Memorial Association of Montgomery, Alabama: Its Origin and Organization, 1860–1870* (Montgomery, Ala.: Alabama Printing Company, n.d.), 10–15; for Bibb see Owen, *Dictionary of Alabama Biography,* 3:1444–45; for Hausman see Cory, *Ladies' Memorial Association,* 10–11; Rable, *Civil Wars,* 137–40; Faust, *Mothers of Invention,* 24–25.

17. Caroline Hausman to John Gill Shorter, October 30, 1862, in Hausman Surname File, ADAH; *Montgomery Post,* August 28, September 11, 1861.

18. Lewellyn Shaver to Mrs. Judge Bibb, October 3, 1863, in Benajah Smith and Sophia Lucy Ann Bibb Papers, ADAH.

19. *Montgomery Mail,* April 21, 1864.

20. Thomas Hill Watts to George Randolph, May 14, 1862, LR (Confederate Secretary of War); *Montgomery Weekly Advertiser,* July 3, 1861; *Montgomery Post,* June 19, 1861; *Montgomery Weekly Post,* June 10, July 17, 1861; Cory, *Ladies' Memorial Association,* 13–22; for Carnot and Sarah Bellingers see Owen, *Dictionary of Alabama Biography,* 3:131; Rable, *Civil Wars,* 121–28; Catherine Clinton, *Tara Revisited,* 83.

21. Samuel Stout to Mary Jarrett Bell, January 19, 1864, Samuel H. Stout Papers, Emory University; *Montgomery Advertiser,* May 5, 1864.

22. Edward Moren to wife, January 26, 1862, Moren Papers, ADAH; for Sarah Herron see Owen, *Dictionary of Alabama Biography,* 3:803; for Mary Ann Phelan, 4:1356; for Eliza Moore see Cory, *Ladies Aid Association,* 11; Clinton, *Tara Revisited,* 88; Faust, *Mothers of Invention,* 92–114; Rable, *Civil Wars,* 121–28.

23. *Montgomery Weekly Advertiser,* September 30, 1863.

24. *Montgomery Advertiser,* June 3, 1864.

25. *Montgomery Mail,* August 25, 1864; Black, *Railroads of the Confederacy,* 38–39.

26. *Montgomery Advertiser,* May 24, 20, August 5, 1864; *Montgomery Mail,* August 12, 1864; for William Bell see Owen, *Dictionary of Alabama Biography,* 3:128; for Albert Strassburger see Strassburger Surname File, ADAH.

27. William Gentry to Samuel Stout, May 11, 1864, Samuel H. Stout Papers, Emory University; *Montgomery Advertiser,* May 5, June 14, 1864; *Montgomery Mail,* May 6, 1864.

28. *Montgomery Advertiser,* May 8, 1864.

29. Ibid., August 18, 1864; *Mobile Advertiser and Register,* July 13, 1864.

30. *Montgomery Weekly Mail,* May 1, 1861; Rable, *Civil Wars,* 103–6.

31. *Montgomery Mail,* November 25, 1862, October 26, 1862; for Norton see Cory, *Ladies' Memorial Association,* 13–14.

32. *Montgomery Weekly Advertiser,* December 17, 1862, April 17, 1863; *Montgomery Mail,* April 30, September 11, 1864.

33. *Mobile Advertiser and Register,* April 22, 1864.

34. *Montgomery Mail,* May 1, 1864.

35. *Columbus Enquirer,* December 23, 1864.

36. *Montgomery Advertiser,* April 17, 20, 1862, June 19, 1864; *Montgomery Mail,* March 6, 1863, January 2, June 23, September 5, 7, 1864; *Columbus Enquirer,* January 5, 1864; Augusta Jane Evans, *Macaria; or, Altars of Sacrifice,* ed., Drew Gilpin Faust (Baton Rouge: Louisiana State University Press, 1992), xv–xviii; Brewer, *Alabama: Her History,* 602.

37. *Montgomery Weekly Advertiser,* April 13, 1861; *Montgomery Advertiser,* March 15, 1861.

38. *Montgomery Post,* August 21, 1861.

39. George G. Pattison to William Lowndes Yancey, September 4, 1862, William Lowndes Yancey Papers, ADAH.

40. Thomas Taylor to Jefferson Davis, June 8, 1863, LR (Confederate Secretary of War); *Montgomery Advertiser,* May 8, 1863.

41. *Montgomery Mail,* November 23, 1864; *Montgomery Advertiser,* October 15, 1864.

42. *Montgomery Mail,* October 21, 1864.

43. Basil Manly to son, August 23, 1861, Manly Papers, University of Alabama; *Montgomery Mail,* May 16, 1864; *Mobile Advertiser and Register,* July 28, 1864; Rable, *Civil Wars,* 206.

44. Edward Moren to wife, March 8, 1862, Moren Papers, ADAH.

45. William Lowndes Yancey to Jefferson Davis, May (2?), 1862, in Jefferson Davis, *The Papers of Jefferson Davis: Vol. 8, 1862,* edited by Lynda L. Crist, Mary Seaton Dix, and Kenneth H. Williams (Baton Rouge: Louisiana State University Press, 1994), 164; Rable, *Civil Wars,* 208–12.

46. *Montgomery Weekly Advertiser,* August 5, 1863.

47. Edward Moren to wife, August 24, 1863, Moren Papers, ADAH; *Montgomery Mail,* August 7, 1864; Rable, *Civil Wars,* 204–14.

48. *Mobile Advertiser and Register,* August 11, 1864; May 19, 1864.

49. Morrissette, "Social Life in the First Capital of the Confederacy," 23; *Montgomery Advertiser,* May 8, 1863, May 30, 1864; *Montgomery Mail,* August 20, 1864.

50. M. J. Solomon's Scrapbook Collection, Special Collections, Duke University, James Gutheim, n.p.; *Montgomery Advertiser,* May 5, 1864; *Montgomery Mail,* August 20, November 15, 16, 23, December 16, 1864; *Mobile Advertiser and Register,* December 31, 1864; Lewellyn A. Shaver, *A History of the Sixtieth Alabama Regiment Gracie's Alabama Brigade* (Montgomery: Barrett and Brown, 1867), 7–8, 61–65.

7. Dissenting Voices

1. Testimony of Johnson C. Davis, Claim #21,355, in Case Files of Southern Claims Commission, RG 217, Records of the Accounting Offices of the Treasury Department, NA, Washington, D.C. Hereafter cited as Claim #21,355.

2. Testimony of William J. Bibb; Walter L. Coleman, Claim #21,355, RG 217, NA.

3. Testimony of David Carter, Claim #5616, in Case Files of Southern Claims Commission, RG 217; NA, Washington, D.C. Hereafter cited as Claim #5616.

4. William Hedges, "Three Years in Montgomery," *Harper's New Monthly Magazine* 29 (July 1864), 196; testimony of David Carter, Claim #5616, RG 217, NA.

5. Hedges, "Three Years in Montgomery," 197; testimony of David Carter, Claim #5616, RG 217, NA.

6. For Unionism in the South and the experience of Southerners living under Federal occupation see Ash, *When the Yankees Came;* Frank W. Klingberg, *The Southern Claims Commission* (Berkeley: University of California Press, 1955), 1–19, 194–209; Gerald M. Capers, *Occupied City: New Orleans Under the Federals, 1862–1865* (Lexington: University of Kentucky Press, 1965), 48, 70, 78, 90–92, 110–11; Durham, *Nashville: The Occupied City,* 6, 90–91.

7. Hedges, "Three Years in Montgomery," 196–97; for Lewis Owen see Owen, *Dictionary of Alabama Biography,* 3:1309; *Alabama State Census, Slave Population: 1860,* 226, 235; *Alabama State Census, Free Population: 1860,* 98; testimony of Samuel Seelye, Claim #5616, RG 217, NA; *Montgomery Mail,* February 13, 1864; *City Directory,* 41.

8. Testimony of Lewis Owen, David Carter, Samuel Seelye, and James Stow, Claim #5616, RG 217, NA; see also Seelye and Stow Surname Files, ADAH.

9. Testimony of Benajah S. Bibb, William Bibb, Johnson Davis, Claim #21,355, RG 217, NA; *Alabama State Census, Free Population: 1860,* 98.

10. Testimony of Shepherd A. Darby, William Bibb, William Coleman, Johnson Davis, Claim #21,355, RG 217, NA; for establishment and operations of the Southern Claims Commission see Klingberg, *Southern Claims Commission;* for description of records see Gary B. Mills, *Southern Loyalists in the Civil War: The Southern Claims Commission* (Baltimore: Genealogical Publishing Co., 1994).

11. Testimony of Israel Roberts, Claim #21,355, RG 217, NA.

12. Testimony of Walter Coleman, Claim #21,355, RG 217, NA.

13. Testimony of Benajah Bibb, Claim #21,355, RG 217, NA.

14. Testimony of C. H. Cheatam, William C. Bibb, Claim #21,355, RG 217, NA.

15. Testimony of James Berney, David Carter, Claim #5616, RG 217, NA; Owen, *Dictionary of Alabama Biography,* 3:135.

16. *Chicago Tribune,* May 2, 1861.

17. George Pendleton Strong, *The Diary of George Templeton Strong,* ed., Allan Nevis and Milton Halsey Thomas (Seattle: University of Washington Press, 1998), 215; testimony of David Carter, Claim #5616, RG 217, NA; *Montgomery Weekly Confederation,* July 3, 1861; for an account of one of the Federal prisoners captured at Shiloh and incarcerated in Montgomery see J. J. Geer, *Beyond The Lines; or A Yankee Prisoner Loose in Dixie* (Philadelphia: J. W. Daughaday, 1863), 75–88.

18. *Montgomery Weekly Advertiser,* August 7, 1861; *Montgomery Post,* August 9, 1861; testimony of David Carter, Claim #5616, RG 217, NA.

19. Testimony of William Bibb, Claim #21,355; David Carter, Claim #5616, RG 217, NA; for the situation of several Unionists in Atlanta see Thomas G. Dyer, "Vermont Yankees in King Cotton's Court: The Case of Cyrena and Amherst Stone," *Vermont History* (Fall 1992).

20. Testimony of James Stow, David Carter, Claim #5616, RG 217, NA.

21. Ash, *When the Yankees Came,* 108–11, 114, 122–23, 127; Ash, *Middle Tennessee Society Transformed,* 146–47; Durham, *Nashville: The Occupied City,* 237–39; Richard H. Abbott, "Civil War Origins of the Southern Republican Press," *Civil War History* 43 (March 1997), 43–50.

22. Testimony of David Carter, Claim #5616, RG 217, NA.

23. Testimony of Milton Safford; testimony of Walter Coleman, Claim #21,355, RG 217, NA.

24. Testimony of Samuel Seelye, Claim #5616, RG 217, NA.

25. Testimony of David Carter, Claim #5616, RG 217, NA; *Montgomery Mail,* March 18, 1863, January 30, 1864; for an example of the pass enforcement system in Montgomery see Arthur James Lyon Fremantle, *Three Months in the Southern States, April–June 1863* (Edinburgh: William Blackwood and Sons, 1863), 134–36.

26. Testimony of James Stow, Claim #5616, RG 217, NA.

27. Testimony of Walter D. Carter, David Carter, Claim #5616, RG 217, NA.

28. *Montgomery Mail,* March 17, 13, 1863; *Montgomery Confederation,* February 29, 1860; testimony of David Carter, Claim #5616, RG 217, NA.

29. Hedges, "Three Years in Montgomery," 196–201.

30. Testimony of David Carter, Claim #5616; testimony of Charles Sheats, Claim #21,355, RG 217, NA; for Sheats see Sarah Woolfolk Wiggins, *The Scalawag in Alabama Politics, 1865–1881* (Tuscaloosa: University of Alabama Press, 1977), 6–7; Richard N. Current, *Lincoln's Loyalists Union Soldiers From the Confederacy* (Boston: Northeastern University Press, 1992), 133–39; Michael K. Honey, "The War Within the Confederacy: White Unionists of North Carolina," *Prologue* 18 (Summer 1986), 74–93.

31. Testimony of Johnson Davis, Claim #21,355, RG 217, NA.

32. Testimony of Samuel Seelye, David Carter, Claim #5616, RG 217, NA; Mears and Turnbull, *Montgomery Directory,* 4.

33. Hedges, "Three Years in Montgomery," 197.

8. Military Preparations Deferred

1. McMillan, *Disintegration of a Confederate State,* 34–37, 53–54; Arthur W. Bergeron, Jr., *Confederate Mobile* (Jackson: University of Mississippi Press, 1991), ix–x, 14, 56; Thomas, *Confederate Nation,* 100–101.

2. *Montgomery Mail,* February 25, 1862; *Columbus Enquirer,* October 7, 1862.

3. *Montgomery Advertiser,* April 30, 1862.

4. *Montgomery Weekly Mail,* May 20, 1862.

5. "Meeting of the Citizens of Montgomery and Surrounding Counties," newspaper clipping, Matthew Blue Papers, ADAH; *Montgomery Advertiser,* April 30, 1862; for P. T. Sayre see Owen, *Dictionary of Alabama Biography,* 4:1507; for military career of Clanton see Wheeler, *Confederate Military History,* 7:398–400.

6. George Randolph to James Forney, May 5, 1862, *OR,* ser. 2, vol. 3, 864; "Special Orders of H. P. Watson," *OR,* ser. 1, vol. 52, pt. 2, 311; John Gill Shorter to Mayor and Council of the City of Montgomery, May 8, 1862, John Gill Shorter Papers, ADAH.

7. Basil Manly to Charles, February 13, 1862, Manly Papers, University of Alabama;

Muster Roll of Alabama Rebels in Montgomery County, also Muster Roll of Montgomery Foreign Guards in Montgomery County, both in Independent Company File (1863–1864), ADAH; G. W. Say to Col. J. F. Morgan, April 21, 1863, LR (Confederate Secretary of War); *Montgomery Weekly Advertiser,* June 6, 1863; *Montgomery Mail,* March 3, May 3, 9, 13, 31, 1863.

8. *Montgomery Mail,* July 14, 16, 1863; *Montgomery Weekly Advertiser,* July 22, 1863.

9. John Gill Shorter to General Dabney Maury, July 6, 1863, in John Gill Shorter Letterbooks, ADAH.

10. James Powell, William Gilmer, George Goldthwaite et al. to James Seddon, January 15, 1864, in *OR,* ser. 1, vol. 32, pt. 2, 561.

11. *Montgomery Weekly Advertiser,* July 1, 1863.

12. Grimsley, *The Hard Hand of War,* 162–166.

13. Charles Dana to E. M. Stanton, *OR,* ser. 1, vol. 30, pt. 2, 71–72; Ulysses Grant to H. W. Halleck, January 15, 1864; *OR,* ser. 1, vol. 32, pt. 2, 100–101; Herman Hattaway and Archer Jones, *How the North Won A Military History of the Civil War* (Urbana: University of Illinois Press, 1983), 476–77, 492–93, 518–19.

14. Braxton Bragg to Jefferson Davis, July 15, 9, *OR,* ser. 1, vol. 39, pt. 2, 713, 695–96.

15. *Montgomery Mail,* June 12, 7, 16, 30, 1864; *Montgomery Advertiser,* May 22, June 3, 1864.

16. William Sherman to Lovell Rousseau, July 6, 1864, in *OR,* ser. 1, vol. 38, pt. 5, 71; Sherman to Rousseau, June 29, 1864, *OR,* ser. 1, vol. 38, pt. 4, 638; Sherman to Rousseau, June 30, 1864, ibid., 648; "Reports of Maj. Gen Lovell Rousseau, U.S. Army of Raid from Decatur, Ala., to the West Point and Montgomery Railroad (July 12–20) and the Wheeler Raid," *OR,* ser. 1, vol. 38, pt. 2, 904–7; see also Stephen Z. Starr, *The Union Cavalry in the Civil War: The War in the West, 1861–1865,* vol. 3 (Baton Rouge: Louisiana State University Press, 1985), 462–64; Edwin C. Bearss, "Rousseau's Raid on the Montgomery and West Point Railroad, 1864," *Alabama Historical Quarterly* 25 (Spring and Summer 1963), 7–48.

17. *Montgomery Mail,* July 21, 24; *Mobile Advertiser and Register,* July 20, 1864.

18. "Report of Lovell Rousseau," *OR,* vol. 88, pt. 2, 907–9; William Sherman to Lovell Rousseau, July 7, 1864, *OR,* ser. 1, vol. 38, pt. 5, 8; Starr, *Union Cavalry in the Civil War,* 462–63.

19. *Mobile Advertiser and Register,* July 21, 1864; *Montgomery Mail,* July 21, 23, 24, 1864; Theodore Bethea Confederate Service Record, Service Record Files, ADAH.

20. Dabney H. Maury to George Whitfield, July 27, 1864, *OR,* ser. 1, vol. 39, pt. 2, 729–30; Calvin L. Sayre to Dabney Maury, August 26, 1864, ibid., 798; Braxton Bragg to Col John B. Sale, July 23, 1864, *OR,* ser. 1, vol. 38, pt. 5, 904; *Mobile Advertiser and Register,* July 26, 29, 1864; Black, *Railroads of the Confederacy,* 251–52.

21. William Sherman, *Memoirs of Gen. W. T. Sherman,* I (New York: Charles L. Webster, 1891), 69.

22. *Montgomery Mail,* July 24, 1864.

23. *Mobile Advertiser and Register,* July 21, 20, 1864; P. T. Sayre to H. P. Watson, February 11, 1864, in "Montgomery Guards File," Montgomery County Independent Company File, 1863–1864, ADAH.

24. *Mobile Advertiser and Register,* September 15, 1864; *Memphis Appeal,* September 20, 1864; *Montgomery Mail,* January 9, August 7, 1864; *Montgomery Advertiser,* August 8, 1864; Thomas H. Baker, "Refugee Newspaper: *The Memphis Daily Appeal, 1862–1865," Journal of Southern History* (August 1963), 326–42.

25. Edward Moren to wife, October 29, 1862, Moren Papers, ADAH.

9. The End Nears

1. *Montgomery Mail,* January 3, 1865.

2. Thomas Caffey to Mary, May 15, 1864, in "Letters From the Front," *Confederate Veteran* 26 (August 1918), 354; Beringer, Hattaway, Jones, and Still, *The Elements of Confederate Defeat,* 148–49, 158–61.

3. Goff, *Confederate Supply,* 218–21; John J. Walker to L. B. Northrop, January 25, 1865, in *OR,* ser. 1, vol. 46, pt. 2, 1220–21; Ball, *Financial Failure and Confederate Defeat,* 253.

4. George Brent to P. G. T. Beauregard, *OR,* ser. 1, vol. 45, pt. 2, 704–5.

5. *Mobile Advertiser and Register,* February 1, 1865, April 21, 1864; E. H. Harris to George W. Brent, January 29, 1865; George Brent Papers, Duke University.

6. *Montgomery Mail,* February 18, 1865, September 7, 1864; *Montgomery Advertiser,* September 6, 1864, February 3, 1865; *Mobile Advertiser and Register,* July 1, August 20, 1864, January 12, 1865; "Post of Montgomery, Ala. Returns of the Post for January 1865," in Returns of Confederate Post Commands (Alabama), RG 109, NA.

7. *Montgomery Mail,* April 11, 1865; December 17, 1864; January 3, 1865.

8. Ibid., March 27, 1864.

9. "Report of J. R. Waddy," January 21, 1865, in George Brent Papers, Duke University; *Montgomery Advertiser,* January 3, 1865, February 24, 1865.

10. William Cole to Samuel Stout, March 17, 1865, William Gentry to Samuel Stout, March 9, 1865, Samuel H. Stout Papers, Southern Historical Collection, University of North Carolina; "Consolidated Morning Report of Surgeon S. H. Stout, Medical Director of Hospitals, Army of Tennessee," Samuel H. Stout Papers, Duke University.

11. William Gentry to Samuel Stout, March 9, 1865, Samuel H. Stout Papers, Emory University; *Montgomery Mail,* March 15, 1869.

12. *Montgomery Mail,* March 8, 12, 15, February 7, 1865; Ellen Blue Diary, entry for March 10, on file at Landmarks Foundation of Montgomery, Montgomery, Ala.; *Montgomery Advertiser,* January 3, March 5, 1865; *Mobile Advertiser and Register,* December 31, 1864.

13. *Montgomery Mail,* March 29, April 11, 1865.

14. Thomas Hill Watts to Jefferson Davis, *OR,* ser. 2, vol. 7, 1223; Goff, *Confederate Supply,* 117–18.

15. M. Lehman and Isaac Tichenor to Ulysses Grant, January, 1865, *OR,* ser. 2, vol. 8, 166; *Montgomery Advertiser,* March 5, 1864.

16. Jefferson Davis to Thomas Hill Watts, March 7, 1865, *OR,* ser. 2, vol. 8, 365; *Montgomery Advertiser,* March 5, 1865.

17. *Montgomery Mail,* March 29, 1865, February 20, 1864.

18. *Memphis Appeal,* February 16, 1865.

19. *Montgomery Mail,* December 29, 28, 1864.

20. *Mobile Advertiser and Register,* February 1, January 21, 1865.

21. *Montgomery Mail,* January 3, 1865, August 19, December 30, 1864.

22. Ibid., January 3, 1865.

23. Ibid., December 17, 1864.

24. Ibid., December 14, 1864; January 10, 1865.

25. Ibid., January 4, 1865.

26. *Mobile Advertiser and Register,* November 2, 1864, February 22, 1865; *Montgomery Mail,* February 8, April 17, 1865; *Montgomery Advertiser,* January 3, 30, 1865.

27. *Montgomery Mail,* December 20, 1864.

28. *Montgomery Advertiser,* January 30, 1865.

29. Earl Schenck Miers, *When the World Ended: The Diary of Emma LeConte* (New York: Oxford University Press, 1957), 4–5.

30. *Montgomery Mail,* December 20, 1864; February 9, 1865; *Montgomery Advertiser,* March 3, 1865.

31. *Montgomery Mail,* February 8, 1865, August 19, September 2, 1864; *Montgomery Advertiser,* January 3, 30, 1865; *Mobile Advertiser and Register,* February 22, 1865.

32. Montgomery City Council Minutes (1861–1866), 305–7; *Montgomery Mail,* December 28, 1864.

33. *Montgomery Mail,* December 28, February 14, 1865.

34. William Sanford to Sallie, July 22, 1864, William Augustine Sanford Papers, ADAH.

35. B. F. Jones to General Cooper, December 12, 1864, in Inspection Reports, reel 9, RG 109, NA; McMillan, *Disintegration of a Confederate State,* 84–87.

36. *Montgomery Advertiser,* January 3, 1865; *Montgomery Mail,* September 2, November 25, 1864; Foreman's Battery was the invention of Colonel John H. Foreman who was connected to the State Artillery in Mobile; William Baldwin Confederate Service Record, Service Records, ADAH.

37. Montgomery City Council Minutes (1861–1866), 315–16.

38. *Montgomery Advertiser,* March 3, 1865; *Montgomery Mail,* March 18, September 4, October 10, 1864; Montgomery City Council Minutes (1861–1866), 305–7, 309, 315.

39. *Montgomery Mail,* December 29, 1864.

40. *Montgomery Mail,* January 3, 1865.

41. Ibid., December 22, 1864; February 7, 24, March 8, 1865; December 27, 1864; *Montgomery Advertiser,* February 22, 1865.

42. John Rozier, ed., *The Granite Farm Letters: The Civil War Correspondence of Edgeworth and Sallie Birth* (Athens: University of Georgia Press, 1992), 234.

43. *Montgomery Mail,* December 22, September 2, 1864.

44. Ibid., January 13, 1865; *OR,* ser. 1, vol. 49, pt. 1, 960–61.

45. R. M. Collins, *Chapters From the Unwritten History of the War Between the States* (St. Louis: Nixon-Jones, 1890), 273–75.

46. *Montgomery Mail,* February 8, 1865.

47. Ibid., March 8, 1865; *Memphis Appeal,* February 16, 1865.

48. *Montgomery Advertiser,* February 22, 24, 1865; *Montgomery Mail,* March 1, 1865.

49. *Montgomery Mail,* March 1, February 18, 1865; *Montgomery Advertiser,* February 22, 1865.

50. *Mobile Advertiser and Register,* March 14, 1865, November 2, 1864; Georgia L. Tatum, *Disloyalty in the Confederacy* (Chapel Hill: University of North Carolina Press, 1934), 25–32, 54–72; Rable, *Civil Wars,* 202–14.

51. *Montgomery Mail,* February 8, 1865; *Mobile Advertiser and Register,* March 3, 1865.

52. Morrissette, "Social Life in the First Capital of the Confederacy," 20; *Alabama State Census, Free Population: 1860,* 98; List of Families in Montgomery County who are Entitled to Relief, in Military Volunteer Association Records, ADAH.

53. *Montgomery Advertiser,* March 3, February 2, 22, 1865; *Mobile Advertiser and Register,* March 3, 1865; *Memphis Appeal,* February 28, 1865; for Woods see Owen, *Dictionary of Alabama Biography,* 3:1804; for Gaines see Wheeler, *Confederate Military History,* 7:283.

54. *Montgomery Advertiser,* March 5, 1865.

55. Ibid., March 12, 1865.

10. A City Surrendered

1. Ulysses Grant to Henry Halleck, Jan 18, 1865, *OR,* ser. 1, vol. 55, pt. 2, 609–10; Henry Halleck to Ulysses Grant, January 18, 1865, ibid., 609; Halleck to Grant, December 30, 1865, *OR,* ser. 1, vol. 55, pt. 2, 419–20; James P. Jones, *Yankee Blitzkrieg: Wilson's Raid through Alabama and Georgia* (Athens: University of Georgia Press, 1976), 3, 22.

2. Richard Taylor to George Brent, Feb 17, 1865, in George Brent Papers, Duke University; James P. Jones, *Yankee Blitzkrieg,* 13.

3. W. F. Bullock, Jr., to Daniel W. Adams, Feb 15, 1865, *OR,* ser. 1, vol. 49, pt. 1, 982.

4. Thomas Hill Watts, "Proclamation to the People of Alabama," Thomas Hill Watts Papers, ADAH.

5. Samuel Stout to William Gentry, March 9, 1865, Samuel H. Stout Papers, Emory University; *Montgomery Advertiser,* March 12, 1865.

6. Stephen Z. Starr, *The Union Cavalry in the Civil War: From Fort Sumter to Gettysburg, 1861–1863,* vol. 1 (Baton Rouge: Louisiana State University Press, 1979), 19–20; Ellen Blue Diary, entry for March 31, Landmarks Foundation, Montgomery, Ala.; *Memphis Daily Appeal,* March 10, 1865; James P. Jones, *Yankee Blitzkrieg,* 3–6; 13, 30–35, 51–96; for Wilson see John T. Hubbell and James W. Geary, ed., *Biographical Dictionary of the Union: Northern Leaders of the Civil War* (Westport, Conn: Greenwood Press, 1995), 595–96.

7. Ellen Blue Diary, entry for April 2, 9, Landmarks Foundation, Montgomery, Ala.; James P. Jones, *Yankee Blitzkrieg,* 99–100.

8. Sam H. Harris to B. F. Jones, December 1, 1864, in Inspection Reports, RG 109, NA; R. H. Moore, to Thomas Owen, in Montgomery County Independent Company File (Watts Cadets); for Adams see James P. Jones, *Yankee Blitzkrieg,* 46; Jon L. Wakelyn, *Biographical Dictionary of the Confederacy* (Westport, Conn.: Greenwood Press, 1977), 67.

9. A. S. Buford to Thomas Hill Watts, April 4, 1865, Watts Papers, ADAH; Montgomery City Council Minutes (1861–1866), 315–18; *Montgomery Mail,* April 8, 1865; *Montgomery Advertiser,* April 22, 1865; James P. Jones, *Yankee Blitzkrieg,* 109.

10. *Montgomery Mail,* April 11, 1865.

11. A. S. Buford to J. C. Breckinridge, April 7, 1865, *OR,* ser. 1, vol. 49, pt. 2, 1216.

12. *Montgomery Mail,* April 11, 1865; *Montgomery Advertiser,* April 18, 1865; Mears and Turnbull, *Montgomery Directory,* 13, 55; for Richmond see Rembert W. Patrick, *The Fall of Richmond* (Baton Rouge: Louisiana State University Press, 1960).

13. *Montgomery Mail,* April 11, 1865.

14. Ibid., April 11, 1865; *Montgomery Advertiser,* April 18, 1865; *Troy Southern Advertiser,* April 14, 1865; *Columbus Sun,* April 6, 8, 1865; Jones, "Journal of Sarah Follansbee," 229.

15. James H. Wilson, *Under the Old Flag* (New York: D. Appleton, 1912), 249–50; "Report of Surgeon Francis Salter, U.S. Army, Medical Director," *OR,* ser. 1, vol. 49, pt. 1, 407; James P. Jones, *Yankee Blitzkrieg,* 101–3.

16. Jefferson Davis to Thomas Hill Watts, April 7, 1865, in Rowland, *Jefferson Davis, Constitutionalist,* 6:536.

17. Jones, "Journal of Sarah Follansbee," 230–31; *Columbus Sun,* April 14, 1865; *Montgomery Mail,* April 17, 1865; Benjamin F. McGee, *History of the 72nd Indiana Volunteer Infantry of the Mounted Lightening Brigade* (Lafayette, Ind.: S. Vater, 1882), 576.

18. *Montgomery Mail,* April 17, 1865.

19. Ibid., April 11, 1865.

20. *Montgomery Advertiser,* April 18, 1865; *Montgomery Mail,* April 17.

21. Charles F. Hinricks, Diary, entry for April 12, Hinricks Manuscripts, Western Historical Manuscripts Collection, University of Missouri, Columbia, Mo.; "Report of Col Wickliffe Cooper," May 3, 1865, *OR,* vol. 49, pt. 1, 433; Wilson, *Under the Old Flag,* 250.

22. Jones, "Journal of Sarah Follansbee," 321; Diary of S. V. Shipman, First Wisconsin Cavalry (1865), entry for April 12, p. 35, Shipman Manuscript, Wisconsin State Historical Library, Madison, Wis.; Wilson, *Under the Old Flag,* 251.

23. *Montgomery Mail,* April 17, 1865; James P. Jones, *Yankee Blitzkrieg,* 116.

24. "Report of Wickliffe Cooper," *OR,* ser. 1, vol. 49, 434; McMillan, *Disintegration of a Confederate State,* 119.

25. "Report of Francis Salter," *OR,* ser. 1, vol. 49, 407.

26. Shipman Diary, entry for April 13, 36, Wisconsin State Historical Library.

27. Wilson, *Under the Old Flag,* 252.

28. Hinricks Diary, entries for April 12, 13, University of Missouri.

29. Lewis M. Hosea, "The Campaign of Selma," *Sketches of War History, 1861–1865: Papers Read before the Ohio Commandry of the Military Order of the Loyal Legion of the United States* (Cincinnati: n.p., 1888), 187–88.

30. "Affairs of Southern Railroads," 39th Congress, 2nd sess., 1867, Report No. 34, 897, 885–86; "Report of Wickliffe Cooper," *OR,* ser. 1, vol. 49, 434; "Report of Col. John H. Peters," *OR,* ser. 1, vol. 49, pt. 1, 498; *Montgomery Advertiser,* April 18, 1865; McGee, *History of the 72nd Indiana Volunteer Infantry,* 577.

31. Testimony of Walter Carter, Claim #5617, Southern Claims Commission, RG 217, NA.

32. J. H. Wilson to Thomas, April 13, 1865, *OR,* ser. 1, vol. 49, pt. 2, 344; "Report of Francis Salter," *OR,* ser. 1, vol. 49, 407–8; *Montgomery Mail,* April 17, 1864.

33. Hinricks Diary, entry for April 13, University of Missouri; Cunningham, *Doctors in Gray,* 67.

34. *Montgomery Mail,* December 3, 1862.

35. Hinricks Diary, entry for April 12, University of Missouri.

36. E. B. Beaumont to R. H. G. Minty, April 12, 1865, *OR,* ser. 1, vol. 49, 332; James P. Jones, *Yankee Blitzkrieg,* 136–38.

Epilogue

1. *Montgomery Mail,* January 15, 1863, May 4, 1864; *Montgomery Weekly Mail,* November 15, 1862; Evans Johnson, "Henry W. Hilliard and the Civil War Years," 109–10.

2. Charles Pollard to Bessie Pollard Lee, February 12, 1863, Thomas Winfrey Olivers III Papers, ADAH; *Montgomery Weekly Mail,* August 1, 1862; *Montgomery Mail,* October 18, 1864; March 15, 1865; *Montgomery Advertiser,* September 6, 1864; Montgomery City Council Minutes (1860–1866), 48, 174.

3. Sam R. Watkins, *"Co. Aytch" Maury Guards First Tennessee Regiment or A Side Show of the Big Show* (Jackson, Tenn.: McCowat-Mercer Press, 1952), 180–81; John Gill Shorter to Dabney Maury, July 2, 1863, John Gill Shorter Papers, ADAH.

4. Sophia Bibb to Abraham Myers, April 28, 1862, in CP, NA.

5. *Montgomery Advertiser,* June 14, 1864.

6. Ibid., April 19, 18, 1865.

7. Walter Coleman to E. J. Newbold, June 28, 1865, in Montgomery City Council Minutes (1861–1865); *Alabama State Census, Free Population: 1860,* 89; Sanford, *The Code of the City of Montgomery,* 89–90; George P. Rawick, *The American Slave: A Composite Autobiography Alabama and Indiana Narratives,* Federal Writers Project, vol. 1 (Westport, Conn.: Greenwood Press, 1977), 177–78.

Bibliography

PRIMARY SOURCES

Documents of the United States

U.S. Bureau of the Census. *Eighth Census of the United States: 1860.* Washington, D.C.

U.S. Congress. House. "Affairs of Southern Railroads." House Report No. 34. 39th Congress, 2d sess., 1867. *Journal of the Congress of the Confederate States of America,* vol. 1. Washington, D.C.: Government Printing Office, 1904.

U.S. War Department. *War of the Rebellion: A Compilation of the Official Records of the Union and Confederate Armies.* 128 vols. Washington, D.C.: Government Printing Office, 1880–1901.

Documents of the Confederate States

Applications for Military Service Exemption File. Manuscript Division, Alabama Department of Archives and History, Montgomery, Ala.

Case Files of Southern Claims Commission. Records of the Accounting Officers of the Treasury Department, Record Group 217, National Archives, Washington, D.C.

Confederate Papers Relating to Citizens or Business Firms, 1861–1865, Record Group 109, National Archives Microfilm Publications, Microcopy 346, National Archives, Washington, D.C.

Inspection Reports and Related Records Received by the Inspection Branch in the Confederate Adjutant and Inspector's Office, 1861–1865, Record Group 109, National Archives Microfilm Publications, Microcopy 437, National Archives, Washington, D.C.

Journal of the Congress of the Confederate States of America (1861). Washington: Government Printing Office, 1904.

Letters and Telegrams Sent by the Confederate Quartermaster General, 1861–1865, Record Group 109, National Archives Microfilm Publications, Microcopy 437, National Archives, Washington, D.C.

Letters Received by the Confederate Adjutant and Inspector General, 1861–1865,
    National Archives Microfilm Publications, Microcopy 474, Record Group
    109, National Archives, Washington, D.C.
Letters Received by the Confederate Quartermaster General, 1861–1865, Record
    Group 109, National Archives Microfilm Publications, Microcopy 344, Na-
    tional Archives, Washington, D.C.
Letters Received by the Confederate Secretary of War, 1861–1865, Record
    Group 109, National Archives Microfilm Publications, Microcopy 437, Na-
    tional Archives, Washington, D.C.

State Documents

Alabama State Census, Free Population: 1860.
Alabama State Census, Slave Population: 1860.
"Descriptive Muster and Pay Roll of Stewards, Ward Masters, Nurses and Cooks
    on duty in the Madison House Hospital at Montgomery, Alabama." In Mus-
    ter Roll for Hospitals, RG 109, National Archives, Washington, D.C.
Muster Roll of Alabama Rebels in Montgomery County. Independent Company
    File, Alabama Department of Archives and History, Montgomery, Ala.
Muster Roll of Montgomery Foreign Guards in Montgomery County. Inde-
    pendent Company File, Alabama Department of Archives and History,
    Montgomery, Ala.
Muster Roll of Montgomery Guards in Montgomery County. Independent Com-
    pany File, Alabama Department of Archives and History, Montgomery, Ala.
"Report on the Committee for Public Buildings." Alabama Historic Commis-
    sion Office, Montgomery, Ala.

City Documents

List of Families in Montgomery County who are Entitled to Relief, March
    1862, October 1864. Military Volunteer Association Records, Alabama De-
    partment of Archives and History, Montgomery, Ala.
Mears, Leonard, and James Turnbull. *The Montgomery Directory for 1859–60, Con-
    taining the Names of the Inhabitants: A Business Directory, Street Directory.*
    Montgomery: Advertiser Book and Printing Office, 1859.
Montgomery City Council Minutes, June 1856–September 1860, ADAH.
Montgomery City Council Minutes, September 1860–December 1866, ADAH.
Sanford, John W. A. *The Code of the City of Montgomery.* Montgomery: Gaines and
    Smith, 1861.

Manuscripts and Archival Materials

Bibb, Sophia Lucy Ann. Papers. Alabama Department of Archives and History,
    Montgomery, Ala.

Blue, Ellen. Diary. Landmarks Foundation of Montgomery, Montgomery, Ala.

Blue, Matthew. Papers. Alabama Department of Archives and History, Montgomery, Ala.

Boyrer, William. *Montgomery Parade March; Composed and Respectfully Dedicated to the Metropolitan Guard.* Mobile, Ala.: J. H. Snow, 1861. (Copy in the Lester S. Levy Collection of Sheet Music. Special Collections, Milton S. Eisenhower Library. Johns Hopkins University, Baltimore, Md.)

Browne, William P. Papers. Alabama Department of Archives and History, Montgomery, Ala.

Burton, James H. Papers. The Center for American History, University of Texas, Austin, Tex.

Brent, George. Papers. William R. Perkins Library, Duke University, Durham, N.C.

Clapp. Surname File. Alabama Department of Archives and History, Montgomery, Ala.

Clay, C. Clement. Papers. Special Collections, William R. Perkins Library, Duke University, Durham, N.C.

Cobb, Howell. Papers. Special Collections Division, University of Georgia Libraries, Athens, Ga.

Cobb, Thomas. Papers. Special Collections Division, University of Georgia Libraries, Athens, Ga.

Davidson, Lucretia Bailey. Papers. Alabama Department of Archives and History, Montgomery, Ala.

Douglas, Stephen. Papers. Special Collections Department, University of Chicago Library, Chicago, Ill.

Durr. Surname File. Alabama Department of Archives and History, Montgomery, Ala.

Fair, Elisha. Papers. Alabama Department of Archives and History, Montgomery, Ala.

Glackmeyer. Surname File. Alabama Department of Archives and History, Montgomery, Ala.

Hausman. Surname File. Alabama Department of Archives and History, Montgomery, Ala.

Herbert, Hillary. Papers. Southern Historical Collection, University of North Carolina, Chapel Hill, N.C.

Hill. Surname File. Alabama Department of Archives and History, Montgomery, Ala.

Hinricks, Charles. Diary. Western Historical Manuscripts Collection, University of Missouri, Columbia, Mo.

Hoole, William Stanley. Papers. W. S. Hoole Special Collections. University of Alabama, Tuscaloosa, Ala.

Hunter, Robert M. T. Papers. Special Collections Department, Alderman Library, University of Virginia, Charlottesville, Va.

Jackson, Jefferson Franklin. Papers. Alabama Department of Archives and History, Montgomery, Ala.

Janney. Surname File. Alabama Department of Archives and History, Montgomery, Ala.

Journal of the Convention of the People of South Carolina Held in 1860–61. Charleston: Evans and Cogswell, 1861. South Carolina Pamphlets Collection, South Caroliniana Library, Columbia, S.C.

Kreutner. Surname File. Alabama Department of Archives and History, Montgomery, Ala.

Lehman, Meyer and Emanuel. Surname File. Alabama Department of Archives and History, Montgomery, Ala.

Lewis, E. Papers. Alabama Department of Archives and History, Montgomery, Ala.

McClellan, Thomas M. Papers. Papers. Alabama Department of Archives and History. Montgomery, Ala.

McIntyre, Archibald. Surname File. Alabama Department of Archives and History. Montgomery, Ala.

Manly, Basil. Papers. W. S. Hoole Special Collections, University of Alabama, Tuscaloosa, Ala.

Minutes of the Presbyterian Church of Montgomery, Ala. (1857–1869). Department of Archives and Special Collections, Auburn University at Montgomery Library, Montgomery, Ala.

Moren, Edward. Papers. Alabama Department of Archives and History, Montgomery, Ala.

Morrissette, Kate. "Social Life in the First Capital of the Confederacy." Landmarks Foundation of Montgomery, Montgomery, Ala.

Olivers, Thomas Winfrey, III. Papers. Alabama Department of Archives and History, Montgomery, Ala.

Prospectus of the Montgomery Military Academy. Montgomery, Ala.: Montgomery Advertiser Book, 1862. (Copy in the Alabama Department of Archives and History, Montgomery, Ala.)

Regulations and Rules of the Montgomery Military Academy, 1861. Montgomery, Ala.: Floyd and Warrock, 1861. (Copy in the Alabama Department of Archives and History, Montgomery, Ala.)

Sanford, William A. Papers. Alabama Department of Archives and History, Montgomery, Ala.

Seelye, Samuel. Surname File. Alabama Department of Archives and History, Montgomery, Ala.

Shipman, S. V. Diary. Shipman Manuscript Collection, Wisconsin State Historical Library, Madison, Wis.

Shorter, John Gill. Letterbooks. Alabama Department of Archives and History, Montgomery, Ala.

———. Papers. Alabama Department of Archives and History, Montgomery, Ala.

Solomons, M. J. Papers. William R. Perkins Library, Manuscript Division, Duke University, Durham, N.C.

Stephens, Alexander H. Papers. Robert Woodruff Library, Special Collections, Emory University, Atlanta, Ga.

Stout, Samuel H. Papers. William R. Perkins Library, Manuscript Division, Duke University, Durham, N.C.

———. Papers. Southern Historical Collection, University of North Carolina, Chapel Hill, N.C.

———. Papers. Tennessee State Library and Archives, Nashville, Tenn.

———. Papers. The Center for American History, University of Texas, Austin, Tex.

———. Papers. Robert Woodruff Library, Special Collections, Emory University, Atlanta, Ga.

Stow. Surname File. Alabama Department of Archives and History, Montgomery, Ala.

Strassburger. Surname File. Alabama Department of Archives and History, Montgomery, Ala.

Wallace, Frances Woolfolk. Diary. Southern Historical Collection, University of North Carolina—Chapel Hill, N.C.

Watts, Thomas Hill. Papers. Alabama Department of Archives and History, Montgomery, Ala.

Weil, Jacob. Papers. Alabama Department of Archives and History, Montgomery, Ala.

Winter. Surname File. Alabama Department of Archives and History, Montgomery, Ala.

Yancey, William Lowndes. Papers. Alabama Department of Archives and History, Montgomery, Ala.

Books and Articles

Bevens, William E. *Reminiscences of a Private.* Edited by Daniel E. Sutherland. Fayetteville: University of Arkansas Press, 1992.

Brewer, Willis. *Alabama: Her History, Resources, War Record and Public Men From 1540 to 1872.* Reprint ed. Spartanburg, S.C.: Reprint Company, 1975.

Brown, Thomas A. *History of the American Stage.* New York: Dick and Fitzgerald, 1870.

Caffey, Thomas. "Letters from the Front." *Confederate Veteran* 26 (August 1918).

Chesnut, Mary. *Mary Chesnut's Civil War*. Edited by C. Vann Woodward. New Haven: Yale University Press, 1981.

Chisolm, Julian. *A Manual of Military Surgery for the use of Surgeons in the Confederate Army*. Richmond, Va.: West and Johnson, 1861.

Collins, R. M. *Chapters From the Unwritten History of the War Between the States*. St. Louis: Nixon-Jones, 1893.

Corsan, W. C. *Two Months in The Confederate States, Including A Visit to New Orleans Under the Domination of General Butler*. London: Richard Bentley, 1863.

Cumming, Kate. *Kate: The Journal of a Confederate Nurse*. Edited by Richard Barksdale Harwell. Baton Rouge: Louisiana State University Press, 1959.

Davis, Jefferson. *The Papers of Jefferson Davis: Vol. 7, 1861*. Edited by Lynda L. Crist and Mary Seaton Dix. Baton Rouge: Louisiana State University Press, 1992.

——. *The Papers of Jefferson Davis: Vol. 8, 1862*. Edited by Lynda L. Crist, Mary Seaton Dix, and Kenneth H. Williams. Baton Rouge: Louisiana State University Press, 1994.

Davis, Varina. *Jefferson Davis Ex-President of the Confederate States of America: A Memoir*. Vol. 2. New York: Belford, 1870.

DeLeon, Thomas C. *Four Years in Rebel Capitals*. Mobile, Ala.: Gossip Printing, 1890.

East, Charles. ed. *The Civil War Diary of Sarah Morgan*. Athens: University of Georgia Press, 1991.

Gordon, John B. *Reminiscences of the Civil War*. New York: Charles Scribners' Sons, 1904.

Grisamore, Silas T. *The Civil War Reminiscences of Major Silas T. Grisamore, C.S.A*. Edited by Arthur Bergeron. Baton Rouge: Louisiana State University Press, 1993.

Harper's Weekly Magazine. "Out of Dixie." June 25, 1864.

Hedges, William. "Three Years in Montgomery." *Harper's New Monthly Magazine* 29 (July 1864), 196–201.

Hill, Luther Leonidas. *Sermons, Addresses, and Papers of Rev. Luther Leonidas Hill*. New York: Fleming H. Revell Press, 1919.

Hilliard, Henry W. *Politics and Pen: Pictures At Home and Abroad*. New York: G. P. Putnam's Sons, 1892.

Hoole, W. Stanley, ed. "The Diary of Dr. Basil Manly, 1858–1867," pt. 1. *Alabama Review* 4 (April 1951), 127–149.

——. "The Diary of Dr. Basil Manly, 1858–1867," pt. 2. *Alabama Review* 4 (July 1951), 221–236.

Hosea, Lewis M. "The Campaign for Selma." *Sketches of War History, 1861–1865: Papers Read before the Ohio Commandry of the Military Order of the Loyal Legion of the United States*. Vol. 1. Cincinnati: n.p., 1888.

Hull, Augustus Longstreet, ed. "The Correspondence of Thomas Reade Rootes

Cobb, 1860–1862." In *Publications of the Southern History Association* (May 1907), 148–185; (July 1907), 233–260; (September-November 1907), 312–328.

———. "Thomas R. R. Cobb: Extracts from Letters to His Wife, February 3, 1861–December 10, 1862." *Southern Historical Society Papers* 28 (1900), 280–301.

Huse, Caleb. *The Supplies for the Confederate Army: How They Were Obtained in Europe and How Paid For.* Boston: T. R. Marvin, 1904.

Jones, James P., and William Warren Rogers, eds. "Montgomery as the Confederate Capital: View of a New Nation." *Alabama Historical Quarterly* 26 (Spring 1964), 1–125.

Jones, John B. *A Rebel War Clerk's Diary.* Vol. 1. Philadelphia: J. B. Lippincott, 1866.

Jones, Virginia K., ed. "The Journal of Sarah G. Follansbee." *Alabama Historical Quarterly* 27 (Fall and Winter 1965), 213–258.

McClean, Margaret. "A Northern Woman in the Confederacy." *Harper's Magazine* 128 (February 1914), 440–451.

McGee, Benjamin F. *History of the 72nd Indiana Volunteer Infantry of the Mounted Lightening Brigade.* Lafayette, Ind.: S. Vater, 1882.

Manarin, Louis H., ed. *Richmond at War: The Minutes of the City Council.* Chapel Hill: University of North Carolina Press, 1966.

Morgan, James M. *Recollections of a Rebel Reefer.* Boston: Houghton Mifflin, 1917.

Owen, Thomas M. *History of Alabama and Dictionary of Alabama Biography.* 4 vols. Chicago: S. J. Clarke, 1921.

Rawick, George P. *The American Slave: A Composite Autobiography. Vol. 6, Alabama and Indiana Narratives.* Westport, Conn.: Federal Writers Project, Greenwood Press, 1972.

Reese, George W., ed. *Proceedings of the Virginia State Convention, 1861.* Vol. 4. Richmond: Virginia State Library, 1965.

Rowland, Dunbar, ed. *Jefferson Davis, Constitutionalist: His Letters, Papers, and Speeches.* Vols. 6 and 9. Jackson: Mississippi State Department of Archives and History, 1923.

Rozier, John, ed. *The Granite Farm Letters: The Civil War Correspondence of Edgeworth and Sallie Bird.* Athens: University of Georgia Press, 1988.

Russell, William Howard. *My Diary North and South.* Vol. 1. London: Bradbury and Evans, 1863.

Semmes, Raphael. *Service Afloat; or, The Remarkable Career of the Confederate Cruisers Sumter and Alabama During the War Between the States.* New York: P. J. Kennedy and Sons, 1903.

Sherman, William. *Memoirs of General W. T. Sherman.* Vol. 1. New York: Charles L. Webster, 1891.

Simms, William Gilmore. *War Poetry of the South.* New York: Richardson, 1867.

Smith, William R. *The History and Debates of the Convention of the People of Alabama.* Reprint ed. Spartanburg, S.C.: Reprint Co., 1975.

Strong, George Templeton. *The Diary of George Templeton Strong.* Edited by Allen Nevins and Thomas H. Miton. Seattle: University of Washington Press, 1988.

Stueckrath, G. H. "Montgomery, the Capital of Alabama." *Debow's Review* 28 (January 1860), 111–14.

Watkins, Sam R. *"Co. Aytch" Maury Guards First Tennessee Regiment or A Side Show of the Big Show.* Jackson, Tenn.: McCowat-Mercer Press, 1952.

Wilson, James H. *Under the Old Flag.* New York: D. Appleton, 1912.

Newspapers

Atlanta Guardian (1861).
Baltimore American and Commercial Advertiser (1861).
Charleston Daily Courier (1861).
Charleston Mercury (1861).
Chicago Tribune (1861).
Columbus Enquirer (Ga.)(1862).
Columbus Sun (Ga.) (1865).
London Times (1861).
Macon Telegraph (1861).
Memphis Appeal (1864–1865).
Mobile Advertiser and Register (1864–1865).
Montgomery Advertiser (1860–1865, 1910).
Montgomery Confederation (1860–1861).
Montgomery Mail (1860–1865).
Montgomery Weekly Advertiser (1860–1863).
Montgomery Weekly Confederation (1860).
Montgomery Weekly Mail (1860–1862).
New Orleans Daily Picayune (1861).
New Orleans Delta (1861).
New York Herald (1861).
Troy Southern Advertiser (Ala.)(1865).

SECONDARY SOURCES

Books

Albaugh, William, and Edward N. Simmons. *Confederate Arms.* Harrisburg, Pa.: Stackpole Co., 1952.

Allen, Lee N. *The First 150 Years: Montgomery's First Baptist Church, 1829–1979.* Montgomery, Ala.: First Baptist Church, 1979.

Armes, Ethel. *The Story of Coal and Iron in Alabama.* Birmingham: Chamber of Commerce, 1906.

Ash, Stephen V. *Middle Tennessee Society Transformed, 1860–1870: War and Peace in the Upper South.* Baton Rouge: Louisiana State University Press, 1988.

———. *When the Yankees Came: Conflict and Chaos in the Occupied South.* Chapel Hill: University of North Carolina Press, 1995.

Ball, Douglas B. *Financial Failure and Confederate Defeat.* Urbana: University of Illinois Press, 1991.

Barefield, Marilyn D., ed. *Alabama Mortality Schedule, 1860: Eighth Census of the United States.* Easley, S.C.: Southern Historical Press, 1987.

Barney, William L. *The Secessionist Impulse: Alabama and Mississippi in 1860.* Princeton: Princeton University, 1974.

Beers, Henry P. *The Confederacy: A Guide to the Archives of the Government of the Confederate States of America.* Washington, D.C.: National Archives and Records Administration, 1986.

Bergeron, Arthur W. *Confederate Mobile.* Jackson: University of Mississippi Press, 1991.

Beringer, Richard E., Herman Hattaway, Archer Jones, and William N. Still, Jr. *The Elements of Confederate Defeat: Nationalism, War Aims, and Religion.* Athens: University of Georgia Press, 1988.

Berlin, Ira. *Slaves Without Masters: The Free Negro in the Antebellum South.* New York: Pantheon, 1974.

Black, Robert C. *The Railroads of the Confederacy.* Chapel Hill: University of North Carolina Press, 1952.

Capers, Gerald M. *The Biography of a River Town; Memphis: Its Heroic Age.* Chapel Hill: University of North Carolina Press, 1939.

———. *Occupied City: New Orleans Under the Federals, 1862–1865.* Lexington: University Press of Kentucky, 1965.

Capers, Henry D. *The Life and Times of C. G. Memminger.* Richmond: Everett Waddey, 1893.

Centennial Lehman Brothers, 1850–1950. New York: Spirol Press, 1950.

Clinton, Catherine. *Divided Houses: Gender and the Civil War.* New York: Oxford University Press, 1992.

———. *Tara Revisited: Women, War, and the Plantation Legend.* New York: Abbeville Press, 1995.

Cory, Marielou Armstrong. *The Ladies' Memorial Association of Montgomery, Alabama: Its Origins and Organization, 1860–1870.* Montgomery, Ala.: Alabama Printing, n.d.

Crawford, Martin, ed. *William Howard Russell's Civil War: Private Diary and Letters.* Athens: University of Georgia Press, 1992.

Crofts, Daniel W. *Reluctant Confederates: Upper South Unionists in the Secession Crisis.* Chapel Hill: University of North Carolina Press, 1989.

Cunningham, Horace H. *Doctors in Gray: The Confederate Medical Service.* Baton Rouge: Louisiana State University Press, 1958.

Current, Richard N. *Lincoln's Loyalists: Union Soldiers from the Confederacy.* Boston: Northeastern University Press, 1992.

Curry, Leonard. *The Free Black in Urban America: The Shadow of the Dream.* Chicago: University of Chicago Press, 1981.

Davis, William C. *"A Government of Our Own": The Making of the Confederacy.* New York: Free Press, 1994.

——. *Jefferson Davis: The Man and His Hour.* New York: Harper Collins, 1991.

DeCredico, Mary A. *Patriotism for Profit: Georgia's Urban Entrepreneurs and the Confederate War Effort.* Chapel Hill: University of North Carolina Press, 1990.

Dill, J. S. *Isaac Taylor Tichenor: The Home Mission Statesman.* Nashville: Sunday School Board Southern Baptist Convention, 1908.

Dormon, James H., Jr. *Theater in the Ante Bellum South, 1815–1861.* Chapel Hill: University of North Carolina Press, 1967.

Durham, Walter T. *Nashville: The Occupied City.* Nashville: Tennessee Historical Society, 1985.

Durrill, Wayne K. *War of Another Kind: A Southern Community in the Great Rebellion.* New York: Oxford University Press, 1990.

Escott, Paul D. *After Secession: Jefferson Davis and the Failure of Confederate Nationalism.* Baton Rouge: Louisiana State University Press, 1978.

Faust, Drew Gilpin. *The Creation of Confederate Nationalism: Ideology and Identity in the Civil War South.* Baton Rouge: Louisiana State University Press, 1988.

——. *Mothers of Invention: Women of the Slaveholding South in the American Civil War.* Chapel Hill: University of North Carolina Press, 1996.

Gallagher, Gary W. *The Confederate War.* Cambridge, Mass.: Harvard University Press, 1997.

Genovese, Eugene D. *Roll, Jordan, Roll: The World the Slaves Made.* New York: Pantheon, 1974.

Goff, Richard D. *Confederate Supply.* Durham: Duke University Press, 1969.

Grimsley, Mark. *The Hard Hand of War: Union Military Policy Toward Southern Civilians, 1861–1865.* New York: Cambridge University Press, 1995.

Harris, William C. *Leroy Pope Walker: Confederate Secretary of War.* Tuscaloosa, Ala.: Confederate Publishing, 1962.

Harwell, Richard Barksdale. *Brief Candle: The Confederate Theater.* Worcester, Mass.: American Antiquarian Society, 1971.

Hattaway, Herman, and Archer Jones. *How the North Won: A Military History of the Civil War.* Urbana: University of Illinois Press, 1983.

Hoole, William Stanley. *Alias Simon Suggs: The Life and Times of Johnson Jones Hooper.* Tuscaloosa: University of Alabama Press, 1952.

Hubbell, John T., and James W. Geary, eds. *Biographical Dictionary of the Union: Northern Leaders of the Civil War.* Westport, Conn.: Greenwood Press, 1995.

Hughes, Nathaniel C., Jr. *General William J. Hardee, Old Reliable.* Baton Rouge: Louisiana State University Press, 1965.

Jimerson, Randall C. *The Private Civil War: Popular Thought During the Sectional Conflict.* Baton Rouge: Louisiana State University Press, 1988.

Johannsen, Robert W. *Stephen A. Douglas.* New York: Oxford University Press, 1973.

Johns, John E. *Florida During the Civil War.* Gainesville: University of Florida Press, 1963.

Jones, Jacqueline. *Labor of Love, Labor of Sorrow: Black Women, Work, and the Family from Slavery to the Present.* New York: Basic Books, 1985.

Jones, James P. *Yankee Blitzkrieg: Wilson's Raid through Alabama and Georgia.* Athens: University of Georgia Press, 1976.

Klingberg, Frank. *The Southern Claims Commission.* Berkeley: University of California Press, 1955.

Korn, Bertram W. *American Jewry and the Civil War.* Philadelphia: Jewish Publication Society of America, 1967.

Lee, Charles R. *The Confederate Constitutions.* Chapel Hill: University of North Carolina Press, 1963.

McCash, William B. *Thomas R. R. Cobb, 1823–1862: The Making of a Southern Nationalist.* Macon, Ga.: Mercer University Press, 1983.

McMillan, Malcolm C. *The Disintegration of a Confederate State: Three Governors and Alabama's Wartime Home Front, 1861–1865.* Macon, Ga.: Mercer University Press, 1986.

McPherson, James M. *The Battle Cry of Freedom: The Civil War Era.* New York: Oxford University Press, 1988.

———. *What They Fought For, 1861–1865.* Baton Rouge: Louisiana State University Press, 1994.

Mills, Gary B. *Southern Loyalists in the Civil War: The Southern Claims Commission.* Baltimore: Genealogical Publishing, 1994.

Mohr, Clarence. *On the Threshold of Freedom: Masters and Slaves in Civil War Georgia.* Athens: University of Georgia Press, 1986.

Parks, Joseph Howard. *General Edmund Kirby Smith, C.S.A.* Baton Rouge: Louisiana State University Press, 1954.

Patrick, Rembert W. *The Fall of Richmond.* Baton Rouge: Louisiana State University Press, 1960.

———. *Jefferson Davis and His Cabinet.* Baton Rouge: Louisiana State University Press, 1944.

Rable, George C. *Civil Wars, Women, and the Crisis of Southern Nationalism*. Urbana: University of Illinois Press, 1989.

Radley, Kenneth. *Rebel Watchdog: The Confederate States Army Provost Guard*. Baton Rouge: Louisiana State University Press, 1989.

Ramsdell, Charles W. *Behind the Lines in the Southern Confederacy*. Baton Rouge: Louisiana State University Press, 1944.

Robertson, James I., Jr. *Civil War Virginia: Battleground for a Nation*. Charlottesville: University Press of Virginia, 1991.

Schott, Thomas E. *Alexander H. Stephens of Georgia: A Biography*. Baton Rouge: Louisiana State University Press, 1988.

Schroeder-Lein, Glenna R. *Confederate Hospitals on the Move: Samuel H. Stout and the Army of Tennessee*. Columbia: University of South Carolina Press, 1994.

Scott, Anne Firor. *The Southern Lady: From Pedestal to Politics, 1830–1930*. Chicago: University of Chicago Press, 1970.

Silver, James W. *Confederate Morale and Church Propaganda*. Tuscaloosa: Confederate Publishing, 1957.

Simms, Henry H. *Life of Robert M. T. Hunter: A Study in Sectionalism and Secession*. Richmond: William Byrd Press, 1935.

Starr, Stephen Z. *The Union Cavalry in the Civil War: From Fort Sumter to Gettysburg, 1861–1863*. Vol. 1. Baton Rouge: Louisiana State University Press, 1979.

———. *The Union Cavalry in the Civil War: The War in the West, 1861–1865*. Vol. 3. Baton Rouge: Louisiana State University Press, 1985.

Sterkx, H. E. *Partners in Rebellion: Alabama Women in Civil War*. Rutherford: Fairleigh Dickinson University Press, 1970.

Sulzby, James F., Jr. *Historic Alabama Hotels and Resorts*. Tuscaloosa: University of Alabama Press, 1960.

Symonds, Craig L. *Joseph E. Johnston: A Civil War Biography*. New York: W. W. Norton, 1992.

Tatum, Georgia L. *Disloyalty in the Confederacy*. Chapel Hill: University of North Carolina Press, 1934.

Thomas, Emory. *The Confederate Nation, 1861–1865*. New York: Harper and Row, 1979.

———. *The Confederate State of Richmond: A Biography of the Capital*. Austin: University of Texas Press, 1971.

Todd, Richard C. *Confederate Finance*. Athens: University of Georgia Press, 1954.

Vandiver, Frank E. *Ploughshares into Swords: Josiah Gorgas and Confederate Ordnance*. Austin: University of Texas Press, 1952.

Wade, Richard. *Slavery in Cities: The South, 1820–1860*. London: Oxford University Press, 1964.

Wakelyn, Jon L. *Biographical Dictionary of the Confederacy*. Westport, Conn.: Greenwood Press, 1977.

Walther, Eric H. *The Fire-Eaters.* Baton Rouge: Louisiana State University Press, 1992.

Warner, Ezra J., and W. Buck Yearns. *Biographical Register of the Confederate Congress.* Baton Rouge: Louisiana State University Press, 1975.

Wheeler, Joseph. *Alabama in Confederate Military History.* vols. 7, 8. Wilmington, N.C.: Broadfoot Publishing, 1987.

Whites, Lee Ann. *The Civil War As a Crisis in Gender: Augusta, Georgia, 1860–1890.* Athens: University of Georgia Press, 1995.

Wiley, Bell Irvin. *Confederate Women.* Westport, Conn.: Greenwood Press, 1995.

Williams, T. Harry. *P. G. T. Beauregard: Napoleon in Gray.* Baton Rouge: Louisiana State University Press, 1954.

Wise, Stephen R. *Gate of Hell: Campaign for Charleston Harbor.* Columbia: University of South Carolina Press, 1994.

———. *Lifeline of the Confederacy: Blockade Running During the Civil War.* Columbia: University of South Carolina Press, 1988.

Wood, Mattie Pegus. *The Life of St. John's Parish: A History of St. John's Episcopal Church from 1834–1955.* Montgomery: Paragon Press, 1955.

Wooster, Ralph A. *The Secession Conventions of the South.* Princeton, N.J.: Princeton University Press, 1962.

Articles

Abbott, Richard H. "Civil War Origins of the Southern Republican Press." *Civil War History* 43 (March 1997), 38–58.

Baker, Thomas H. "Refugee Newspaper: *The Memphis Daily Appeal,* 1862–1865." *Journal of Southern History* 29 (August 1963), 326–344.

Barbee, David R., and Milledge L. Bonham, Jr. "The Montgomery Address of Stephen A. Douglas." *Journal of Southern History* 5 (Fall 1939), 527–52.

Bearss, Edwin C. "Rousseau's Raid on the Montgomery and West Point Railroad, 1864." *Alabama Historical Quarterly* 25 (Spring and Summer 1963), 7–48.

Berney, Saffold. "Major Henry Churchill Semple." *Alabama Historical Quarterly* 14 (1952), 163–169.

Donald, W. J. "Alabama Confederate Hospitals." *Alabama Review* 15 (October 1962), 271–281.

Donnelly, Ralph W. "Scientists of the Confederate Nitre and Mining Bureau." *Civil War History* 4 (December 1956), 69–92.

Dyer, Thomas G. "Vermont Yankees in King Cotton's Court: The Case of Cyrena and Amherst Stone." *Vermont History* 60 (Fall 1992), 205–229.

Faust, Drew Gilpin. "Altars of Sacrifice: Confederate Women and the Narratives of War." *Journal of American History* 76 (March 1990), 1200–1228.

Gerson, Armand J. "The Inception of the Montgomery Convention." *Annual Report of the American Historical Association* (1910), 179–187.

Honey, Michael K. "The War Within the Confederacy: White Unionists of North Carolina." *Prologue* 18 (Summer 1986), 74–93.

Hoole, W. Stanley. "John W. Mallet and the Confederate Ordnance Laboratories, 1862–1865." *Alabama Review* 26 (January 1973), 33–72.

Jacobs, Joseph. "Some of the Drug Conditions During the War Between the States, 1861–5." *Southern Historical Papers* 33 (1905), 161–187.

Johnson, Evans. "Henry W. Hilliard and the Civil War Years." *Alabama Review* 17 (April 1964), 102–12.

Johnson, Ludwell H. "Fort Sumter and Confederate Diplomacy." *Journal of Southern History* 26 (November 1960), 441–77.

Long, Durward. "Political Parties and Propaganda in Alabama in the Presidential Election of 1860." *Alabama Historical Quarterly* 25 (Spring and Summer 1963), 122–30.

———. "Unanimity and Disloyalty in Secessionist Alabama." *Civil War History* 11 (March 1965), 257–73.

Mills, Gary. "Miscegenation and the Free Negro in Antebellum 'Anglo' Alabama: A Reexamination of Southern Race Relations." *Journal of American History* 68 (June 1981), 16–34.

Napier, John W., III. "Martial Ante-Bellum Military Activity." *Alabama Historical Quarterly* 29 (Fall and Winter 1967), 107–31.

———. "Montgomery During the Civil War." *Alabama Review* 39 (April 1988), 103–31.

Ramsdell, Charles W. "The Control of Manufacturing by the Confederate Government." *Mississippi Valley Historical Review* 8 (December 1921), 231–249.

Rogers, William Warren, Jr. " 'In Defense of Our Sacred Cause': Rabbi James K. Gutheim in Confederate Montgomery." *Journal of Confederate History* 7 (Fall 1991), 112–122.

Shofner, Jerrell H., and William Warren Rogers. "Montgomery to Richmond: The Confederacy Selects a Capital." *Civil War History* 10 (June 1964), 155–66.

Templeman, Eleanor Lee. "In the Beginning . . . " *Arlington Historical Magazine* 1, no. 4 (October 1960), 43–49.

Walker, Alan L. "Three Alabama Chaplains, 1861–1865." *Alabama Review* 16 (July 1963), 174–184.

Wight, William E. "The Churches and the Confederate Cause." *Civil War History* 6 (December 1960), 361–373.

Williams, Benjamin B. "Nineteenth Century Authors." *Alabama Historical Quarterly* 37 (Summer 1975), 136–145.

Theses and Dissertations

Beatty, Frederick M. "William Lowndes Yancey and Alabama Secession." M.A. thesis, Auburn University, 1990.

Fisher, John E. "Statesman of the Lost Cause: The Career of R. M. T. Hunter, 1869–87." M.A. thesis, University of Virginia, 1966.

Johnson, Evans. "A Political Life of Henry W. Hilliard." M.A. thesis, University of Alabama, 1947.

Krug, Donna Rebecca. "The Folks Back Home: The Confederate Homefront During the Civil War." Ph.D. diss., University of California at Irvine, 1990.

LeGrand, Phillis LaRue. "Destitution and Relief of the Indigent Soldiers' Families of Alabama During the Civil War." M.A. thesis, Auburn University, 1964.

Long, Durward, Jr. "Alabama in the Formation of the Confederacy." Ph.D. diss., University of Florida, 1959.

Wible, Hazel B. "History of Montgomery, Alabama, 1860–1865." M.A. thesis, Auburn University, 1939.

Index

Abercrombie, Edmond, 86
Abercrombie, John, 77
Abercrombie, Sarah, 148
Abolitionism, fear of, 10–12, 15–16, 18–19, 78, 89, 91, 100–101, 111
Adams, Daniel, 139–50 passim, 140
Alabama: secession of, 10–20; threatened by Federal forces, 116–23
Alabama Arms Manufacturing Company, 70, 118, 132, 141
Alabama River, 1, 5, 18, 21, 24, 32, 57, 66, 77, 100, 117–18, 121–22, 125, 127–28, 131, 142
Alabama State Agricultural Fair, 6
Albright, Gustav, 63, 148
Albright, Sarah, 64
Alcohol, prevalence of, 2–3, 9, 68–69, 73, 78–79, 84, 86–87, 143–44, 155. *See also* Restaurants and bars
Aldrick, C. S., 108
Alexander, J. C., 90
Alexandria, Vir., 45, 90
Ambrage, T. J., 50, 59
Anaconda Plan, 125
Anderson, Robert, 36
Anderson, William, 3
Antietam, battle of, 68
Appomattox Courthouse, 87, 152
Armaments, production of, 47, 51, 58, 128–29. *See also* Alabama Arms Manufacturing Company
Arnold, Frank, 28
Arrington, Samuel, 15, 25
Artesian Basin, 1–2, 74, 83, 111, 132
Athens, Ala., 116
Atlanta, Ga., 17, 25, 48, 56, 58, 97, 101, 121–22, 124–26, 136, 152, 155
Auburn, Ala., 150
Augusta, Ga., 87, 128, 136, 152

Bacon, Henry, 62
Baird, Harlon, 123
Baldwin, Edwin, 61
Baldwin, Mary, 133
Baldwin, William, 4, 6, 63, 108, 132, 133
Baldwin, Willie, 133
Banks: Bank of Montgomery, 4, 70; Central Bank, 4, 67, 121
Banks, Edwin, 16
Bard, Sam, 99
Barton, Benjamin, 131
Baton Rouge, La., 60
Beaumont, Eugene, 150
Beauregard, P. G. T., 32, 36, 127
Becker, Nick, 4
Bell, John, 15–18, 105, 115
Bell, Mary Jarrett, 96
Bell, William, 97–98
Bellinger, Carnot, 96
Bellinger, Sarah, 96
Belser, Edwin, 84, 118
Bemiss, Samuel, 55
Benton, Ala., 145
Berney, James, 108
Bethea, Eugenia, 124
Bethea, Theodore, 124
Bethea, Tristam, 17, 33, 124
Bevens, William, 86
Bibb, Benjah, 33–34, 107, 135–37
Bibb, Sophia, 33–34, 94–96, 107, 154
Bibb, William, 104–15 passim, 146, 147, 154
Bihler, Joseph, 69, 79–80, 131
Bingham, J. St. Maur, 130
Bird, Caroline, 8
Black Belt, 20, 50, 114, 139, 145
Blacks, free, 2–3, 9, 74, 85, 156. *See also* Slavery; Slaves
Blaum, Stephen, 4
Blind Tom, 64

About the Author

WILLIAM WARREN ROGERS, JR., is Associate Professor of History at Gainesville College, Georgia, and is the author of *Black Belt Scalawag: Charles Hays and the Southern Republicans in an Era of Reconstruction* (1993). He received his master's and doctorate degrees from Auburn University, Alabama.